Political Ideals in Medieval Italian Art

The Frescoes in the Palazzo dei Priori, Perugia (1297)

Studies in the Fine Arts: Iconography, No. 1

Linda Seidel, Series Editor

Associate Professor of Art History
University of Chicago

Other Titles in This Series

Political Ideals in Medieval Italian Art

The Frescoes in the Palazzo dei Priori, Perugia (1297)

by
Jonathan B. Riess

UMI RESEARCH PRESS

Ann Arbor, Michigan

Produced and distributed by
UMI Research Press
an imprint of
University Microfilms International
Ann Arbor, Michigan 48106

Library of Congress Cataloging in Publication Data

Riess, Jonathan B.
  Political Ideals in Medieval Italian art.

    (Studies in fine arts. Iconography ; no. 1)
    "Revision of the author's thesis, Columbia University,
  1977"–
    Bibliography: p.
    Includes index.
    1. Mural painting and decoration, Italian—Italy—
  Perugia. 2. Mural painting and decoration, Medieval—
  Italy—Perugia. 3. Allegories. 4. Politics in art.
  5. Palazzo dei Priori (Perugia, Italy) 6. Perugia
  (Italy)—Palaces. I. Title. II. Series.

  ND2757.P4R5   751.7'3'0945651   81-12950
  ISBN 0-8357-1238-9   AACR2

Contents

List of Figures and Plates

Preface

This study is an iconographic examination of a cycle of murals in the Sala dei Notari of the Palazzo dei Priori in Perugia, dated 1297. The thirty-two murals, only a part of what was originally an even more extensive undertaking, are among the most imposing survivals of the political art of late medieval Italy. Several of the frescoes can be attributed to the Circle of Pietro Cavallini, others to artists of the Umbrian School.

The groundwork for the examination consists in establishing the general historical and cultural setting in Perugia. In the light of this setting, the murals can be seen as pronouncing the victory of the *popolani* and of republican institutions that arose through the evolution of the government during the last third of the Duecento. As control of civic patronage passed more directly into the hands of republican forces in the city, the ever more ambitious undertakings in secular art and architecture became charged with new political meanings. The fresco cycle is indeed the central and most unequivocal aspect of a unified program of administrative palace, cathedral, and fountain situated on the primary communal square of the city.

Each component of the mural decorations is treated separately, and each is related to complementary aspects of the contemporary political setting.

The first three groupings of frescoes, those drawn from the Old Testament, illustrate how the commune sought to ground its independent course in a theological statement that lent the gloss of a religious crusade to its policies and to the dedication of its citizens and rulers. The political mission of the State is equated with the sacred mission of Moses and Gideon. Political service is freed from evil and repressive implications by adopting several crucial tenets of the late thirteenth century Aristotelian revival: notably the belief that the State is natural, necessary, and beneficial, and that good citizenship is the highest expression of the "good life." Good citizenship, in its Christian-political transmutation, is put forth as a prerequisite for salvation.

Aesop murals provide a practical and popular underpinning for the more profound abstract political truths of the Biblical scenes. The manner in which these truths can be translated into a pragmatic statecraft is the chief motif of the fables. The significance of the scenes as a popular teaching or propagandistic-political medium in the proclamation of republican principles and of martial values is shown to derive from the contemporary status, or understanding, of animal fable and lore.

The final murals, a series of astrological representations, highlight the primary meaning of the preceding scenes by demonstrating that wise leadership and military prowess are the twin foundations of the successful State. The singling out of two planets associated with these ideals, Saturn and Jupiter, is a means of offering guardianship to the city in its efforts to create a utopian political life.

The concluding section of the study suggests that a sharper understanding of the frescoes can be achieved by defining some of the broad tendencies in the civic-political art from about 1100 to 1300. Civic-political art is that art which expresses the philosophy of the free city-state, the nature of its institutions, and the relationship between the citizen and the State. The Perugia murals represent a *summa* of the themes in the communal art during this period and are linked with several of the town hall decorative programs of the last decades of the thirteenth century.

Acknowledgments

For the development of this study, and for whatever contribution it might make to the study of art history, I owe the greatest debt to Professor James H. Beck, my teacher, guide, and friend. Without his encouragement, his prodding, his kindness and understanding, many of the ideas contained in the following work would have remained, in large measure, unrealized. My debt to Professor Beck goes beyond help offered in the research and writing of this book. Throughout my career at Columbia, and later, his interest in my work has been constant and strong. And for this too I should like to thank him here.

In addition to encouragement and sound advice the researcher must of course be provided with the means, as well as the environment, to pursue his research. Here I mention, in grateful appreciation, the support of a Fulbright Fellowship (1974-1975), a Whiting Fellowship from Columbia (1974-1975), and a Harvard Fellowship to work at I Tatti in Florence (1975-1976). At I Tatti I received inestimable assistance from Ms. Anna Terni, the librarian, and was the guest of a most considerate Director, Professor Craig Hugh Smyth, and his gracious wife, Mrs. Barbara Smyth. While in Italy, and especially during my regular vistis to Perugia, I was fortunate in finding a generous friend, Professor Roberto Abbondanza of the University of Perugia, who was of immense help in acquainting me with all aspects of the field of Perugian studies. For archival work at Perugia I must thank Dr. Gino Corti for his assistance.

I am also happy to acknowledge the valuable critical and stylistic advice of Professor Eugene Rice, Professor Richard Goldthwaite, Professor Howard Hibbard, and, most importantly, Professor David Rosand for examining the worth and logic of almost every element in the study.

But even with all these friends and helpers, not much could have been accomplished without the cheerful and enduring patience and the moral support of my parents, Chester L. Riess and Marion Riess, and of my wife, Michele Morgan.

1

Scope and Theme: an Introduction

The historian Peter Gay has written fairly recently on the problem of causation in the genesis of a work of art. Although the following passage from his study by no means represents a novel statement of the problem, I should like nevertheless to cite Gay's words for reasons that will be clear shortly. He writes,

> The complex of causal determination occasions no surprise when a work of art is crowded with meanings. For a viewer ignorant of the Fascist rebellion in Spain, the career of twentieth-century painting, and Picasso's ambivalence toward politics, art, and himself, *Guernica* is incomprehensible or, at the least, impoverished.[1]

Few works in the history of art, I imagine, can be said to spring from such incontestably political sources as *Guernica*. But what Gay says of the relation between modern political history and Picasso's painting has of course a far more general truth and application. The present study calls upon political and artistic evidence from the late thirteenth century in Italy to suggest the wide applicability of such perceptions. It will deal, specifically, with the sources and iconography of the cycle of frescoes in the Palazzo dei Priori in Perugia dated 1297.

The Perugia frescoes are, like *Guernica,* political in theme, and illustrate, as we would expect, not so much an individual artist's largely personal reactions to the confluences of his time, but rather, aspects of communal reactions. A further distinction concerns the question of causation. The frescoes are inextricably interwoven with the texture of the political culture of the age; unlike *Guernica,* they cannot be said to derive solely from any clearly defined historic events.[2]

The general nature of that cultural setting may be summarized as follows. During the late thirteenth and early fourteenth centuries important changes occurred in the political thinking of several of the North and Central Italian communes. This development was concerned with the mythical and popular foundations of the state, the re-definition of good government, the character of the ideal ruler, the nature and justification of his power, and the proper functions, powers, responsibilities, and rewards of the governed. It is a development that results in a new order, one distinguished by an unusually intense conjunction of religious and secular modes of thought—good citizenship, for example, becomes a pre-requisite for salvation.

These new currents, interests, and predilections were not synthesized—at least not explicitly—in the work of any single thinker, so that we must call upon evidence from a wide range of fields in order to reconstruct the components of what can be viewed as the heightened civic consciousness of the time. And it is precisely because of the changing and ill-defined political setting of the late thirteenth century that this study assumes a special significance. Ernst Kantorowicz has written that "things difficult and circumstantial to describe in words are sometimes more easily and succinctly expressed by an iconographical formula."[3] The truth of this statement is perhaps especially evident in the study of the great civic monuments of the thirteenth century. At a moment when the actuality lacked the great ordering and theoretical mind of a Bartolus of Sassoferrato (1314-1357) or of a Marsilius of Padua (d. 1342), the secular decorations for the civic palaces and cathedrals of the communes most "succinctly" express and order the major thrusts of a charged and rapidly changing political environment.

Among these decorative schemes, the thirty-two murals in the Sala dei Notari in the Palazzo dei Priori in Perugia are the most significant civic monuments of the age and stand as the clearest and most formidable embodiment of a new political orientation. The communal propaganda so forthrightly expressed in the Perugia frescoes marks an important development both in the history of art and in the history of politics, a cross-fertilization of immense consequence. Indeed, these frescoes can be said to rank alongside the far better known and more fully studied decorations of Ambrogio Lorenzetti in the Palazzo Pubblico in Siena (c. 1337-1339). These so-called scenes of the *Effects of Good and Bad Government* were thought to be the most notable expression of political ideas in medieval Italian art, but they are rivaled by the Perugia frescoes.

Given the importance of the Perugia frescoes and of the related civic projects of the thirteenth century, it is rather difficult to understand why no general history of the political art of the communes has yet been written. Several specialized studies exist, but all treat the later and more developed political art of the fourteenth and fifteenth centuries and, with only one or two exceptions, none deals with the ways in which the political content of the art represents a transformation of the historical setting.[4] (References to these studies are cited appropriately throughout this work.) It is also curious that in spite of this lack of critical study in early communal or political art, a determined effort has been made to demonstrate the existence of what I believe to be a far more tenuous connection between the artistic style of the late thirteenth century and the growth of communal self-awareness.[5]

The paucity of research in this sphere is in no sense redressed by more encompassing studies of the secular art of late medieval Italy. Here too the bibliography is hardly rich.[6] Quite apart from the intrinsic worth of an examination of the Perugia murals, then, the more general state of art-historical scholarship points to the need for such a study.

The history of research concerning the murals in the Sala dei Notari is dealt with in the Appendix (p. 91). The little that has been written almost exclusively treats the problem of attribution. The "Circle of Pietro Cavallini," or the master himself, is the agreed upon attribution. Yet the iconography of the cycle has hitherto been discussed in only the most summary fashion: in fact, little more than a description of the subjects of the scenes constitutes the "iconographic" investigation in most cases. And the accepted identifications are not without problems, for at least six of the scenes have been incorrectly interpreted.

The Sala dei Notari (Plate I), the site of the frescoes, is a vast space on the first story of the Palazzo dei Priori. There are at present three entrances into the room, only one of which is a feature of the original or Duecento fabric, that on the north wall which opens onto a porch facing what is now designated as the Piazza IV Novembre (Plate II).[7] The room is rectangular and is twenty-seven meters in length, fourteen meters in width, and thirteen meters in height. It deviates slightly from a perfect rectangle, as the south wall is one meter longer than the north wall.

The ceiling is supported by the eight elliptical arches that bear the murals. The arches spring from points that correspond with the tops of the windows on the east wall. The spandrels of the arches are decorated on both sides with the murals, with the exception of the southernmost arch which is painted only on the northern side. Each of the scenes is about two meters long and from one to two meters high. Aside from the contemporaneous *stemmi* painted on the arches, most of the coats-of-arms were added in the sixteenth and seventeenth centuries and appear on the south and west walls.[8] The frescoes were uncovered between 1860 and 1865.[9] Recently, Dr. Francesco Santi, *soprintendente* of art and architecture in Perugia, supervised the restoration of the works.[10]

As for the placement and subjects of the frescoes in the Sala dei Notari, twenty-eight of the frescoes occupy the spandrels of the eight elliptical arches in the hall, three are on the north wall, and one is found above the windows between the fifth and sixth arches (counting from the south wall; see Figure 1). The subjects of the decorations are as follows: four scenes from the stories of Moses and Gideon, three illustrations from the story of Adam and Eve, three representations drawn from the story of Cain and Abel, a scene of Saint George and the Dragon, eleven representations of the fables of Aesop, and eleven astrological representations (at least two additional astrological works have been lost).

As far as the documented history of the frescoes is concerned, there can be little doubt that the works were completed in 1297. Progress on the construction of the Palazzo dei Priori, as well as a documented allusion of 1297 relating to the *stemmi* to be placed in the hall, point to this date.[11] This conviction, however, is based entirely on circumstantial evidence; no surviving contemporary reference to the narrative murals has been discovered.[12]

2

The Cultural and Historical Setting of the Perugia Frescoes

The embellishment of the Palazzo dei Priori was related to a nexus of elements in the political culture of Perugia. If the decorations are viewed as a direct outgrowth of the political situation of the period, then their subject matter as well as the problem of why the works were commissioned in 1297 would appear to be readily understandable. While I do not propose to explore, beyond occasional reference, the social and institutional underpinnings of other major civic decorative projects of the period, I believe that this approach should be the starting point for the study of these related works as well. The fact that the mood and disposition of the civic society underwent similar transformations throughout Northern and Central Italy during the late thirteenth century should alert us to the fact that the many civic monuments of the age may have sprung from analogous origins.[1] The model for this approach is Wilde's study of the construction and decoration of the Hall of the Great Council in Florence.[2] As Wilde isolated the salient political and historical conditions that underlay the Florentine project, so I wish to achieve a similar end at the outset of this study of the Perugia frescoes.

The Palazzo dei Priori in Perugia stands on the southern side of what is presently named the Piazza IV Novembre (Plate II).[3] This enormous structure, one of the most impressive examples of the civic architecture of the Middle Ages, is situated at the center of the major architectural complex in the city, on a site that since the Etruscan age has been the focal point of the life of the city.[4] We shall see shortly how the physical situation of the frescoes, placed as they are in so centrally important a location and executed at a time when the city had a clear sense of the meaning and possible symbolic import of its appearance and history, lent a kind of inevitability to the themes of the frescoes in the council hall.

The relevant aspects of the building history of the palace will be discussed in the following chapter. I note for the present that the structure was begun in 1293 and was completed in 1575.[5] The main body was constructed during the initial phases of work—1293 to 1297 and 1333 to 1358. An important aspect of each of these phases is a major decorative project. During the first period of construction the Sala dei Notari was frescoed, and during the second period the sculptures of the portal on the long, eastern flank of the palace were executed.[6]

We are of course concerned here with the initial decorative undertaking. Yet the fact that there is a complementary program of embellishments for the later work on the building is in itself of some moment. Together with the local Fontana Maggiore of 1278 (Plate III), the murals and sculptures for the town hall form a remarkable and unparalleled continuum of major secular monuments for the last quarter of the thirteenth century through the middle of the fourteenth century. The effort to account for this phenomenon will be one aspect of the following discussion of the political situation in the city during late Duecento.

A brief bibliographic comment is needed first. The Umbrian communes that composed the Papal State of the thirteenth century, and of which Perugia was undoubtedly the leading member, have been the subject of scant, now largely dated, study.[7] This generalization is true not only for the social, political, and economic history of the papal towns, but for the examination of the art and culture as well. Primarily for this reason any study that attempts to redress the gross imbalance of interest in favor of more celebrated centers, such as Rome and Florence, begins almost of necessity from a somewhat defensive standpoint. Perugian studies, while hardly an exception to the weak scholarship in the field, are in fact distinguished by two fine, although old, general histories: Pellini (1664), and Heywood (1910).[8] More recently, Sarah Rubin Blanshei has offered a detailed examination of the struggles between the *popolani* and the *magnati* in the late thirteenth and early fourteenth centuries in Perugia.[9]

A reading of Pellini and Heywood and the basic modern studies is sufficient to discover the fundamental ways in which Perugia followed the course of the more carefully and thoroughly examined towns of the thirteenth century.[10] In a more general sense, I might add, even the most cursory study of the political history of the period suggests that the analogy often made between the diversity of the institutional development of the communes and of the ancient Greek city-states has been overdrawn. The close political and economic ties as well as the competitiveness among the Italian towns, in addition to the presence of a professional class of short-term rulers and judges, suggests that a roughly parallel development among the communes should be anticipated. The manifestation of this parallel institutional development is apparent in the construction of town halls for common organs of government in approximately the same periods for most of the towns.[11]

What is important in the present investigation is one distinguishing theme in Perugian history during the thirteenth century, a theme that helps to account for the subjects of the murals in the Sala dei Notari and that might also help to explain the general, highly evolved level of secular art in the city: Perugia, although a leading member of the Papal State, was largely a nominal participant, and she chose to follow, for the most part, an independent course. An important consequence of such independence was the extraordinary attention given to the concept and definition of civic liberty and to the evils of tyranny, both of internal and external origin.

Bartolus of Sassoferrato, the great Perugian political theorist and jurist, wrote in about 1340 that one of the major motifs in the history of the city was the fact that *quod civitas Perusiana non subsit Ecclesiae ned imperio,* a statement which must be considered correct from perhaps the early 1100's.[12] But the assertion is accurate not only in the narrow legalistic sense that the city was freed by privilege from both the emperor and the pope at this early date, but also by virtue of specific actions and policies. Thoroughly pragmatic policies, justified only by frequent reference to, the primary importance of the freedom of the city and its citizens, distinguished the conduct of the city. If Garrett Mattingly's description of Bartolus as the first jurist to encourage the "interest of his practical-minded students in the actual law of their contemporary world" is correct, then surely Bartolus owes somewhat more than has generally been acknowledged to his native city.[13] The fact that the political milieu of thirteenth and early fourteenth century Perugia generated this first true advocate of communal republicanism—Marsilius of Padua notwithstanding—is in itself indicative of the same highly active political society that also generated the frescoes in the Sala dei Notari.

The pragmatic and vigorous political life of the city may be described further as follows. Although Perugia was often one of the closest and most dependable supporters of the pope within the Papal State—a loyalty and devotion demonstrated by her preponderant contribution of soldiers and funds to many papal causes, a devotion rewarded in part by the frequent choice of the city for papal conclaves[14]—Perugia not infrequently opposed papal policies; moreover, it enacted strong anti-clerical legislation, actions to which the pope more than once responded with excommunication.[15]

Such independence was of course possible not because it flowed theoretically from any political philosophy of the sort later codified by Bartolus, and in which cities that acted like Perugia were designated "empires in miniature,"[16] but because of the extraordinary power and wealth of the city. As early as 1250 Perugia was a free policy maker of an importance recognized in many ways, perhaps most clearly in that she was often called upon to mediate disputes among other communes.[17] And by the late 1290s her power and influence were such that one of the major ends of Boniface's reign was the break-up of the alliance among Perugia, Narni, Todi, and Spoleto.[18] Boniface's generally liberal policy toward the communes was obviously abused by Perugia, a city only second in wealth and population to Rome within the Papal State.[19]

Before Bartolus the broadest characterization of the self-sufficiency of the city is found in the first codification of the communal statutes and in the contemporary iconographical program of the Fontana Maggiore (Plate III) of the late 1270s. This concordance of statutes and fountain was not accidental; its causal origins will be examined shortly. Suffice to say at the moment, the grouping of the monument with the statutes is lent rather secure justification by the fact that the fountain itself soon assumed a pseudo-legalistic function. This function is apparent in the citation the fountain received in the first revision of the legal code in 1342.[20]

The sculptures of the fountain describe the particular relation between Perugia and the Church and set this relation within an historical and Biblical framework of encyclopedic proportions. On the upper basin of the fountain the complex and close-knit interactions of Old Testament figures, personifications of *Roma* and *Roma Ecclesia* and *Augusta Perusia,* effigies of the contemporary *capitano del popolo* and *podestà,* and heroic figures from Perugian history and legend, glorify the city and the benefits that it confers upon its citizens.[21] The importance of the Church is affirmed only insofar as it grants a fiat to the civic accomplishment. The ecclesiastical imagery on the fountain is in fact, remarkably scant. The clear emphasis is on local imagery and the transmutation of Biblical themes into civic-political ones. (This transmutation will be treated again later, because the same kind of adaptations are to be found in the frescoes in the Sala dei Notari.) The figure of *Roma Ecclesia* alone stands as a shorthand designation of the precedence of the Church. But opposed as it is by many secular personifications of a Perugian political meaning, the figure of the Church seems to lack any transcendent import. The sculptures offer a kind of mechanism for Perugian self-assertion. Bartolus's belief that the free city should act as an "empire in miniature" is here expressed in art, and is amplified through a theological and historical justification and foundation. It would seem also reasonable to assume that one important and specific aim of the fountain sculptures was to inspire good citizenship by demonstrating the legendary importance of the city and its economic wealth (one relief represents Chiusi, the granary of the city, another represents Lake Trasimene, the fishery), and by representing images of exemplary citizens. (In general, the emphasis given to how the communal art was meant to impress other cities has been overdrawn and too little attention has been given to the more immediate communal world.)

Although the civic statutes of 1279 did not touch upon the conduct of affairs with other cities, they confirmed the ascendent position of the government in internal as well as in external matters. The disassociation of the Church from the workaday life of the city was clearly a leading aspect of the political self-assertion of the time.[22] The freedom of the commune, placed within a setting of universal, divine, and human history in the program of the Fontana Maggiore, was thus countenanced and advanced by a contemporary legal confirmation.

Two other subjects relating to the late thirteenth-century history of the city may now be treated: the general physical evolution and embellishment of the city during the last quarter of the thirteenth century, and the accompanying institutional evolution. Much of the development of the city during the last third of the thirteenth century was surely due to its growth in population and in wealth. But the form that this development assumed points unmistakably to the manipulation of the civic environment as an expression of communal principles. The proclivity to use art, in this instance, the Fontana Maggiore, to encapsulate political ideals will be seen again at the end of the century in the Palazzo dei Priori murals.

The center of Perugia presented an extraordinarily simple, uncluttered, and rational arrangement, an urban space that was essentially unchanged from the design of the ancient city.[23] The walls of the Etruscan and Roman town remained the formal boundaries through the Duecento. Only during the first quarter of the fourteenth century did extensive construction of new walls begin.[24] The five principal gates of the town were also of Etruscan origin.[25] During the 1260s a street was laid from each of the gates to the central piazza, later the site of the Palazzo dei Priori. The five streets, as Heywood has characterized them, may be thought of as the radii of a single circle with the communal square as its center.[26]

As suburban areas spread beyond the walled center of the city a distinction persisted in Perugia, as in several other towns, between the *città vecchia* and the *terra nuova* or *borghi*.[27] Although this distinction was likely drawn primarily for administrative purposes, it does speak also of the burgeoning sense of urban self-consciousness for which we will find evidence elsewhere as well. The precise implications of what might be simply a semantic distinction cannot, however, be determined. At the same moment that the communal properties in the ancient center were being further developed and embellished there was an effort to draw the outlying districts into the daily functioning of the city.[28] It is possible that the decoration of the central square and the construction on it of new symbols of communal power, such as the Palazzo dei Priori, were thought necessary because the city was now making an overt attempt to draw an increasingly dispersed entity around a better defined core. Most revealing is that, although the new palace was constructed in the historic locus of political power in Perugia, many ceremonial events involving the citizenry were moved to squares in other parts of the city.[29] In this context the contemporaneous interest in establishing communal origins[30] appears as an element of the same civic tendency to express shared ideals. This developed urban and historical self-awareness was one essential pre-condition for the commissioning of the subjects depicted in the Sala dei Notari.

If the basic design of the central part of the city remained essentially unaltered during the thirteenth century, the era, as already remarked, was nevertheless one of expansion and of construction for Perugia no less than for other thriving communes. Briefly, the first phase of the construction of the Palazzo dei Priori, 1293 to 1297, coincides with a second period of noteworthy development within the city. The first period of urban undertakings extended from about 1260 to 1280. Associated with each of these phases of development is a changed institutional and political context that helps to explain the distinctive nature that the two periods assumed.

The evolution of the political life throughout the century exhibits a fairly continuous growth in the representative nature of governmental institutions.[31] A not unimportant aspect of this political change was the increasing refinement with which civic construction and embellishment were dealt. As the organs of government that regulated urban change became more representative, so did the intensity and range of construction and decoration grow.

The earliest surviving records of the commune date from the middle of the eleventh century and relate to the submissions of neighboring towns.[32] The first document of institutional reference—that regarding the creation of the office of the *podestà* in about 1170—indicates that a fairly advanced bureaucratic evolution accompanied this early importance and power of the city in the region.[33] Little is certain regarding the beginnings of the commune but it would appear that the city was governed initially by a group of ten consuls and a general council of citizens that had little real power and that assembled principally for ceremonial purposes.[34]

These observations are germane in several ways. First, the fact that Perugia was traditionally independant and free in both a legal and practical sense from papal and imperial control appears now as the logical consequence of a long and uninterrupted political evolution. Unlike Padua, for example, where a period of heightened civic consciousness followed an era of tyrannical rule, Perugian chauvinism was a product of a continuous tradition of liberty and independence.[35]

A second and more immediate sense in which the political changes noted earlier are important is the bearing they have on urban development. One of the functions that accrued to the *podestà,* perhaps to the loss of the consuls, was the task of general urban administration. As defined and ordered in the statutes of 1279, the *podestà* was charged with the care and repair of the city towers, fountains, castles, and walls.[36] That such tasks were assigned initially to the consuls can only be hypothesized. The fact that the Nine Governors of Siena, a group of approximately the same structure as the consuls of Perugia, were concerned with civic construction and maintenance throughout the thirteenth century lends some support to such an interpretation.[37]

Whatever might have been the official distribution of responsibilities in the two cities, however, the general council of citizens played at least a formal or symbolic role in many decisions involving such seemingly simple duties as repair and construction work.[38] Indeed, Zdekauer is perhaps correct in the belief that the two most important obligations of government related to military and urban questions.[39] And because of this it was surely useful that the illusion of direct control of civic development be maintained as the powers of the *podestà* were extended. As we shall see later, the actual control of communal construction quickly returned to a more representative institution than that of the *podestà*.

The creation of the position of *capitano del popolo* between 1250 and 1255, and the social and political energies that were released partly as a result of this action, also had enormous consequences in shaping the physical evolution of the city.[40] Thus, during the last half of the century the city instituted many innovations that weakened oligarchic control, and during this same period there occurred the two most substantial phases of change in the appearance of the city; the first phase, again, extending from about 1260 to 1280, the second from about 1290 to 1300.

The office of *capitano del popolo* in Perugia, as elsewhere, represented, in Hyde's words, "the coping stone of the new structure of *società d'armi* and trade guilds that emerged in the city during the first half of the thirteenth century."[41] The principal duty of the captain was to act as a liason between the re-invigorated corporations and the *podestà*. The office in large measure simply legitimized what by mid-century had become a *de facto* situation: the middle class was the predominant force within the city.[42] So weakened was the old power structure that by the last third of the century its ultimate collapse may be implied in a revised oath for the *podestà*. No longer did he swear fealty to the *Constitutum*, but rather he swore loyalty to the *Statuta Communis et Popoli e reformationes Artium*.[43]

The power of the captain, again as elsewhere, was soon usurped by the more directly representative consuls of the arts and priors. How this shift of power came about is not too clear because the early history of the two groups of officials is most uncertain. The first known reference to the office of prior, the leader of a corporation, is dated 1259.[44] Although the duties of these new civic functionaries were not institutionalized until 1303, together with the consuls whose main roles they appear to have paralleled, power had most assuredly passed into the hands of the middle class. This process of ever-widening the base of power reached its highest point during the last quarter of the century, a time in which the priors became in everything but official sanction the supreme magistrates of the city.

Indication of the nearly complete overthrow of the *magnati* and of the institutions that had served their interests is the steadily increasing size of the major government councils and committees, which thus became more truly representative.[45] As might have been expected, strong anti-*magnati* legislation was enacted during the 1290s by these more open associations.[46]

After about 1260 the administration of the city, in particular matters relating to construction, cleaning, and repair, came more directly under the jurisdiction of the citizens as the *podestà* surrendered some of this authority to representatives of the guilds.[47] But even before this transfer of power a significant change is apparent in the form or character of civic programs, a change that coincides with what we have already seen to be a moment of widening the foundation of rule. Among the first acts of the *podestà* after 1250 was the opening of discussions relating to the construction of the Fontana Maggiore[48] and the intitiation of a system of coinage.[49] (Perugia was among the first cities to have such a system.) The two acts reflect not only the growing commercial wealth and importance of the city but suggest also a new concern with the symbols as well as the substance of power. On the coins of this early period there were depicted San Ercolano, patron saint of the city, and the griffin, symbol of Perugia. The Saint's life of civic commitment and sacrifice was perhaps read as an exemplum.[50] Interpreted in such fashion, the coin images epitomize an essential didactic function of the later sculpture of the Fontana Maggiore.

A crucial element in the image of communal justification and defense on the Fontana Maggiore is the place of Moses as a kind of titular head of the government and as an emblem of the independent theocratic foundation of the state.[51] Situated among the effigies of the civic officials, with an inscription that underlines his own position as leader, the statue of the patriarch lends Biblical support to the claims of communal political power and, by inference, to freedom from papal and imperial control.

The establishment of a system of coinage and the first discussions concerning the fountain came within what has already been described as the earliest notable phase of urban development during the Duecento. Apart from planning the Fontana Maggiore, the period is marked by wall repair and decoration, street and square paving, the construction of fountains in the major districts, and the earliest references to the building of the Palazzo del Priori.[52] The language of these first notices concerning the palace is most informative. The relevant documents are classic examples of the sort first isolated by Braunfels. The argument for the project is advanced largely on the assumption that a splendid new civic hall would bring honor and fame to the city.[53] This manner of conceiving the palace should not be surprising, however, as it is of a piece with the manifest patriotic, almost evangelical function of the coin imagery and of the fountain decorations.

The painting of representations of the Madonna and Child and of scenes from the lives of local saints on the city walls and fortifications is perhaps the most noteworthy innovation among these early programs.[54] Such a development illustrates how the scope of old forms of civic construction and maintenance was widened to incorporate a more pronounced emblematic communal meaning. The sculptural decorations of the fountain might of course be cited once more as the most unified and powerful example of this new propensity to advertise civic pride.

The cityscape of Perugia was changing in at least one other respect during this period. The last third of the century witnessed the construction of a large number of churches. This phenomenon, while not reflecting any consciously pursued civic policy, was surely an expression of the same prosperity and self-confidence responsible for the newly aroused interest in the repair and general restoration of the city.[55]

Before turning to the second epoch of civic development, one note regarding the local university might be cited to summarize the new communal spirit as well as the general nature of the initial stage of about 1260 to 1280. Although the custom of inviting scholars to Perugia began early in the century, well before the official foundation of the university in 1297, by the 1290s the scholars of the city came to serve as communal historians.[56] The interest of the government in an expanding university is of course not without precedent,[57] but the encouragement given to the concept of communal history as a propagandistic tool is apparently unique and is related to the same chauvinistic roots from which much of the urban development sprang.

This brief era of institutional and urban change was in some measure possible only because it was an era of peace as well.[58] But during the early 1280s peace within the Papal State ended and, for Perugia, this new decade of conflict coincided with a hiatus in the initiation of civic projects. By the early 1290s, however, the Perugians, fresh from diplomatic and military triumphs, re-dedicated themselves to the embellishment of their city. The revived interest is apparent in the resumption of the routine work of maintenance and repair and in the grander scale and richer variety of communal projects.

In every facet of the life of the city during the last decade of the century, construction and cultural programs projected earlier were now begun or rapidly developed. The building of the Palazzo dei Priori, only broached during the 1270s, was completed within an extraordinarily brief period of time. The university, which was evolving in a rather ad hoc fashion between 1260 and 1280, became a fully functioning institution lacking only the formal and official approval of papal accreditation.[59] The study of early communal history, initiated two decades before, was granted a mythic dimension through the composition of an epic and self-congratulatory poem entitled the *Eulistea,* describing the legendary foundation and early history of the commune. The work was commissioned by the government, an act that demonstrates a continued interest in the exploitation of an imaginatively re-created past.[60] Another and more mundane aspect of this same period of civic enhancement is that whereas in 1268 the roads of only two of the five districts were paved, in 1298 it was resolved to pave all the streets in the city.[61]

Other activities, unanticipated during the earlier phase of change, may be cited. First, the greater commercial importance and size of the city is reflected in the need for a new granary, which was built between 1295 and 1298.[62] A second major undertaking, one that perhaps has more obvious significance in the context of the varied manifestations of the civic spirit of the period, was the beginning of a new church for the city's patron saint, San Ercolano.[63] Throughout the thirteenth century the most important communal cere-monies, apart from the submissions of conquered cities, were those dedicated to the Saint. Expressions of devotion to San Ercolano were also the primary channel for patriotic demonstrations. A new church dedicated to the Saint is both evidence of the prosperity of the city and of the love for propagandistic display.

The interest in the ceremonial and artistic symbolism of the city is reflected in a quite different sense in two important aspects of the communal legislation of the period. First, rigid regulations were drawn up in the 1290s regarding where and by whom the emblems and standards of the city and its major parties might be shown.[64] A second relevant theme in the ordinances is the many controls that were placed on the ceremonial games and rituals of knights of the city.[65] The city apparently was endeavoring to control and monopolize all forms of public display.

The passion for civic display was certainly an inspiration for the enlargment of the Cathedral in 1300. In language that recalls the references to the Palazzo dei Priori in 1279, the following declaration was made, in the name of the citizens, regarding the Cathedral:

> Cercando il Commune di Perugia con ogni solecitudine i decoro della città, sia dei Palazzi del Commune e del Piazza, è conveniente che la communità nostra, la quale fra tutte le altre d'Italia si distinse per la serenità della sua fede, debba far bella la Chiesa Maggiore dove ogni giorno si celebrano i divini misteri. Per la qual cosa stabiliamo, che il Commune di Perugia debba edificcone della fondamente la sua Cattedrale, à lode del nome di Dio e dei glorisi Martiti Lorenzo ed Ercolano ai quali fu gia intitolata la detta Chiesa Maggiore.[66]

Here are isolated some fundamental aspects of the communal consciousness of the late Duecento in Perugia: the intermingling and mutual reinforcement of religious and civic ideals, the desire to honor the community through the honoring of local saints, and finally the synthesis and embodiment of all these elements in an artistic or architectural undertaking.

The general explanation for the highly evolved sense of civic pride and loyalty during the 1290s was the success of the challenge to oligarchic power. The local pride achieved its most intense expression during the decade when matters relating to civic beautification and maintenance came more directly within the control of the citizens. With the more broadly representative institutional organization of Perugia, we should expect a greater interest in the encouragement of communal undertakings and in public pronouncements of shared ideas.

That the Palazzo dei Priori held a special place among the various communal pronouncements of the decade is evident not only because of its size and architectural dignity but also because it was the first project to be started and the first to be completed. Such priority is even apparent in the above-cited statement of 1300 concerning the Cathedral. Of central interest here also is the construction and decoration of the palace. The broadening of the political administration had reached its greatest advance in this period, and the palace was the most popular and appealing symbol and artistic consummation of the strength, independence, and prosperity of the citizens.

3

The Artistic Transformation of Political Life and Thought

The Palazzo dei Priori and its setting within the city will now be examined in some detail. We shall see shortly that the political content of the frescoes in the Sala dei Notari is functionally related to the communal purposes inherent in the placement and design of the palace. The early history of the buildings on the piazza in fact indicates that the frescoes were to be one element in a large program that included palaces, churches, and a public square.

The Setting of the Palazzo dei Priori

As observed earlier, the piazza was a sharply distinguished space within the city from the time of its Etruscan origins (Plate II, Figure 2). The five converging roads leading from the gates to the square that were constructed during the communal epoch served only to enhance the already predominant role of the area in the design and life of the town. Although encroachments on the square after the thirteenth century have reduced somewhat the extent of the original space, and other centers of political, economic and ecclesiastical activity have developed within the city,[1] the piazza remains one of the most impressive medieval civic survivals in Italy. The very designation of the square during the late thirteenth century is itself suggestive of the special significance of the zone: the piazza was generally designated the *Isola del Comune*.[2] For a city of Perugia's population during the thirteenth century such an ascendent position for one space appears to have been without parallel. Perhaps the main square in Todi is at least comparable but Todi was neither the size nor the importance of Perugia.[3]

On the southern side of the square stood the nucleus of the Palazzo dei Priori (see Figure 2.1). Situated within the space of the then open ground floor loggia was the central market.[4] Attached to the west side of the palace was the Church of San Severo (Figure 2.2). (This building was incorporated within the palace in the fourteenth century.[5]) On the western end of the piazza is the Palazzo del Vescovo (Figure 2.3). (The present appearance of the building is only an imperfect image of the Duecento structure.[6]) Linked to the northwest corner of the Bishop's Palace was a tower (Figure 2.4) and adjoining this was a vaulted passageway (Figure 2.5) that led to the Palazzo dei Consoli on the northwestern corner of the square (Figure 2.6).[7] Above the vault was a large council hall, referred to as the *palatium novum*, which was apparently treated as an independent administrative center, although it was accessible only through the Palazzo dei Consoli. A large stair ramp set sideways to the square (Figure 2.7) provided entry into the *piano nobile* of the Consul's Palace.[8] These stairs surely helped to give the square a greater uniformity, as they balanced the stairs that led into the Palazzo dei Priori on the opposide side of the Piazza.[9] The sense of public space flowing into the communal structures must have been more readily perceived before the stair ramp was removed.

Attached to the eastern façade of the Consul's Palace was the Canonica (Figure 2.8) which was joined, in turn, to the Duomo (Figure 2.9). The Cathedral of Saints Ercolano and Lorenzo, as the structure was known before its transformation in the early fourteenth century, was only about one fourth its present size, but the Cathedral was, nonetheless, the prominent feature in the medieval communal complex.[10] Accentuation of its importance was offered by the cylindrical campanile, the highest tower in the city, which was at this time a part of the Cathedral fabric.[11] At the base of the campanile were stone steps sheltered by a loggia. Here the magistrates gathered when the *parlementum* assembled.[12] The eastern end of the square was open, as it is now. Finally, the Fontana Maggiore (Figure 2.10) is at the approximate center of the grouping, slightly favoring the Cathedral side. Because of the smaller size of the surrounding structures and the greater openness of the square, the fountain was thus more dominant a monument in 1300 than it is at present, and more apparent too was the sense that the fountain provided the public, iconographic centerpiece for the square.

The square has changed much from its Duecento appearance through later construction and natural disaster; a few of these transformations have been noted above. The impression of a unified grouping must, in any event, have been far more pronounced for reasons also mentioned earlier: notably the stair ramps on either side of the square, the clearer focus around the fountain, and the more uniform scale of the buildings. The temptation to regard the assemblage as an example of proto-Renaissance planning should, with one or two qualifications, however, be resisted.[13] This point is a crucial one in calculating the level of communal awareness during the late thirteenth century, a problem of the first order in the effort to define the kind of self-image from which arises the themes of the palace frescoes. No more certain evidence could be found of the translation of a chauvinistic preoccupation into art than in the conscious manipulation of the major civic and ecclesiastical structures of the city for symbolic purposes.

Perugia, like most of the major Umbrian towns, is built on an irregular outcropping. The natural impulse to establish a primary space as a response to such topological disorder is easily understood. In fact, the orientation of the thirteenth century nucleus of the Palazzo dei Priori is itself to be accounted for in part by the ridge-like topography of the central area of the city.[14] The short, piazza side of the palace was almost of necessity the main façade. A second point contradicting the belief that the square is an example of controlled rather than organic or pragmatic growth is the fact that Perugia was originally a fortified Etruscan town, and thus the most easily defended space within the city naturally was predominant.[15]

But perhaps an even more serious, and surely more frequent error than this imposition of proto-Renaissance ideals, is the effort to discover some political meaning in the fact that the Cathedral and the civic palace are on the same square, unlike the more typical Tuscan pattern of a separate center around each of the buildings.[16] Such reasoning denies these same topological exigencies that were imposed on the builders of Umbrian cities before the original towns had grown sufficiently beyond the perimeters of the "historic" nucleus to permit the establishment of new foci elsewhere.

The problem, however, is more subtle than thus far indicated; there is evidence that does suggest a regard for, and a sensitivity to, a planned and meaningful interaction of buildings and fountain. The plain fact that the sculptural program of the fountain included local references is revealing in itself. For although fountains are frequent features in urban spaces of Umbrian towns,[17] none of the earlier examples includes the clearly emblematic decorations of the Fontana Maggiore. With the Perugia monument it is apparent that something is intended beyond the simple and traditional implication of the life-sustaining role of the government as the bringer of water to the citizens.[18] Further, none of these earlier examples is of the size of the Perugia fountain, nor are any placed with such deliberate regard for their setting. These last points indicate that although the pre-eminence of the square is admittedly unrelated to any determined and overt planning scheme, it is nonetheless possible that the nature of the construction on the square demonstrates an awareness of the symbolic-propagandistic possiblities of the setting.

The most important confirmation of this view is that the history of the complex in the late thirteenth century reveals a systematic and calculated unfolding of an overall scheme. A second supporting point is the design of the palace, which, to an extraordinary degree for the age, expresses through the iconography of the architecture and through the sculptural embellishment an appreciation of the possible emblematic uses of a communal structure. The palace, in short, serves a function similar to that of the fountain. Both these points will be developed below.

A revealing aspect of the design of the assemblage is that a primary entrance to the Cathedral, in addition to the traditional one on the western façade, is the portal on the side facing the square. The articulation of the Cathedral wall on the piazza is in harmonious relationship with the façade of the Palazzo dei Priori and differs from the articulation of the rest of the Cathedral.[19] This departure from conventional church architecture is evidence of the desire to contribute to the creation of an integrated totality of structures.

The Design of the Palazzo dei Priori

The following discussion of the design of the palace will center around the question of how the structure realizes or subsumes certain authentic transformations of political ideals. Ventures such as this into architectural iconography are fraught with problems.[20] Nonetheless, one can observe in the form and embellishment of the building communally-charged meanings responding to a new and heightened awareness of the citizen's relationship to his government.

The Duecento section of the palace is but a fragment of the present massive structure, which is largely the product of additions made in the fourteenth and fifteenth centuries. On the short, piazza side of the palace, the main face before the expansion of the succeeding century, three windows rather than the present five were the coordinates of the façade. (See reconstruction, Fig. 3.) On the long side, that facing what has subsequently developed into the main artery of the city—now the Corso Vanucci—ten windows rather than the present sixteen defined the limits of the structure.[21] (A distinct line marking the termination of the thirteenth century fabric can still be seen in the masonry.) The upper two stories of the building were built above what was once an open ground-floor loggia. Placed against the short, closed side of the palace was a double ramp staircase. At the top of this grand approach is the present porch from which the main portal opens directly into the council hall.

Any impression of heaviness and compactness is relieved by light, florid triforium windows, and by the coloristic contrasts between the *pietra rossa* and the more dominant shades of gray and white.[22] The impression of simple and unembellished bulk is further enlivened by the decorative battlements.

The effect presented by the original piazza façade was likely that of a modest and steep rectangular block that was strikingly distinguished from the attached church of S. Severo. The present Palazzo del Capitano in Todi offers perhaps the closest surviving impression of the original palace. The chronologies of the two structures are, however, too vague to permit theories as to which might represent the formative influence.[23] The sense of an interrelation between the two palaces is further strengthened by the parallels between the design and decorative schemes of the two main council halls. One is tempted to ascribe such parallels to the strong political ties between the two cities.[24] Such hypotheses are of course tenuous, but Perugia and Todi together formed one of the several stylistic centers in Umbria, and the design relationships between the palaces are but one expression of a far more thorough-going artistic interchange.[25]

An important parallel between the Palazzo dei Priori and another contemporary structure might also be attributed in part to a political source. Judging from pictorial and descriptive evidence, the Senator's Palace of 1299 in Rome was, like the Perugia and Todi palaces, a simple rectangular block set on an open loggia with a prominent exterior ramp leading directly into the main council hall.[26] Furthermore, there are decorative links among the three structures. The adaptation of the Perugia-Todi model may be explained in part by the fact that Boniface VIII, who commissioned the Rome palace, would naturally wish his architects to look first at the monuments in the towns of two of his most important allies. That the Senator's Palace was part of a general program of artistic undertakings connected with the Jubilee and that one goal of the celebrations was to strengthen the political and spiritual bonds among the papal cities, would appear to underscore the appropriateness of such an architectural choice. The profusion of papal imagery, and of portraits in particular, throughout the Papal State during the reign of Boniface is proof enough of the close tie at this time between art and the pope's attempt to enhance and broadcast his position—or political importance—among the Umbrian communes.[27]

To understand something more of the emblematic meaning of what can now be considered the Palazzo dei Priori type, we might look briefly at one coeval architectural antithesis, the Palazzo della Signoria in Florence. The cyclopean rusticated masonry of this other major palace of the age, and the general and frequently noted fortress-like appearance of the structure, provides a striking contrast to the more decorative masonry and to the sense of openness and ease of entry into the council hall that are suggested by the monumental exterior ramp and centralized portal at Perugia. Florence, no less than Perugia, was an aspiring republic, so that such stylistic polarities have very little relation to the structure of government in the two cities. Perhaps the differing forms of the palaces are more closely related to the tradition of internal conflict in Florence, as opposed to the tradition of relatively greater internal peace in Perugia.[28] But whatever the reason may be, populist-motivated ideals seem to have been more purposefully translated into architectural forms in Perugia than in Florence.

To pursue such characterizations a bit further, the more pronounced effort to order the components of the Perugia façade and to underplay the height of the structure, as well as its possible use for military defense, would appear symptomatic of what Becker has called the "gentle" effort of the commune at this time to direct the actions of the citizen in the public life.[29] The progression from the ground floor loggia to the upper two stories is a sharply drawn and measured one. The regularly spaced windows of each of the stories have a distinct form on each level of the structure. Two sharply protruding cornices separated by a plain, flat area of masonry, lend an emphatic coherence and order to the fabric. The height of the wall appears deceptively low because the tops of the first level of windows run along the lower string course, and the bottoms of the upper windows adjoin the upper cornice. Because the original palace did not have a tower, the impression of a simple clarity linked with a modest structural profile must have been even more distinct a feature of the piazza façade than it is at present.

A further reduction of the severity of the building's design is the result of an element of plagiarism of church design in the structure. The contemporary church of San Ercolano is the most direct reflection in Perugia of the portal articulation and of its relation to the whole of the northern façade. In both structures the monumental entryway is a centralized and organic member of the wall. The fenestration of the second and third stories of the palace sets the portal within a symmetrical framework. On the second floor the windows are placed at equal distances from the entrance, which itself bisects the façade. The windows of the upper story are also balanced, and the middle one is directly above the door thus lending an additional accent. The original double ramp that led up to the portal of the palace and that was placed in symmetrical relation to it, must have further highlighted the entry. The centrality and grandeur of the portal, so like a cathedral, is complemented by the fact that another close parallel to the conception are the portals on the west façade of the Todi Duomo. These elements of ecclesiastical design are enhanced by the council hall itself, which is more suggestive of the nave of an Umbrian church than anything found in secular architecture.[30]

There is a final aspect to this accommodation of the design and embellishment of the façade to incorporate a communal symbolism: the large bronzes of the Guelph lion and the Perugian griffin set symmetrically above the portal. The sculptures contribute first to the framing and emphasis of the portal but, more important, they are an extraordinary example of monumental, organically incorporated sculpture within the façade of a civic structure.[31] Here is the clearest expression of the use of the structure as vigorous and explicit advertisement of the power and function of the commune. The only close parallel use of sculptural decoration on the exterior of a contemporary civic palace is found at Narni, Ancona, and Arezzo. But reference to these examples serves only to underline the unique strength and purposefulness of the Perugia decorations. In each of these other instances the sculptures are small relief works of far less visual consequence than the Perugia bronzes. A second difference is that the subjects of the related works in the three other communes lack the local connotations of the Perugia sculptures. The palace bronzes make the same local reference as do certain sculptures on the fountain. The grouping of piazza structures and monuments presents an impression of unity because of its formal or stylistic relationships and because it presents a series of repeated thematic motifs. We shall see that the frescoes in the council hall—into which one enters directly through the cathedral-like, sculpturally enframed portal—represent yet another elaboration and glorification of the "gentle *paideia*" of Perugia.

The Early History of the Palazzo dei Priori

The history of palace construction in Perugia follows a pattern similar to that of many other communes. As the institutional evolution of the free towns followed the same general histories, so too did the efforts to satisfy practical needs by providing appropriate meeting places and palaces for new officials. Perugia is thus no exception to this general rule.

The Palazzo dei Priori was the third civic hall to be built in the city. Before the first palace was constructed, meetings of the general assembly of citizens were first held on the central square.[32] At the same time that the large gatherings of citizens were meeting on the square, the consuls and the *podestà* met in the major churches of the town.[33] This custom appears not to have been specifically related to the Guelph ties of the city, for it was a common practice throughout Italian communes, including both Guelph and Ghibelline.[34]

In about 1205—the chronology is uncertain here—the first civic structure for which there are any known records was constructed: a building called the Palazzo dei Consoli.[35] In 1289 a second palace was constructed above the vault that led from the Palazzo del Vescovo to the Palazzo dei Consoli. There has been much confusion about the use of this palace, one designated simply as the *palatium novum*.[36]

The precise date of the beginning of construction of the Palazzo dei Priori has not been established. Certain only are the original uses of the building: the palace was the residence of the *capitano del popolo* and the location of the two major council halls—the hall later designated the Sala dei Notari and the room above—which functioned as meeting places for the guilds and their representatives.[37]

Speculations as to the start of construction vary from an early date of 1271 to a late one of 1293.[38] The later year is the most generally accepted because the first known payments date from this time.[39] The documents record a series of payments made initially to Giacomo di Sevadio and later to Giovanello di Benvenuto. These payments end in 1297, leading to the assumption that the palace was completed in that year. A *terminus ante quem* of 1297 or of 1298 is suggested by the additional knowledge that the decoration of Sala dei Notari was finished, and that planning for the enlargement of the palace had been initiated in 1298.

The year, then, in which the palace was begun remains problematic. My own belief is that the widely accepted date of 1293 for the beginning of the palace is somewhat too late; more probable is 1289. Mention of the council hall above the vaulted passageway in 1289 is a crucial fact for the resolution of the issue. The payments of 1293 to 1297 refer to both the *palatium novum* and to the *palatio communis*, or Palazzo dei Priori. A second connection between the palaces is suggested by the parallel course followed by the associated decorative undertakings. In 1297, the year in which the frescoing of the Sala dei Notari was completed, it was decreed that the wall below the *palatium novum* be painted with figures of the Virgin, S. Lorenzo, S. Ercolano, and S. Cristoforo.[40] The implication would appear to be fairly clear: unless the parallel histories of the course of the buildings are purely coincidental, both were begun in the same year, 1289.

If this assumption is correct, then the impression of the *Isola del Comune* as an integrated whole is given some reinforcement. The point is central to an understanding of the sources and meaning of the frescoes in the Sala dei Notari. For these works, it would now appear, derive from a civic milieu in which art and architecture were accepted forms of communal glorification. To have studied the frescoes apart from the general communal setting and the immediate urban context would have implied that they constitute a kind of scholastic argument. In fact, the frescoes are themselves the emblematic touchstones of the piazza complex.

4

Moses and Gideon as Political Leaders

In Milton's poem of sin and redemption, Moses is conceived as God's worldly "mediator," an embodiment of "civil Justice" who brings the "laws and rites" of heaven to earth.[1] Moses as a divine hero is the counterpart of the Pharaoh, who is cited as an exemplar of earthly tyranny.[2] Finally, shortly following the characterization of Moses, Gideon's name stands out in the catalogue of leaders who insured the survival of Israel, the ideal worldly state.[3] Milton of course was no mere theologian and for this politically-committed poet, Moses and Gideon were intended to stand as personifications of perfect forms of political and military action.[4]

The meaning of the scenes drawn from the lives of these Biblical figures in the Sala dei Notari sets the frescoes within the same tradition from which Milton's view of the Old Testament as a political tract derives. This theme will be developed in the course of a study of the following scenes, listed here in the order in which they appear beginning with the arch closest to the end or north wall of the council hall: *Gideon Squeezes Dew from the Fleece at the Command of an Angel* (Plate IV); *God Appears to Moses in the Burning Bush* (Plate V); *Moses and Aaron before the Pharaoh* (Plate VI); *The Pursuit of the Israelites by the Egyptians* (Plate VII).[5]

That Biblical events and figures should be depicted in a town hall at this time should come as little surprise. Political theory was simply a branch of ethics, and the most important sourcebook for the knowledge of ethics, and thus for political behavior, was of course the Bible.[6] The Bible may be considered a political treatise in the sense that it expresses divine law; and law is the foundation of the earthly no less than of heavenly city.[7] The citation of scriptures for the legitimization of political behavior pervades the literature of the late thirteenth century, from the writing of the encyclopedists, philosophers, and chroniclers, to that of papal publicists.[8] The ultimate source of this theological predilection was perhaps expressed most memorably by Augustine, who wrote that there existed a "law of nature that was written in the hearts of the godly" and that from this eternal law was copied the law given to the Jews through Moses.[9] Milton and the designers of the Perugia cycle illustrate two of the applications given to such a legalistic and political understanding of the Bible.

The juxtaposition of the scenes of the *Burning Bush* (Plate V) and *Gideon with the Fleece* (Plate IV) on the far, northern arch of the hall, establishes an iconographic keystone for the cycle of murals. The scenes come at the beginning of the natural order of the frescoes and occupy what must be considered the most important arch in the hall, corresponding as it does with the placement of the speaker's platform. Although I do not believe that it is possible to relate the subject of the scenes directly to the nature of the business conducted beneath them—such an interpretation has recently been proposed as an explanation for the placement of the sixteenth century decorations in the Palazzo Ducale in Venice[10]—the location of these crucial works does at least speak of an awareness of the implications of setting and of balance within a scheme of representational decorations that is extraordinary for the time.[11]

There is first a compositional congruence between the two works that underlies the iconographic parallels. In both depictions the field is divided by two confronting elements with a mediating form placed between them. Gideon and the angel face one another while the figure of God, the fleece, and the bowl act as a bridge between them. Moses looks toward God, and the landscape and the sheep link these primary components of the narrative. The potential for a balanced representation of the scenes was fully exploited through this simple and reductive depiction of the two events.

The placement and stylistic analogies between the works suggest that the mission of Moses may be equated with that of Gideon. Represented in the scene drawn from the story of Moses is a crucial moment in the narrative. Moses has already removed his shoes at God's command and is depicted in the act of raising his arm, perhaps in a mixture of awe before the sight of God and of surprise at the mission with which he has been charged. The mission is of course a political one: the "sons of Israel" are to be rescued from tyrannical rule (*Exodus* III, 2-10).[12]

The task with which Gideon is charged is similar (Judges VI, 1, 37-38).[13] When Gideon is first informed that he must deliver his people from tyrannical rule, he is reminded that Israel had once before been rescued by the "Lord ... who brought us out of Egypt" (*Judges*, VI, 13). Gideon's initial reaction is, like that of Moses, one of skepticism. Indeed, the moment depicted is not the divine assignation, but the demonstration of the fact that Gideon is destined "to free Israel" (*Judges*, VI, 14).

Two other important links between the stories further our understanding of why the scenes were grouped together and were clearly intended to be understood as a distinct unit within the program. First, the Israelites in both instances asked for help from God. The advent of Moses and of Gideon is the fulfillment of their plea. The Israelites had to understand, or be reminded of, the nature of tyranny in order to dedicate themselves, and later to rededicate themselves, to the ideals enshrined in their theocratic state. Second, Gideon and Moses were not only warrior-saviors; they became political leaders of their people and embodiments of ideals wholly opposed to those of their former oppressors.[14] Once more the implication is obvious: the works illustrate the subject of victory over an evil government by divinely chosen instruments of good government. In the first instance, the perfect state was founded, and in the second instance the perfect state was re-established so that a golden age of justice and liberty could begin again.

In this definition of the essential Biblical meaning of the scenes the greater magnitude and importance of the story of Moses is readily evident. Moses's achievement is the more illustrious and consequential in part because his mission is the prototype for Gideon's. The following scenes bring the Perugia cycle still more firmly within the focus of the story of Moses. As his calling was an *exemplum* so the depiction of *Moses and Aaron before the Pharaoh* (Plate VI) is amplified into a more generalized confrontation between two notions of government, and the *Pursuit of the Israelites by the Egyptians* (Plate VII) translates into a symbol of deliverance from tyranny.

The representation of *Moses and Aaron before the Pharaoh* depicts what is perhaps one of the least dramatic moments in *Exodus* (VII, 8-11). No divinely aided miracles have yet been performed; Moses and his brother—holding the staff that will soon be transformed into the serpent—simply present the Pharaoh with God's message.[15] The narrative and characterization of the figures are set forth through a sharply drawn contrast in physical types. The movements of Moses and Aaron are bold: Moses extends his right arm in a speaking gesture, stressed by its repetition in the posture of Aaron. The Pharaoh draws back; he occupies only the far corner of the throne and his arms appear to be hidden in his garment. His withdrawn and secretive aspect is reinforced by the tightly inward turning attendant who stands behind the throne. The scheming and closed mien of the Egyptians is further enhanced though the contrast between their small scale and the openness and dominance with which Moses and Aaron are presented.

Emphasis is placed on distinguishing between two expressions of leadership. The very moment chosen focuses on Moses as leader and spokesman of the Israelites and draws us from the supernatural implications of the narrative. The fact that the scene is paired with the *Pursuit of the Israelites* gives added force to the description of the leadership of Moses.[16]

In this second scene the cavalry of the Pharaoh follows the Israelites across the Red Sea (*Exodus*, XIV, 23-26).[17] The first doubts about victory have spread among the men. Although the lance of the first horseman gives the group a strong forward surge, the final impression is one of a slackening movement, accentuated by the more upright direction of the second lance. As in the scene of *Moses before Aaron*, the moment represented comes immediately before the punishment of tyrants.

Discussion of the frescoes, limited for the moment to their specific Biblical reference, permits the following deductions: the cycle opens with a pronouncement of praise for patriarchial government and with a condemnation of tyranny. Two individuals are called upon to serve their people, to rescue them from evil government and to restore liberty and justice. The implication is quite certain, given the context of the murals as decorations of a civic palace. The government of Perugia should devote itself to the pursuit of a policy based on the ideals that inspired Moses and Gideon. As the role of Moses as a military leader was model for the actions of Gideon, so his leadership is perhaps also intended to inspire the citizens and leaders of Perugia in the leadership and defense of their city.

That Biblical figures and events were given a political life and gloss during the Middle Ages has prepared us in a general, although an admittedly circumstantial way for the depiction of Moses and Gideon as political and military heroes in a civic hall. More direct support for an almost exclusively political interpretation of the murals is that the antithesis between Moses and Pharaoh was an especially favored one in the theo-political literature.

Augustine's writings summarize the essential nature of this tradition. In the course of an examination of how the Church should act toward evil-doers, Augustine broached the broader problem of the meaning and uses of punishment, and he cited the contrast between the Pharaoh and Moses as the central proof in his argument. He wrote:

> Pharaoh oppressed the people of God by hard bondage [while] Moses afflicted the same people by severe correction when they were guilty of impiety: their actions were alike; but they were not alike in the motive of regard to the people's welfare—the one being inflated by the lust of power, the other inflamed by love.[18]

The spirit in which the ruler corrects the errors of his subjects is a key to understanding the spirit and nature of his government. Moses appears as the personification of good rule; the Pharaoh as the personification of bad rule. The opposition between these figures was conceived as one between the forces of the "power of God's spirit and magic."[19] The struggle, according to Augustine, was not unlike that between the "false" gods of the Romans and Christian martyrs.[20]

In Salvian's *On the Government of God*, written shortly after *The City of God*, the inherent political and social application and thrust of Augustine's pairing of Moses and the Pharaoh becomes more nearly a political manifesto.[21] Also significant is the fact that, as in the frescoes, the story of Gideon is introduced here as a companion tale to that of Moses.

For Salvian—and for many other later medieval writers on this subject—the Biblical account of Moses was an illustration above all else of God's "care for human affairs."[22] His discussion of the contrast between Moses and Pharaoh emphasizes not the struggle between true and false religion or magic, but rather the manner in which earthly society is managed. When Salvian recounts the story of the wandering of the Jews through the desert and the establishment of the Israeli nation, God is conceived only as a divine comrade and overseer. The theological meaning of the story is of little consequence as the specifically political content came to the fore. While the prosperity enjoyed by Israel is cited as an example of how a pious people can flourish, the difficulties and trials that Egypt underwent are a warning to all tyrants.[23] The opposed conceptions of the two rulers is an analogue to the differences between Rome and Israel,[24] while for Augustine the conceptions are analogues of the polarity between a "false" and a true divinity. By implication the Biblical story was for both a prototypical instance of the sources of political decline and good fortune.[25]

The account of Gideon is even more overtly political. The parallel with the Roman state is a primary aspect of Salvian's approach. In the end, the downfall of Rome and the triumph over the Midianites prove that "merit" rather than strength prevails.[26]

The persistence of such ideas in the theo-political literature and the full development of their potential as political pronouncements are most apparent in the writings of Aquinas. A key statement on the question comes in the course of his exposition of the belief that a danger of democratic government is its susceptibility to tyrannical change.[27] The full horror of tyranny is evident, Aquinas notes, in the Pharaoh's treatment of the Jews.[28]

The singling out of Pharaoh as a paradigm of evil rule is noteworthy largely because of the novelty of its context. The Biblical story remains an historical account from which lessons may be drawn. Now, in the setting of Aquinas's study of politics, the story is a foundation for the defense of a particular form of government,[29] and the Moses-Pharaoh typology assumes a more emphatic stamp of historical authenticity. In the evolution of political institutions, the theocracy of Moses was unique only in that it represented the perfect fulfillment of Aquinas's ideals. These beliefs are founded on the conviction that the "object of human society is the virtuous life;" and such a conviction is the measure to which all government must be subject.[30]

This levelling or equalizing of all governments of the past and present in the attempt to write a true or standard "history" and to discover the drift of evolutionary patterns is apparent in the chronicle tradition of the time as well. In Otto Freising's *The Two Cities: A Chronicle of Universal History*, for example, the narrative of Moses is a major part, as it was in other universal histories of the age.[31] Once more the government that Moses established is seen as the archetypical pattern against which all other states are judged. Also typical of these histories is Otto's effort to underline the importance of the Biblical account of Moses by citing other supporting literary sources.[32] The way was prepared for a Villani and, still later, for a Machiavelli to refer to Moses as an ideal ruler and to place his government in a position of first importance in their polemicising histories.[33] In a more general sense, because the chroniclers of the thirteenth and early fourteenth centuries described all events as manifestations of divine will, the placing of the government of Moses alongside present governments appears as an understandable and defensible procedure.[34]

The appropriateness of Moses and Gideon as civic heroes for Perugia is evident in several ways, and perhaps the most obvious of these is the most crucial: both were political as well as military leaders, and thus they personify the dual effort of the city at this time to codify and to justify its legal foundations and to consolidate its military and political position within the Papal State. The pronounced religious tone that the communal military and political programs assumed was summarized by the figurehead leadership of the Biblical rulers.

   To further support this interpretation, it is necessary to examine a variety of relevant issues before returning to the political and artistic situation in Perugia. Largest among these issues is the conception of the ruler in imperial art and thought and the mechanism of the communal realization of this conception.

   References to Moses as the incarnation of good government are found in Byzantine, imperial, and papal literature and art.[35] The view of a ruler in terms of his supposed Biblical prototype was fairly common, although Moses was not always chosen as the standard Old Testment hero. Yet the Moses typology has the longest history of the Biblical *exempla*, one that has been traced back to the rule of Constantine.[36] The Franks, for example, placed their ideological roots in Israel rather than in Rome, considered themselves the successors of the Chosen People, and thought of their rulers as successors of Moses and David.[37] They saw their armies, as Kantorowicz has expressed it, as the "columns of Israel leaving Egypt under the guidance of an angel," and as the small army of Gideon that defeated the Midianites.[38] Comparison of the ruler with Moses was a part of a thorough-going resurrection of the ideals and history of the state of Israel, so that the Empire came to conceive of itself as Israel reborn. In the political literature, an often generalized or passing reference to the perfection of the state founded by Moses is contrasted with the evils of Babylon or of Egypt.[39]

   The expression of these currents of thought in art took various forms. Most striking is a series of imperial Bibles in which portraits of the ruler were paired, like diptychs, with scenes drawn from the lives of the partriarchs.[40] Common in Byzantine and papal representations was the bringing together of scenes from the life of the ruler with analogous events in the lives of Solomon, David, and Moses. One favored pairing was the *Crossing of the Red Sea* with a military victory of the emperor.[41] The Biblical-ruler typology, in brief, was a common one, one that with some modification readily lent itself to a communal or popular adaptation. We should expect, in fact, that for the Italian city-states of the twelfth and thirteenth centuries, citation of the Old Testament must have held a strong appeal in the general endeavor to prove that the independent city was founded on at least an equal theocratic standing to that of imperial power.

We have already observed how in Perugia reference to ideal rule is to be associated with reference to evil leadership as personified by Pharaoh. The associated or matching depiction of the two notions in art occurs rarely and apparently most frequently in the scene of contrasting personifications of good and bad rulers. Often the figures in the Biblical scene are labelled as an opposed virtue and vice, an interpretation that gives further force to the allegorical meaning proposed for the confrontation.[42]

The definition of tyranny in imperial thought was, like the perception of ideal government, closely allied with Biblical personages and concepts. The *Moralia* of Gregory I was a frequently cited text, and Gregory's statement that "unchristian" behaviour was the primary criterion for bad govenment was about as precise a definition as was generally offered.[43] An early legalistically-inspired statement about the meaning of tyranny was made by Bartolus. His conception, it should be noticed, underscores the importance of Moses in the late medieval view of rule. For Bartolus, the best way of determining the existence of a state of tyranny was to determine whether the leader obeyed the laws.[44] This reasoning follows the assertion, one perhaps influenced by his reading of Ambrose, that the Mosaic Law was needed because man had disobeyed the natural law of God. The law that Moses brought to man marks the beginning of the notion of the original rationale for government.[45] The suitability of the representation of the life of Moses for a civic palace would seem more strikingly appropriate in the light of this common interpretation of the Mosaic Law.

In considering the application of the Moses typology to the communal setting, it is important to bear in mind that, in the borrowings from imperial theory, notions that had earlier referred solely to the glory of the emperor took on a more generalized reference and became descriptive of attributes of the community rather than of a single individual.[46]

There are many indications in civic art and literature of this shift in emphasis. As for the Moses typology, the most important is that in the so-called "*podestà* literature" of the twelfth century—a kind of "Mirror of

Princes" for the just civic leader—the leadership of Moses is cited as the ideal toward which all civic officials should strive. This ideal is advanced not because it might be taken as a sign of the assumed divinity of the ruler, but because the government of Moses was a fair one and is thus a suitable model for a contemporary ruler.[47] The chief interest in these civic writings is with an ascending view of government; how, in other words, the power that the ruler holds is founded on the approval of the ruled and is, therefore, an extension of the power of the ruled. Allusions to Moses are, then, only in one sense a reflection on the nature of the man who holds office. Like the imperial guides for good leadership, the ruler is thought of first as a model Christian. If the ruler leads an upright life, then he will successfully maintain order and dispense justice.[48] In the communal guides for good government, however, the first concern is with the political organism and not with the character of the ruler as a part or function of that organism. The leader, again, is important, is worthy of being obeyed, only insofar as he conforms to and expresses the true spirit of the *polis*.

Although comparison with Moses was not expressed in the political literature of Perugia during the thirteenth century, the Perugian theorist Bartolus later employed the Moses analogy for his republican leader,[49] and those sections of the statutes of 1279 that present the general nature of rule place it securely within this ascending, Christian view of leadership.[50] Lacking any direct reference to the rule of Moses, the statutes reflect, and perhaps derive from, the communal and imperial interest in Biblical typologies.

If the statutes leave open the question of Moses as an embodiment of just rule, the exactly contemporary decorations of the Fontana Maggiore illustrate the importance of Moses in Perugian political thought. The figure of Moses is placed near the effigy of the *podestà* of Perugia on the upper basin. Immediately below is the emblematic griffin of the city.[51] From the point of view of sculptural proximity and setting alone, the associations of the statue of Moses surely include an element of local allusion. The inscription beneath the figure—*MOYSES CUM VIRGA ET LEGA*—suggests more precisely how Moses relates to civic concerns. In the dual role conceived for him, the legalistic aspect of his mission carries the implication that he was considered a legitimizer of the civic government.[52] The leading function of the fountain sculptures is, as I have observed, to define the independence of the commune and to defend it against the pope and the emperor. By adapting the trappings of more acceptable and established political systems, the commune strove to legitimize itself as well.[53]

In Moses's role as leader of the Israelites, the second aspect of his rule described on the fountain—symbolized by the rod with which he parted the waters of the Red Sea and brought water forth from the rock—he stands as a prototype for the actions of the Perugian commune under the direction of the *podestà* and *capitano del popolo.*[54] Herein is distilled the essence of the first frescoes in the Sala dei Notari.

One of the most telling artistic expressions of the paradigmatic significance of the life of Moses in imperial art was his inclusion in illustrations of the "Nine Worthies." This popular decoration for palaces presents in its setting an antithesis to the public display of Moses on a communal fountain and in a communal council hall.[55] Once more we see evidence in Italian communal art of the de-emphasis of the imperial use of the typology as descriptive of an individual rather than of a people. Another similar transformation in meaning among fountain sculptures is that the personification of the city of Perugia is not meant to represent a goddess, as do the ancient and imperial personifications of localities, but represents, as does the figure of Moses, the body of citizens.[56]

We have already observed how in imperial political thought the Moses typology was only one element of an interplay of ideas in which the ruler and his subjects were considered a Chosen People with a divine mission to fulfill on earth. The earliest school of historical thought in the communes, that of Pisa, was marked by a similar set of associated notions. The pre-eminent aspect of this school of historiography that developed during the early twelfth century was the conviction that all successes of the city were owed to divine favor; the Pisans were a virtuous people and were therefore rewarded by God.[57] The providential framework of the later chronicle of Giovanni Villani is here predicted in its coarsest outline.[58] But the Pisans went further than Villani in altering the texture of their history to conform with a divine meaning. They thought of themselves as being no less than "the chosen instruments of God," a role evident to the historians because the city had played a major role in the crusades.[59] Parallels were drawn between the campaigns of the city in North Africa and the campaign of Gideon against the Midianites. A specific parallel was presumed to exist between the booty taken by the Pisans from the towns of Africa and that taken by the Israelites as they left Egypt. So thoroughgoing was this evocation of the tales of Moses and of Gideon as a precedent and justification for their own history that comparison was made by at least one historian between a spring of water discovered by the Pisans and the water that Moses brought forth from a rock.[60] The Frankish conception of history, noted earlier, was resurrected by the commune, the major alteration being of the same order as the adaptation of other parts of the imperial philosophy: emphasis was given to the Pisan people rather than to their rulers.

The Pisan situation in the twelfth century is exceptional in that the crusading ideal as a distinguishing aspect of the local civic chauvinism was carefully and fully delineated. By the late thirteenth century, the crusading ideal had for the most part degenerated into a frequently evoked propagandistic ingredient in purely political undertakings, such as Martin IV's campaigns against Aragon or Boniface's struggle with the Colonna family.[61] Combined with this distortion of the original crusading impulse was the revival of papal pamphleteering against the infidel and the consolidation of anti-European power in the Holy Land that had come with the fall of Acre to the Egyptians in 1291. A leading argument in this pamphleteering, as in much of the papal rhetoric of the 1290's, was the frequent reference to the acts of Gideon and Moses, as well as the frequent invocation of the Moses typology, for the rule of the pope.[62]

Perugia played an important part in all these efforts. Perhaps more than in any other aspect of the papal political activities of the time, the struggle against the Colonna involved direct military assistance from the members of the Papal State, and Perugia's share was the preponderant one. The granting of indulgences, as in the earlier crusades against the infidel, was one important stimulus to Perugia's aid.[63]

As for Perugia's share in Boniface's reversal of papal indifference in dealing with the Saracens, there is little to say. While the city did take an active role in the consolidation of the pope's power in Italy, most of the direct help for the renewed attacks on the infidel continued to come from Northern Italy. By the early fourteenth century, however, there are several instances of Perugian involvement in the attempt to regain parts of the Holy Land.[64]

The point is that it is not unlikely that Perugian policies had been given the aura of a crusade to accompany the invocation of the Moses and Gideon ruler typology. The first murals of the cycle can be understood on several levels, all of which point toward a divine or religious intention for the "mission" of the city, its rulers, and its citizens. In 1292 Bonifazio da Verona composed a pretentious epic poem in fulfillment of a government commission in Perugia. The work, as remarked earlier, was entitled the *Eulistea* after one of the legendary heroes of the city. Bonifazio describes the divine origin and career of the city's patron and symbol, the griffin, and the destruction of the enemies of the city by this sacred beast.[65] By inference, the citizens of Perugia, under the protection of their totemic image, share in this heavenly association.

5

Adam and Eve and the Foundation of the State

The next group of frescoes is comprised of the following three scenes: *The Creation of Adam* (Plate VIII),[1] *The Creation of Eve* (Plate IX),[2] and *The First Labor of Adam and Eve* (Plate X).[3] These murals follow the representations of *Moses and Aaron before the Pharaoh* on the west spandrels of the second and third arches. The east spandrels of the arches are decorated with scenes of the fables of Aesop and with a depiction of *St. George and the Dragon*.

The placement of these scenes within the overall scheme suggests, as did the examination of the first sacred depictions, that something other than the simple illustration of Biblical narrative was the leading intention of the Sala dei Notari decorators. The inclusion of the story of Adam and Eve outside its proper narrative sequence—the story follows, again, the scenes of Moses and Gideon—makes clear that a rather novel interpretation is to be made of the frescoes. The modification of the normal or traditional order of the narrative coincides with the particular political content of the frescoes.

A second general and unanticipated aspect of this part of the decorations—unanticipated, that is, after the organization of the Moses and Gideon scenes—is that the story of the First Parents evolves on a single side of the arches and appears to make no specific reference to the opposing murals. The remaining spandrels of the hall are decorated in the format of the Adam and Eve cycle, so that the story of Moses and Gideon is a uniquely integrated grouping in the decorations. In such fashion the customary importance of the Creation scenes is further lessened.

With only two exceptions depictions of the story of Adam and Eve are, so far as I can determine, without precedent among the embellishments of a civic palace.[4] As in the example of the Moses-Gideon scenes there is the problem of accounting for this civic borrowing of an ecclesiastical decoration. The political meaning of the works, might now be briefly summarized: political and social actions are set within a moral framework that derives from an

Aristotelian view of the origin and functions of the state, and these actions are defended because of their redemptive character.

The artist who executed the Moses-Gideon frescoes would seem to have carried out this group of works as well, although the figures perhaps lack the fullness of the figures in the first murals. The compositional simplicity of the *Creation of Adam* is close to that found in the opening scenes. The form of the spandrel, more clearly here than in any other scene, is transformed into an ideal container for a landscape that molds and establishes hierarchies in the figural grouping. The counter-balanced relationship between the figures creates two opposed diagonals on the picture plane, and the gestures, as in the first scenes, establish reciprocal movements. The sphere on which God sits becomes a focal ordering principle of the fresco, echoed, as it is, by the semicircular form of the stone upon which His feet rest, and by the great circle of drapery which envelopes the body. These elements create a cascading movement of round forms that radiate from His body and help to build up a tightly unified composition.

The compositional structure of the *Creation of Eve* and of *Adam and Eve at Work* is repeated in the *Creation of Man* on the opposite spandrel, although the scheme of the *Creation of Eve* is enlivened somewhat by the gesture of God straining forward to reach out to the equally animated figure of Eve. The parallel compositional devices, features that characterize the entire series of decorations, give special force to the iconographic unity and continuity of the scheme. Despite the fact that there were clearly several artists of differing abilities engaged in the project, this uniformity of design suggests that a single artist was responsible for the overall scheme.

That the sequence of scenes does not conform with the Biblical narrative suggests a visual, shorthand reference to the belief that government is a benign necessity not dependent on the Fall, as we will see more fully. (The more common belief had been of course that government is an evil and repressive necessity.) The fact that the story of Moses and Gideon begins the cycle of Biblical representations indicates, I believe, that the state is accepted as axiomatic. Thus a particular concept of leadership and citizenship is the quintessential subject of the decorations.

The uniqueness of the scenes of Adam and Eve can perhaps most immediately be appreciated by citing two related decorative schemes on civic palaces: an earlier one of about 1270, in Ancona, and a later one of about 1410, in Venice.

In the original decorative scheme of the Palazzo degli Anziani at Ancona, a sculptured representation of *Adam and Eve* was to be found on the façade together with reliefs of *Lamech Killing Cain* and of the *Judgment of Solomon.*[5] The occurrence of the scene of Lamech, extremely rare for the time, together with a depiction of the First Parents, is the most obvious point of correspondence between the decorations and the murals at Perugia. But the sole emphasis at Ancona is with the role of the state as an enforcer of justice. The portrayal of Lamech is an example of how justice is meted out; the *Judgment of Solomon* reinforces such an interpretation by standing as a symbol of the actions of the ideal judge or ruler.[6] The representation of Adam and Eve is, I believe, simply a reminder that original sin is the source for the foundation of the earthly state, as well as a source for the record of sin that followed, and of which Cain's murder of Abel is the first example. At Perugia attention is drawn away from the role of sin and the Fall. The illustration of the *First Labor* shows us that redemptive work on earth can atone for original sin.

A somewhat similar union of subjects is to be found in the sculptural decorations on the Piazzetta corner of the Doge's Palace in Venice. The grouping of *The Fall* and the *Judgment of Solomon* parallels the expression of the role of government as the suppressor of wrong-doing found at Ancona. As God dealt justly with the disobedience of the First Parents, so did Solomon's fair rulings continue the reign of justice on earth, as is perhaps implied by the so-called *Justitia* capital below.[7] By inference, the leaders and judges of the commune carry forth and make plain Solomon's theocratic ideals. The contrast at Perugia comes again in the emphasis placed on the value of the redemptive behavior in man and, as a consequence, the accompanying lack of stress on the Fall.

This contrast between the Perugia murals and the two related civic programs at Ancona and Venice is a distinction that is also to be found with ecclesiastical cycles. Throughout the thirteenth and early fourteenth centuries representations of scenes drawn from Genesis do not lead directly, as they do at Perugia, to the depiction of *Adam and Eve at Work*. The theme of the Fall—Warning, Sin, Apprehension, and Expulsion—was generally more fully evolved.[8] At Perugia this ecclesiastical path is rejected. Consequently the emphasis is on the positive aspects of the labor of Adam and Eve and on the belief that the state would have been necessary even without original sin.[9] The murals depart here even from the most important local example. On the Fontana Maggiore the traditional ecclesiastical theme is followed in summary fashion with the representations of *The Temptation* and *The Fall*.

In at least three later civic-political monuments—first in the early decorations for the Florence Campanile (c. 1335)—the direct progression from the Creation to the First Labor suggests a similar political reformulation of Genesis. At Florence the redemptive spirit of work for the state is given greater importance than at Perugia through the depiction of the seven Liberal Arts and of the practitioners of the arts, sciences, and works of man. Here is outlined for the viewer the various types of virtuous and productive action.[10]

Further indication of the association of useful work within a program of propagandistic decorations are the so-called frescoes of *Good and Bad Government* at Siena (1338-9). In the borders of the representations of ideal town and country life are representations of the *artes meccaniche*.[11] Again, the kinds of constructive activity in human society are defined.

Perhaps the most transparent expression of the relation of service to the community and its corollary theme of redemption is the cycle of the trades on the soffit on the third arch of the central porch of San Marco in Venice (c. 1300). The cycle has been described by Otto Demus as the "most complete and lifelike representations of the Trades in medieval art," and the emphasis is on local Venetian crafts and professions.[12] These mundane pursuits are infused with a redemptive significance by their proximity to the representation of the Last Judgment in the lunette of the porch. The implication, as at Perugia and Siena, is the celebration of the inherent nobility of labor without reference to the wages of sin. That such labor helps the state is sufficient justification in itself.

The Florence Campanile and San Marco sculptures of course differ in at least one important way from the Perugia murals. The Florence works include allusions to the sacramental role of the Church, the Venice sculptures point to the relationship between divine judgment and earthly behavior, and thus both plans of embellishment have a more traditional theological foundation as programs outlining the means to salvation.[13] All such reference is absent at Perugia where the idea of a kind of secular salvation is upheld without qualification.

In order to understand more completely the political significance of the murals, we must turn first to the question of how creation and original sin were conceived in the contemporary political literature. The writings of Paul and Augustine are among the most noteworthy of the early medieval statements regarding the relation of the First Parents to the creation of the state. In this interpretation the beginnings of political society coincide with and are necessitated by man's disobedience.[14] The political order represents a corruption of the natural and innocent state of man; in Carlyle's words, a loss of the "happy anarchy of the primitive world."[15]

The belief that the state was a corrupt body because it was not included in the original divine scheme received its seminal elaboration in the writings of Augustine. For Augustine, all the crimes and evils that marked the course of human society since the Fall are a consequence of a moving away from God; or, expressed in more Augustinian terms, a consequence of the abuse of God-granted free will.[16] Government is an invention, or compromise, that is at once necessary and evil. Government is necessary in order to thwart the unleashed evil in the world and is itself evil because the state perverts the natural order.[17]

This strong disapproval of the earthly city is mitigated in part by the conviction that a true Christian leader can make the best of what is fundamentally a bad thing.[18] But the negative implications are overwhelming. As man has proved himself to be wicked, so political institutions can be only punitive in nature. To avoid a condition of universal anarchy, man's inherent evil must be restrained by the political order.[19] Some individuals, it is true, are marked from birth for salvation, but most are damned.[20] And one cannot avoid this damnation by virtuous earthly behavior; for the most part, such behavior is not even acknowledged and the wide gulf between the uncorrupt heavenly state and corrupt earthly state remains eternally fixed.[21]

The traditional medieval notion of the state, then, was inevitably linked to the Fall. Adam and Eve were directly to blame for the creation of the state. Yet, at Perugia we have seen a rather different explanation for the advent of political institutions. The Fall is not a dominant theme, as we might expect it to be; the state as an enforcer of justice is the subject of the scenes.[22] In this context original sin is simply paradigmatic of the kind of unjust or evil action that the state strives to expunge.

A major source for the change in the concept of the origins and role of political institutions was the Aristotelian revival of the thirteenth century, a revival strongly influenced at the beginning by the translation of Aristotle's *Politics* from Greek into Latin by William of Moerbeke in 1260.[23] There is, however, at least one point of contact between the earlier tradition and that of the later thirteenth century: Augustine, like Aristotle, did concede that man was a gregarious or "political animal."[24] This point of correspondence is important for an understanding of the murals. At a time in which a clearly defined and isolated political realm did not exist, such general issues as the duties of man among his fellows were of great import in a still relatively primitive political consciousness. The adjoining Aesop scenes, as we will see, direct attention even more sharply to the fact that the designers of the Perugia program were concerned first with general patterns of behavior in society and not with any specifically political action. As the political theory of the age, even after the translation of Aristotle, remained theological in orientation, it is natural to expect that guides for ideal political behavior, such as the Perugia frescoes, would be moral and ethical in nature. Augustine's belief in the need for society, and its Aristotelian reinforcement through Aquinas, are notable early phases of what was still a general study of the nature and moral limits of man, rather than evidence, as it is sometimes held to be, of a "modern" political outlook.

Partly as a result of the Aristotelian revival of the thirteenth century, the political order was buttressed with the same justification that inspired the acceptance and defense of society itself: the political order too was now held to be natural and inevitable.[25] In light of this point of view, the location of the frescoes representing Adam and Eve after those of Moses and Gideon takes on a special meaning and import. For if the traditional view of the relation of the Fall to the origin of the state were being proposed at Perugia, then it would be logical to anticipate that the story of Adam and Eve would come before that of Moses and Gideon, works that glorify action in the service of the state and a particular type of rule. The implication of the existing order is then further proof that the state is accepted as necessary and that a main subject of the murals is the celebration of ideal political behavior and leadership.

As Augustine expounds and typifies the early medieval conception of the relation of the Fall to the state, so Aquinas expresses the neo-Aristotelian interpretation as expressed in the frescoes. "When we consider all that is necessary to human life," Aquinas writes,

> "... it becomes clear that man is naturally a social and political animal. ... One man alone would not be able to furnish himself with all that is necessary, for no man's resources are adequate to the fullness of human life. For this reason the companionship of his fellows is naturally necessary to man."[26]

After completing this largely derivative rehearsal of how man is able to sustain and to fulfill himself only among his fellows, Aquinas states—in the first pages of the *De Regimine Principum*—that a transcendent or ordering principle must be superimposed so that society functions for the equal and just benefit of all its members:

> For if a great number of people were to live, each intent only upon his own interests, such a community would disintegrate unless there were one of its number to have a care for the common good: just as the body of a man or of any other would disintegrate were there not in the body itself a single controlling force, sustaining the general vitality of all its members.[27]

The need for order in human affairs is not, therefore, a consequence of original sin, but rather it is a natural and rational impulse to advance "the common good."

One of the routes by which Aquinas arrived at his conclusion regarding the necessity for government indicates a more precise and direct parallel with the scheme of the Perugia murals. Aquinas refers often to the ways in which mankind differs from, or is similar to, the animal kingdom. As animals need some ordering pattern in their lives so too does man.[28] The balancing of the Biblical scenes with representations of Aesop's fables at Perugia indicates a like defense and rationale for the state. This matter will be more fully expounded in an examination of the Aesop representations.

The prevalence of this pseudo-evolutionary doctrine, and its kinship with the political climate of Perugia, is apparent in many ways, the most noteworthy perhaps being in the propaganda advanced on behalf of Boniface

VIII.[29] In strongly pro-papal Perugia the thinking of the most important among these papal defenders, Egidius Colonna (1246/7-1316), must have had some impact. Following Aquinas's example, Egidius declared that the state is natural to man because it represents a predictable and inevitable development from the family and village.[30] The Fall does not figure in what one might term an anthropologically-focused theory of the beginnings of the state.

Another indication of the currency of Aristotelian ideas regarding the creation of the state suggests that these notions enjoyed a fairly widespread circulation long before the reappearance of the *Politics*. Despite the fact that there is no real precedent in art for their expression, there is ample indication that varying forms of the philosophy were of some influence in the political life and thought of late medieval Europe.

As early as the first *renovatio* of the Empire after the fall of Rome, an event signaled by the crowning of Charlemagne by Pope Leo III, the Church admitted in fact what its defenders might have continued to deny in theory: that the earthly city was necessary for the propagation of the Christian message throughout the world.[31] Imperial propagandists, unsurprisingly, granted an important place in their writings for the expression of the belief in the natural need for government. The Constitution of Melfi (1231), for example, opens with a statement of how the ruler is a direct descendent of Adam in the sense that the just ruler must attempt to re-establish the ideals of Adam's rule before the Fall.[32] Not only did government exist before the sin of Adam and Eve, but it embraced an ideal that all benevolent rulers should attempt to revive. Francis Yates has described this tendency in the imperial thought of the thirteenth century as "Adam mysticism." This "mysticism" included a redemptive, Christ-like role for the emperor and a belief that an earthly paradise might be created anew through the leadership of the emperor.[33]

One further aspect of the "Adam mysticism" of the thirteenth century reveals most fully how the Augustinian taint had been removed from the role Adam played in the theory of the creation of the state during the thirteenth century. Associated with the greater objectivity with which Adam was conceived, was the belief in a kind of profane corporation of men embodied in Adam, a companion notion to the spiritual corporation thought to be embodied in Christ.[34] This imperially derived notion was also of importance in the thinking of Boniface's defenders.[35] Like almost every other political ideal of the age, "Adam mysticism" was an extremely useful and adaptable concept.

There is no evidence to suggest that Perugia was directly touched by the imperial legalistic concepts or political theology that exercised an influence on papal thinking. There is at least one indirect indication, however, that the city was not unaware of general tendencies in imperial thought. Contacts between the university in Bologna and the developing one in Perugia were numerous and included the employment of many Bolognese teachers of law in Perugia. The legalistic philosophy of the empire would be known in Perugia through these close relations with one of the most important centers for the study of imperial law in Europe.[36] Briefly, the justification for imperial law was founded on three ideals: *Necessitas, Justitia,* and *Providentia.* In other words, a ruler was necessary to direct the state, a divine law maintained that such rule would be just, and divine providence guaranteed that this necessary and just ruler was the emperor.[37] The Perugia frescoes already discussed reflect this transcendent and imperial outlook. The Moses and Gideon murals uphold divinely supported leadership. Together with the frescoes of Adam and Eve and the defense they provide for the idea of government as a natural function, the parallels become even stronger. The scene of *Adam and Eve at Work* proclaims the final, redemptive aspect of imperial political theory.

There is one other dimension to the ideas associated with Adam during the thirteenth century that is of relevance here: the contemporary position of Adam and Eve in the chronicles and world histories. The texts begin with reference to the creation as marking the beginning of human history.[38] This "historical" centrality of Adam and Eve was one necessary foundation for the belief that all men are embodied in Adam. As far as more specifically political considerations are concerned, the granting of an historical primacy to Adam was also essential before he could be given a place in the evolution of government. To stress his historical role was also to recognize that he was a man like other men, and that the controls imposed on his liberty by the state and society were as crucial to his welfare as they were to the well-being of the thirteenth-century citizen of an Italian commune.

The inclusion of the scene of *Adam and Eve at Work,* together with the de-emphasis on Temptation and Fall, indicates that participation in society and the state was considered virtuous or praiseworthy behavior. The interest in earthly labor as a means for attaining salvation is related to the Thomistic belief in the possibility of secular redemption.[39] For Aquinas the Cardinal or Earthly Virtues and the Theological Virtues were equally important. Before one ascended to the Heavenly Virtues, it was necessary to live a life dedicated to the Cardinal Virtues.[40] The correct way of attaining earthly virtue was by working for the common good. As the common good was synonymous in Aquinas's thought with the ideal state, the whole issue was transformed into a political one. The notion of the common good was interchangeable with that of political justice; one was the precondition and evidence of the other.[41] The faith, as stated by Aquinas in the *Summa,* "That all men being a part of the city they cannot be truly good unless they adapt themselves to the common good" represents the center of this philosophy.[42] David Herlihy's apt phrase for this outlook—"civic Christianity"—immediately evokes its distinguishing aspects.[43]

Before returning to the Perugia murals it is essential that we understand the transformation of Aquinas's monarchic politics into a supportive theory for the communes. The Florentine Remigio dei Girolami (active *c.* 1295) was the leading figure in the movement. He is said to have been trained by Aquinas himself, although there is no convincing evidence for this, and in turn to have been an instructor of Dante.[44] Remigio developed, even more fully than did Aquinas, the doctrine that man finds fulfillment only in the state. "If Florence were destroyed," Remigio wrote, "he who was a Florentine citizen, no longer could be called a Florentine. . . . And if he no longer is a citizen, he no longer is a man, because man is by nature a civic animal."[45] The passage of course has familiar Aristotelian overtones. Only through participation in the *polis,* Remigio continued in the spirit of his ancient mentor, can man lead a virtuous life. Finally, the participation of the individual in the life of the city is a just and proper end in itself, needing neither the blessings of the pope nor the aegis of the emperor to be sanctified through transcendent purpose. While Aquinas's Aristotelianism was a rather tentative alteration of a fundamentally theological perspective, Remigio's Aristotelianism appears to have been quite literally intended.

A forthright acceptance of neo-Aristotelian views is expressed through the placement and choice of the scenes of Adam and Eve at Perugia. The state is accepted as a necessary and benign force, and virtuous, productive labor is put forward as the model form of behavior in the state; that is, the behavior by which men achieve earthly and heavenly reward.

Cain and Abel and the Concept of Political Justice

The group of murals derived from the Old Testament concludes with two scenes from the story of Cain and Abel: *The Offering* (Plate XI) on the southeast face of the fourth arch[1] and *The Slaying of Abel* (Plate XII) on the southwest spandrel of the fifth arch. These Biblical episodes are supplemented by the apochryphal *Death of Cain* (Plate XIII) on the northwest face of the fourth arch. Together with the two preceding cycles of Biblical depictions, the scenes of Cain and Abel represent what appears to be a unique conflation of sacred histories.[2] This fact in itself points to the special sense in which the program must be understood and is one indication that a theological accounting is unsatisfactory.

The representations are, individually, conventional enough, and appear to subscribe to traditional formulas. The basic compositional pattern and the figure style are closely related to the preceding murals.[3] The impression of an overall unity of conception assumes greater force here in the uniform orientation of the narratives toward the middle of the hall. As the eye moves from one fairly inaccessible spandrel to the next, this shared feature gives the design a strong sense of continuity and flow. Overcoming to as great an extent as possible the difficulties inherent in the location of the frescoes was surely a major end of the painters throughout the decorative program.

The scenes illustrate, first, a part of sacred history. It may be remarked here that the same is true of the other Biblical murals—all are representations of "historical" events.[4] Because the Old Testament often appears at this time to have been, in Meyer Schapiro's words, a "secular history with memorable tales of war, adventure and love,"[5] we have perhaps a sufficient justification for the location of Biblical murals in a political setting. That the communes were searching for what can be thought of as an ideologically supportive past might tend to sustain this point of view.[6] The ramifications of political symbolism and allegory, of course, divert us from a purely literal interpretation of the frescoes.

The political coloration impressed upon Cain and Abel at Perugia stems in part from the fact that the theme of original sin is not directly treated. The most common late medieval meaning of the story of Cain and Abel was as a prefiguration of Redemption.[7] But as Redemption was a necessary consequence of the Fall, lack of any overt reference to original sin would imply that we must search for an alternative interpretation.

The single other example of the depiction of Cain and Abel among the decorations of a public palace, the reliefs at Ancona, has little direct relation to the Perugia murals as the sculptures represent a more straightforward appropriation of the conventional theological intent of the Biblical story.[8] The significance of the pairing of the *Death of Cain* with *The Temptation* and the *Judgment of Solomon,* would appear to be, as we have seen, that the sin of the First Parents is equated with that of Cain, and that Cain's death is a just retribution. The wisdom of this divine punishment is an inspiration for the rule and judgment of Solomon.

Although the meaning of the representation of Cain and Lamech is similar at Perugia—that is, a model for wise governance and judgment—the fact that *The First Labor* rather than *The Temptation* precedes the episodes gives the works a somewhat different thrust. The actions of Cain and of Adam and Eve are not equated at Perugia. The First Parents redeemed themselves through work. Cain's crime, on the other hand, marks another stage downward in the course of fallen man and is an act that cries out for vengeance.[9] While the Biblical story is meant to demonstrate that no man is beyond the charity of God, the apocryphal tale of Cain's death was surely more in accord with popular sentiment and thus was appropriate for the public context of a town hall.

There is little direct evidence to suggest a political side to the medieval conception of Cain and Abel that might corroborate what has been here proposed as an interpretation of the Perugia murals. It would be helpful, however, to isolate several central themes in the theological literature pertaining to the two Biblical figures.

The first theme is best exemplified by Aquinas who cites God's forgiveness of Cain as proof of divine goodness.[10] A second theme, one found primarily in the chronicle and world history tradition and one with Biblical precedent as well, is somewhat more political in nature: Cain is depicted as the founder of the earthly city.[11] In the *City of God* this motif receives one of its earliest and fullest treatments; this connotation of the Biblical story is of first importance to Augustine.[12] The fact that Aquinas does not note this earlier tradition, and the fact that by the early fourteenth century the belief was no longer the common historiographic topos that it had been earlier, indicates that the view of Cain as city-founder had lost its former importance. In any event, it is unlikely that such an outlook would have been canonized in a program of decorations, such as that at Perugia, in which political power and the course of government were held to be the result of natural rather than supernatural forces. Cain as the founder of an earthly city of sin is incompatible with the Aristotelian background of the Adam and Eve story.

Another strain in the medieval idea of Cain and Abel more closely coincides with the Perugia frescoes. Although far less common a typology than that of Moses as ideal ruler, Abel too provided an important model for just leadership.[13] Reference to this conception is confined to the literature of the thirteenth and fourteenth centuries and there is no associated visual tradition. The model was employed by papal propagandists as a proof of the assertion that there had never been a king without a papal contemporary. Abel was, in this tradition of Biblical exegesis, seen as the first pope and Cain as the usurper of his legitimate power.[14] At the core of this school of interpretation was the belief that the popes were the descendents of Abel and that all secular rulers were descendents of Cain. As Abel was born a member of the City of God and was thus only a "sojourner" on earth, papal rule is legitimate in the sense that the leader of the Church is, as the first citizen of heaven, God's representative on earth.[15] Another meaning of the *Death of Cain* would now appear evident. The act of Lamech re-establishes legitimacy in government. Cain's murder of Abel appears more clearly as the act of a political usurper, and Lamech's act as that of a political assassin.

One may remark further of Abel that because of his moral purity he was unique in being untainted by original sin, although he lived in the shadow of the Fall. Abel was in fact the personification of virtue and righteousness, his own death a prophecy and parallel to Christ's. The appropriateness of according Abel a position of prominence in the council hall would seem, therefore, to go little beyond the argument that, like Moses and Gideon, he was a suitable symbol of the attributes of ideal citizenship and leadership.[16]

The death of Abel may be interpreted as a crime or action against the social order that makes political organization essential. The state is needed if such crimes are to be prevented or the guilty punished. The scene is both a warning to the potential committer of unlawful and unjust acts and a reminder of the need for political institutions to control man's baser instincts. One should recall that a chief preoccupation of the commentators and chroniclers of the communes was with order, order which insured peace by outlawing strife and crime.[17] These points are, of course, common principles in almost all utopian visions of good government, but never before the communal epoch did these visions assume such importance, and seem so practical, attainable, and historically sound.

The obsession at this time with order and with the expunging of crime has many sources.[18] For Perugia, perhaps most important was that the ending of all civil disorder would help the city in solving the problem of external strife; in other words, would contribute to the effort to consolidate and strengthen its position in the Papal State and in Umbria.[19] A pre-eminent subject of the communal legislation of the 1290s was in fact the enforcement of civil order and, in particular, the curbing of the crimes of the *magnati* who had long been a favorite target of the republican political associations in the city.[20]

The point is that we may take the scenes of the *Murder of Abel* of the *Death of Cain* as indications of the special sense in which government was regarded as the enforcer of civil peace and order during the communal age. In the struggle of the communes to justify their independence from the more established centers of power, the pope and the emperor, no argument was more pressing than that internal rather than external institutions were more fit to establish a peaceful society.[21] Pointing to the existence of crime and disorder was as much a conventional theoretical argument for the theologians and "political scientists" of the age to justify the existence and power of local government as it was an element of communal self-justification.

The key mural for the pronouncement of how in the ideal state the individual's drive for power and the individual's tendency to commit acts against the common good must be controlled by moral and political authority is the *Death of Cain*. In one sense the mural is a kind of *pittura infamante,* a warning to the potential criminal of the fate that awaits him.[22] The scene, as noted, was extremely rare. One earlier Italian example may, however, serve to indicate its relation to the communal ideal of concord: on the west façade of the Cathedral at Modena is a relief representation of the same subject, attributed generally to Guglielmo and dated about 1180.[23] The work is related to a contemporaneous part of the same program of decorations for the Cathedral complex, a capital at the east end of the fifth story of the Campanile depicting an allegory of good and bad judges. The carvings show how man is oppressed by injustice and how the upright judge, he who has learned the *Code of Justinian,* is the foundation of the good commune. Although this connection between two disparate aspects of the Modena sculptures might be questioned, the pervasive emphasis throughout the late twelfth century decorations points to the interlinking of sacred history, romance, and secular history.[24] In this sense the death of Cain may stand at Modena, as at Perugia, as an exemplum of a wise and just meting out of punishment.

The further implication of the *Death of Cain* relates the scene to the notion that the murder of Abel represents a usurpation of Abel's power. The slaying of Cain may then signify the overthrowing of unjustly held, tyrannical rule. An important principle in the Aristotelian political atmosphere of the thirteenth century dealt with the moral or political justification for regicide.[25] Aquinas, returning to a theme that John of Salisbury had already revived, expressed his approval for the murder of a ruler who had obtained his power through violence. The power of all rulers, Aquinas maintained, stems from the people; if their interests are abused, they then have the right, through violent means if necessary, to reclaim their power. Thus the *Death of Cain* is as much a warning to the rulers of Perugia to govern wisely as it is a pronouncement of the sacredness of the ideal of righteous leadership modelled on the life of Abel.[26]

This association in the popular imagination of the death of Cain with justly motivated violence is seen in at least one other legend of the time: Cain's death was said to illustrate the inadequate way in which man defends himself if he is dependent only on weapons, as Cain was. Lamech, on the other hand, was dependent more on God for his defense.[27]

In the larger context, the political content of the Cain and Abel scenes relates to the redemption of the earthly city, its return to fair and just control through the murder of its Biblical founder. *The Death of Cain* is allied to the representation of *Adam and Eve at Work* in that both re-assert the inherent worth of the secular realm. Such an interpretation is in accord with the significance ascribed to the murals of Moses and Gideon. For the conviction that the state conducts business in the spirit of a holy crusade is of a piece with the justification of Lamech's divinely-inspired violence. Lamech's act is a metaphor for the actions of the enemies of the state, just as Cain's crime is a metaphor for the actions of the enemies of the state.

Aesop and the Pragmatic Justification and Bases of Rule

The next group of murals is the largest thematically unified assemblage in the Sala dei Notari: eleven representations of the fables of Aesop that begin on the northeast side of the second arch and, but for the depiction of *Saint George and the Dragon* on the southeast side of the third arch, unfold without interruption on the eastern part of the hall (Plates XV-XXV). The representation of fables by Aesop in a public palace is both without precedent and without later adaptation. But the murals of Aesop are extraordinary in other, more significant ways.

The depiction of the fables may be considered, in general, a rather rare phenomenon in the art of the Middle Ages. There are extant only a small number of illustrated manuscripts of Aesop and an even smaller number of known or surviving monumental programs.[1] Apparently there was a slight increase in the illustration of certain selected fables at the end of the thirteenth century.[2] The murals at Perugia may be considered a part of this trend. Among these contemporary works—most are French and are confined by and large to manuscript illumination[3]—there is no group of depictions of such prominent public importance nor of so ambitious a scope as those at Perugia. To be sure, some of the same individual fables are found elsewhere, but the grouping of scenes at Perugia is extraordinary among the surviving works.

Representations of Aesop were more commonplace in Umbria than in other regions of Italy. At Spoleto, Assisi, and Perugia itself on the Fontana Maggiore, fairly modest cycles of animal fables constitute a context for the scenes in the council hall.[4] But because none of these decorations can in any sense be considered a source for the murals, we must seek elsewhere for their origin. Further, as the representation of the fables was subject to general textual influences that tended to standardize their form, the similarity of several of the frescoes with earlier occurrences proves little in itself.[5] The fact that there are some precedents in Umbria suggests only that the area was open to an appropriate pattern of artistic and literary influences. These precedents and the distribution of Aesop texts in Italy during the late Middle Ages have been discussed by others and lie beyond the problem at hand for it will be seen shortly that such "influences" do not account for the Aesop frescoes.[6] A final note, however, about an important point common to all the Umbrian representations of Aesop: the fables are part of, and subordinate to, larger decorative undertakings, ones that include Biblical scenes.

Despite the general absence of artistic example, texts were common and their application was extremely varied and widespread.[7] Before dealing with the sources and expressions of this interest, the subjects of the eleven Aesop frescoes must be described. For each of the scenes the subject of the narrative will be followed by the appropriate moral, as they are recounted in the Daly edition, a modernization of medieval texts.[8]

On the northeast side of the second arch is the illustration of the fable of *The Wolf and the Lamb* (Plate XV):

> A wolf saw a lamb drinking from a river and decided to find a plausible reason for making a meal of him. So from where he stood upstream he began to complain that the lamb was muddying the water and not letting him get a drink. When the lamb said that he was no more than touching the water with his lips and that besides, from where he was standing downstream, he could not possibly disturb the water above him, the wolf, failing in his complaint, said, "But last year you made unpleasant remarks about my father." Then, when the lamb said he was not even a year old, the wolf said to him, "Am I to be cheated out of eating you just because you are so glib with your excuses?"[9]

> MORAL: The fable shows that those who are set on doing wrong are not to be deterred even by a legal argument.[10]

The scene of *Saint George and the Dragon* (Plate XIV) follows. The fresco, as will be clear shortly, is central to the interpretation of the fables and should, moreover, be thought of as thematically related to the Aesop murals.

The Dog Carrying Meat (Plate XVI) is on the northeast side of the third arch:

> A dog with some meat was crossing a stream when he caught sight of his reflection in the water and thought it was another dog with a larger piece of meat. On this supposition he dropped his own meat and started to go and get that of the other dog. As a result he lost both, since he could not get the one because it did not exist and the other was carried away by the stream.[11]

> MORAL: The fable is appropriate for greedy men.[12]

The story of *The Wolf and the Crane* (Plate XVII) follows in the southeast spandrel of the fourth arch:

> A wolf had swallowed a bone and was going around looking for someone to be his doctor. When he met a heron, he begged him to remove the bone for a fee. The heron put his

head into the wolf's jaws, pulled out the bone, and asked for the pay they had agreed on. The wolf replied, "My good fellow, aren't you satisfied with getting your head out of a wolf's mouth whole without asking for pay besides?"[13]

MORAL: The fable shows that the greatest return for good service to bad men is not to be wronged by them in the bargain.[14]

On the northeast face of the fourth arch is the fable of *The Fox and the Crow* (Plate XVIII):

A crow had stolen some meat perched in a tree. A fox caught sight of him and, wishing to get the meat, stood there and began to praise him for his size and beauty, telling him that of all the birds he might most appropriately be kind, that he certainly would be if he had any kind of voice. The crow wanted to show the fox that he did have a voice so he dropped the meat and raised a great croaking. The fox ran up, seized the meat, and said, "Friend crow, if you had any kind of sense, you would be completely equipped to be king of all."[15]

MORAL: The fable is appropriate for a senseless person.[16]

The Fox and the Grapes (Plate XIX) follows in the northeast spandrel of the fifth arch:

A hungry fox saw some grapes hanging from a vine in a tree and, although he was eager to reach them, was unable to do so. As he went away, he said to himself, "They're sour grapes."[17]

MORAL: So it is with men, too. If they cannot get what they want because of their own inability, they blame it on circumstances.[18]

The Old Lion and the Fox (Plate XX) is on the northeast face of the fifth arch:

A lion who was growing old and could not get his food by force decided he would have to get it by wit. So he went into a cave where he lay down and played sick. When the other animals came to visit him, he would eat them. After many animals had been done away with, a fox, who had seen through his trick, came along and, standing at a distance from the cave, asked him how he was. When the lion said he was not well and asked him why he did not come in, the fox said, "Why, I would if I did not see so many tracks going in but none coming out."[19]

MORAL: So it is that intelligent men sense danger from signs in advance and avoid it.[20]

The following fable, on the southeast face of the sixth arch, is too generalized to permit an unequivocal identification. I have suggested two alternatives as the subject of the scene. The first is that of *The Dog and the Wolf* (Plate XXI):

The wolves said to the dogs, "Why, since you are like us in every way, don't you show a brotherly spirit towards us? The only difference between us is one of principle. We live a life of freedom together but though you slave for men, all you get from them is beatings; you get collars put around your necks, and have to guard their sheep. But when you eat, all they throw you is bones. Why don't you listen to us? Turn the flocks over to us; we will share everything and have all we want to eat." So the dogs did as they said, but as soon as they got into the shelters where the sheep were kept, the dogs were the wolves's first victims.[21]

MORAL: That those who betray their own countries get an appropriate recompense.[22]

The second alternative subject of the same scene is the fable of *The Dog in Pursuit of the Wolf:*

A dog was chasing a wolf and was feeling proud of his swift-footedness and strength. At the same time he thought that the wolf was running from him out of weakness. Then the wolf turned around and said to the dog, "It is not you I am afraid of; I am afraid of being run down by your master."[23]

MORAL: This shows that one ought not take credit for good qualities that belong to others.[24]

The next identification is a more certain one—*The Fox and the Dog* (Plate XXII) on the northeast side of the sixth arch:

A fox slipped into a flock of sheep, took one of the suckling lambs, and pretended to be mothering it. When the dog asked, "What are you doing here?" she replied, "I am suckling this lamb and playing with it." Whereupon the dog said, "And now, if you do not let the lamb go, I'll give you some pups to suckle."[25]

MORAL: The fable is appropriate for a clumsy, inept thief.[26]

The fable of *The Fox and the Eagle* (Plate XXIII) is found on the southeast spandrel of the seventh arch:

An eagle and a fox that had struck up a friendship decided to live close to one another and made their living together a pledge of the friendship. The eagle flew up to a very tall tree and had its brood there, while the fox went into the thicket below and bore her young. Once when the fox went out to hunt, the eagle, having no food, flew down to the thicket, snatched up the young foxes, and helped its nestlings to devour them. When the fox returned and realized what had been done, she was not so much troubled by the death of her young as she was with revenge. As an earthbound creature she could not pursue her winged neighbor and therefore stood and cursed her enemy from a distance, which is the only resort of those who are weak and impotent. But it turned out before long that the eagle paid the penalty for her violation of the friendship. Some men were making a sacrifice in the country, and the eagle flew down and carried off a piece of burning entrail from the altar. When she brought this to the nest, which was made of old dry sticks, a strong wind caught it and started a bright fire. The nestlings, who were still unfledged, were caught in the fire and fell to the ground. The fox ran up and ate them all before the eagle's very eyes.[27]

MORAL: The fable shows that those who violate friendships do not avert the vengeance of God, even though they may escape punishment by those they have wronged because the latter are weak.[28]

The subject of the mural on the northeast face of the seventh arch is also difficult to identify with certainty. There are two fables that I would like to propose as possibilities (Plate XXIV):

A hog and dog were bickering with one another. When the hog swore by Aphrodite that he would tear him apart with his tusks if he did not stop, the dog said that was just where he showed his ignorance of Aphrodite, for she hated him so much that even if the man had eaten pork, she would not let him into her shrine. But the hog had an answer and said, "Oh yes, but you know she does not do this because she hates me. She is looking out for me so that no one will sacrifice me."[29]

MORAL: So it is that clever public speakers often turn the names they are called by their enemies into praise.[30]

A second suggested fable is the following:

A sow and a bitch were arguing about how easily they bore their young. The bitch said that she was the only four-footed animal that brought them forth so quickly. The sow replied, "Yes, but when you say this you must realize that they are still blind when you bear them."[31]

MORAL: The story shows that accomplishments are not judged by speed but by completeness.[32]

The final fable is found in the southeast spandrel of the eighth arch, *The Thief and the Dog* (Plate XXV):

A thief came in the night to break into a house. He brought with him several slices of meat that he might pacify the house dog. As the thief threw him the piece of meat the dog said, "This gift will only make me more watchful."[33]

MORAL: Fair words, presents, and flatteries are the methods of treachery in courts as well as in cottages; only the dogs are truer to their masters than the men.[34]

Before returning to the purpose of the murals in the overall program, let me point out that the style of the Aesop scenes is similar to that of the Biblical representations. A primary principle appears again to be the achievement of the sharpest impact of the narrative by means of the reduction of all extraneous elements. Another link with the Biblical depictions, and a further way in which the impression of an overall direction and meaning is given to the vast program, is that the fables are composed with a view toward accommodation to the irregular form of the spandrel and with an effort to orient them toward the center of the hall.[35]

The scenes are extraordinary in the vivid naturalism of the animals and settings. The fable of *The Dog Carrying Meat* (Plate XVI), for example, includes perhaps the earliest representation of a reflected image in water.[36] Although one might argue that the particular demands of the story led to this advance in the direct observation of nature, or that the realism might be related to traditions in the representation of Aesop, as it surely is, such qualifications in no way lessen the achievement. In many of the other scenes there is an equally impressive realism.[37]

The educational adaptations made of the Aesop texts during the late Middle Ages, including the moral and philosophical lessons to be drawn from them, partly account for the inclusion of the scenes among the Perugia murals. Beginning in the classical age the fables were used widely in the schools not only for their obvious moral value, but also because theoreticians and philosophers found them useful for the study of grammar and rhetoric or argument.[38] The fables served, in short, a serious instructional function sharply at variance with the present view of Aesop as light or childish diversion. By the thirteenth century, Aesop and similar collections of animal lore had become so popular and so valued that their veracity was the frequent object of debate among educators, some of whom had come to believe that the stories enjoyed an unreasonably important status and that students were being indirectly subjected to false knowledge.[39] The animal frescoes thus should properly take a place beside the Biblical stories in the Perugia council hall as a major source of wisdom. That Aesop was accorded an elevated position in the city cannot be doubted, for a generation earlier the fables represented on the Fontana Maggiore were grouped with the Liberal Arts as a fountainhead of knowledge.[40]

The effectiveness of the fables as a didactic vehicle would seem to be broadened through their representation in the council hall.[41] This brings us to a further, general ramification of the Aesop murals. In his study of animal fables during the Middle Ages, Klingender proposes a connection between what he describes as the increasing popularization of knowledge during the thirteenth century and the employment of animal symbolism which is seen as a means to make knowledge more easily accessible.[42] Perhaps, then, one indication of the republican temper of Perugia at the end of the thirteenth century is the use made of the fables. Aesop, as a compendium of a folk or popular wisdom, had always been associated with a disguised opposition of the folk to privilege and aristocratic power; and the popular effort to restrain the power of the nobles was, as we have observed, a characteristic of the political situation in Perugia in the late thirteenth century.[43]

When one bears in mind that Perugia was not alone in the utilization of the popular wisdom of the bestiary as a motif in the decoration of a civic palace, the relevance of Klingender's hypothesis seems more persuasive. Two diverse examples of such decorations might be mentioned here. Although neither one is derived from Aesop, the application of animal lore is an echo of the murals in Perugia.

The first example was the representation of a lion looking tenderly upon its young, an image that was painted above the main exterior portal of the Senator's Palace in Rome in 1300.[44] In an effort to inspire compassion and magnanimity, every senator was ceremoniously brought before the mural when inducted into office. Beneath the image was the following inscription:

IRATUS RECOLE QUOD NOBILIS IRA LEONIS
IM SIBI PROSTRATUS SE NEGAT ESSE FERAM.[45]

Thus, the behavior of the lion toward its cubs is intended as a model for the paternal behavior of the leader toward his subjects. The function of the Aesop fables at Perugia is much the same: the stories are meant to influence the thinking and behavior of the city rulers. Further, the decorations in the two palaces inform the citizens of the righteous and moral goals to which their government is dedicated. It is possible that the parallel is even more precise than I have thus far implied; the Aesop murals, too, may have played some role in the political rituals of the city as the lion mural did in the political rituals of Rome.[46]

Further dimension to the context for the fables at Perugia is offered by the sculptural decorations on the façade of the Palazzo del Podestà in Narni dated about 1280.[47] A generalized scene of battling knights is given allegorical extension through the representation of a dragon struggling with a lion. Narni, a leading city in the Papal State, is symbolized by the Guelph lion, while the dragon is a sign of the evil force of the enemies of the state. The neighboring relief of *The Beheading of Holofernes* indicates that the sculptures might be invested with a fervent populism. Janson and Wind have demonstrated how the Judith episode came to allude in the fifteenth century to the conquest of civic republican virtues over tyranny; the Narni sculpture might represent a precedent for the Quattrocento.[48] In any case, like the emblematic or allegorical image of the lion and its cubs at Rome, the Narni decorations at least suggest the possibility of a connection between the use of animal symbolism and metaphor in the proclamation of communal principles.

As further, general support for the "folk" or popular nature of the animal legends, it should be noticed that the illustration of Aesop and the lore of the bestiary received their first monumental expression in the public art of the exteriors of the Romanesque French cathedrals.[49] The popularization of ethical principles through the representation of animal fables placed on cathedral façades seems as related and as natural an occurrence as the erosion of the power of the aristocratic families in an age that witnessed a general broadening of the foundation of political and economic power.[50] The famous controversy between Suger and Bernard of Clairvaux on the question of the secularization of ecclesiastical imagery, and in particular on the matter of the appropriateness of animals as decorative devices, is the clearest barometer of how the depiction of such subjects was an aspect of the tendency of the time to use secular motifs in the expression of moral and workaday truths.[51]

The direct association of Aesop with the popular religious movements of thirteenth-century Italy is yet another indication of the effort to reach a larger and less educated audience through a more popular and easily grasped subject matter. As in the cathedral decorations, animal fables were cited by Dominican and Franciscan preachers in order to translate the moral truths of the sermons into a vulgar or popular currency.[52] Preachers were advised by Vincent of Beauvais to apply the animal fables in this way, so the practice even carried a theoretical sanction.[53] Animal stories were also widespread in the margins of manuscript illuminations during the late thirteenth century and thus served the same purpose as in the sermons: general theological or ethical theorems and texts were made more accessible, or at least more vivid, to the semi-literate reader.[54] In monumental art, aside from the cathedral sculptures, the fables and legends of the bestiaries were also popular and widespread. For example, animal allegories are depicted in the border medallions in the Arena Chapel at Padua, distilling in simple form the meaning of the murals.[55]

A related and more manifest political function of the fables was their use, in the form of extended similes, as proof of political assumptions in the literature of the thirteenth century.[56] The practice would seem to have been common in the neo-Aristotelian circle of Aquinas, the group whose thought was vital in shaping, however indirectly, the meaning of the Biblical murals at Perugia.[57] The reason that tyranny is to be condemned, Aquinas writes, is that it opposes the natural order of things; in other words, a state of tyranny denies what he believes to be true among the lower animals.[58] Through the study of the social habits of animals, Aquinas says, the features of human society can be best understood.

Closer to the spirit in which the fables are employed at Perugia are the animal similes in handbooks compiled for the guidance of princes and the related practice of inserting advisory material in bestiaries.[59] Typical of this material is the proposal that when sovereigns have erred they should erase their misdeeds through humble repentance and through greater beneficence for their citizens "as the lion escapes pursuit by obliterating footprints with its tail."[60] Another popular simile or parallel runs as follows: as the lion's whelps lie three days dormant after they are born, so the monarch must give heed to three matters before arriving at a decision, the three matters being the advice of his councilors, the comparison of their differing views, and the adoption of the best advice.[61] Although the fables of Aesop were apparently never used in these handbooks, one meaning of the Perugia frescoes was that they too included practical instruction for the leaders of the city.

Other evidence of the direct relation between the wisdom of the bestiaries and the policies of government comes in the form of popular political tales with animal characters. One widespread folk story dealing with the emperor was popularized by Dante. The legend concerns a giant dog that was said to rule over Asia but had designs on the Western world. A variation of the tale dealt with the prediction that a dog would come to deliver nations from oppression by defeating the evil of the she-wolf who ruled over the West.[62]

Comparison with the famous tale of the Wolf of Gubbio shows how these variant tales followed a rather conventional line: a confrontation between evil, symbolized in both tales by a wolf, and a symbol or embodiment of goodness.[63] Klingender has summarized the message of the story of the Wolf of Gubbio as follows:

> Beneath the popular, anecdotal appeal of the story is the deeper symbolism of bestial, uncontrolled nature transformed by sanctity, and an anagogical identification of the wolf with brigands, heretics and other outlaws from society redeemed by Saint Francis's all-embracing compassion and courtesy.[64]

It seems clear that all the political folk tales can be reduced to such commentaries on contemporary conditions. As the wolf was thought to be unlawful and mendacious, no stronger negation of the obsession with control and concord could be found. And the wolf is one of the leading characters in the Aesop murals at Perugia, figuring prominently in four of the scenes.

But to appreciate the special significance of the fables at Perugia, one must also observe their general association with scenes of combat. A generalized scene of combat at Perugia, aside from the battle representations in the areas flanking the main portal of the council hall, is the representation of *Saint George and the Dragon* (Plate XIV) in the southeast spandrel of the third arch. Once the association of animal fables with scenes of combat is recognized, the intrusion of the story of Saint George among the fables appears entirely reasonable.

Two rather disparate monuments may be cited to summarize the nature of the tradition from which the Perugia murals spring. The first is the Bayeux tapestry (1066-1082), the second is the Porta della Pescheria at Modena (c. 1150). Several fables of Aesop are represented on the upper and lower borders of the Bayeux tapestry. The inclusion of the fables in the commemoration of an historical event was quite commonplace.[65] The significance of the particular battle was thereby enhanced and it became an instructive or exemplary action. Just as the scene of the confronting animals at Narni carried the representation of the battle into an allegorical sphere, so the fables on the tapestry transfer the victory into a far more generalized context as descriptive of the behavior of the victors. Success in war is seen as dependent first on the virtue and common sense of the combatants.[66] The fables exemplify principles that guided the victors, and the victory itself is transformed into a demonstration of the efficacy of these principles.

At Modena the fables of Aesop are found on the lintels beneath the representation of an Arthurian conflict.[67] That the fables may be somewhat later in date is in itself no proof that a connection between the allegories and the scene of conflict was not intended. The fables were possibly added to the original core of the program with a view toward enrichment and expansion. The theme at Modena, as on the Bayeux tapestry, is to show how victory in war is possible only if the knights are guided by an ethical and practical standard of conduct. The fact that this meaning is expressed on the Cathedral in conjunction with a mythic rather than historic conflict implies, more clearly than in the tapestry, the relation between war and chivalric ideals.[68] The Arthurian conquest emerges both as an illustration of exemplary victory and as a reference to the character of the ideal warrior.

The tapestry and the sculptures summarize the nature of the range of monuments in which war and animal fables are linked. An actual victory is commemorated in the first instance, while in the second, an epic or mythic event is charged with more general significance through the introduction of the allegories. The historical event and the poetic fantasy are also revealed as metaphors and as sources of inspiration for the actions of the state.

We have already observed how in the stories of Gideon and Moses communal warfare was introduced as an important aspect of the decorations at Perugia. The theme of communal crusade becomes even more important with the depiction of *Saint George and the Dragon*. The mural is itself an emblem of war and of ideal martial values.[69] In the late Middle Ages, Saint George had come to stand increasingly as a kind of patron figure for soldiers and as a guide for real as well as for literary heroes. Roland, for example, was commonly called the "new" Saint George, and following his sacred model, the writers of the epics and romances proclaimed that the hero was a man of courage and was dedicated to upholding the chivalric code.[70] These same ideals were regularly invoked in the still partly feudal world of the free commune.[71]

Saint George as the champion of lost and noble causes, as the conqueror of evil—such variants on the theme of the Saint as exemplar of the knightly ideal were prominent aspects of his fortunes during the thirteenth century throughout Europe, especially in Italy and France.[72] This attribute of the

Saint's meaning was also well adapted to the contemporary mood of the communes, in particular to the crusading *apologia* that justified nearly all its military ventures. The Saint was conceived at the time as the titular leader of the effort to liberate the Holy Land, so his name and feats were invoked in the most important crusades of the day.[73] Again and again he miraculously appears in a literary description or representation of a crusader conflict, not surprisingly on a splendid white horse, to turn the tide of battle in favor of the Christians.[74]

In Rome, notably at the papal court, interest in Saint George as a crusader-savior was especially keen. Manuscripts were produced extolling his special virtues, and at least one major monument, a mural representing the Saint in armor on his white horse, was commissioned in about 1295. There is no doubt that this fresco in S. Giorgio in Velabro was painted by a member of Cavallini's circle, perhaps by the master himself, and thus there is a strong stylistic link with the Perugia mural.[75] It is tempting to explain this stylistic and thematic connection as an expression of the close ties between the two cities and of Perugia's pre-eminent position as defender of the papacy.[76] And, to be sure, the crusading spirit of the two cities at the end of the thirteenth century was intense partly because each helped to sustain the strength of the crusading spirit in the other.

But the appropriateness of the mural for the Perugia program appears to extend beyond its immediate relation to the fables of Aesop. Saint George joins the list of civic heroes of the time. With Gideon and Moses, the Saint was meant to inspire in the citizens a zealous and aggressive sense of chauvinist pride and bravado.

Before returning to the Aesop illustrations, a word should be added about the dragon that the Saint battles. If the role of Saint George at Perugia was in accord with contemporary papal thinking and interests, then the dragon also was a popular denotation for the enemies of Rome. In papal art as early as the twelfth century, the dragon had assumed an overtly political function as a symbol of evil counsel and satanic power.[77] The story of Saint George must have appeared all the more irresistible given this conception of the beast vanquished by the Saint. I do not mean to imply that this role of the dragon in papal art is unusual; the dragon as a symbol of Satan was universal. What is notable here is that the pronounced political meaning accorded to the papal dragon is perhaps one source or precedent for the political role that the story of the Saint plays in Perugia. An earlier communal adaptation of the dragon is the relief already noted at Narni. The image of *Saint George and the Dragon* was, in short, a highly charged political symbol.

As for the specific implications of each of the Aesop scenes, little can be said with absolute certainty. There is no direct relation that I have been able to discern, as noted earlier, between the fables and the opposed Biblical representations. The relationship perhaps does not go beyond the general one of the fables offering a practical or mundane kind of translation of the Old Testament stories. For example, in a broad sense the first fable of *The Wolf and the Lamb* might be said to have some direct bearing on the scene of *Moses and Aaron before the Pharaoh*. Both stories teach that reasonable and just arguments cannot sway an unreasoning individual. For the most part, however, without invoking too strained an argument, the fables should be considered independently.

Something more can be said about the general choice of fables. The first, that of *The Wolf and the Lamb,* touches a moot point in legal argument and its effect on those set to do wrong. The story is a fitting one for the beginning of the cycle of Aesop because it relates to an issue fundamental to the whole program: the necessity, when all else fails, to use force against the enemies of the state.

The following fable, *The Dog Carrying Meat,* complements this first lesson with a more practical kind of reminder to the legislators. Painted at a time when the commune had become an imperial force in Umbria, the fable enjoins the leaders of the city not to over-extend its resources and to hold their own ambitions within bounds.

The Wolf and the Crane repesents another lesson in practical statecraft. One must always be vigilant and cautious in dealing with potential enemies. A tough and watchful conduct is advised, backed always by a strong and ready military. The following three scenes—*The Fox and the Crow, The Fox and the Grapes,* and *The Old Lion and the Fox*—are variations of the same motif. Never trust the envious rivals of the state is the clear message here as well. The error of the crane in trusting the wolf is not repeated by the fox because of his skeptical attitude.

The illustrations of *The Dog and the Wolf* (or *The Dog in Pursuit of the Wolf*), *The Fox and the Dog,* and *The Fox and the Eagle,* all concern the responsibilities of the leader to those in his charge. The didactic import of these first fables, especially their relation to the political conduct of Perugian citizens, is demostrated through a series of exempla.

The last fables—*The Hog and the Dog* (or *The Sow and the Bitch*), and *The Thief and the Dog*—treat another aspect of good and wise government: the ethics of the leaders themselves. The illustrations set forth clear ideals for public behavior on questions regarding how officials should deal with criticism, how civic goals and accomplishments should be judged, and why leaders should be wary of those who seek to curry favor with them.

Erich Auerbach, in his essay on the *Mystère d'Adam,* explored the almost universal medieval practice of relegating the profound to the everyday, of "hiding" religious truths in the simplest and most mundane affairs.[78] In this sense the general appeal of Aesop is readily appreciated. Here was a perfect vehicle for a forthright yet veiled, and yet sometimes amusing and highly dramatic expression of basic laws of social and political behavior.

A second point that Auerbach makes is that such transformational art cannot be considered truly secular, for the "everyday" character of, in this instance, the fables of Aesop, is, by its very nature, capable of expressing profound truths. "A real secularization does not take place," Auerbach writes, ". . . until the secular action becomes independent; that is, when human actions outside of Christian world history, as determined by Fall, Passion, and Last Judgment, are represented in a serious vein."[79] In this sense, the fables, as one element of a religious-based program that unites the state to a divinely-inspired mission, are themselves transformed into "religious" images that express Christian ideals in the popular style of the everyday. The Biblical images establish the goals of the policies and actions of the commune, while the fables add the element of shrewdness and practical wisdom necessary for the carrying out of public purpose.

8

The Astrological Frescoes and Planetary Protection

The astrological subjects of the final group of murals is the most original and unanticipated aspect of the program; "unanticipated" in that the first analogous cycle in Italy has previously been thought to be Giotto's lost work for the Palazzo della Ragione in Padua, dating from about 1309 to 1313, or some ten years after the Perugia frescoes.[1] The Perugia murals are thus important not only in their own right in adding one other sphere of meaning to the overall scheme but also in representing a striking precedent, perhaps a source, for what shortly became a common motif in civic palace decorations in Italy.[2]

For the first time in this discussion the problem of loss discloses an unfortunate lack of evidence. As suggested by a few remaining fragments, the now destroyed murals originally on the south and northwest faces of the sixth arch, and the frescoes that were painted below the windows on the east side of the hall, must have been all a significant part of the grouping of astrological scenes. (I will have a suggestion to make regarding the possible subjects of these murals.) The nine surviving astrological scenes are the following: the personifications of the months of *January and February* (Plate XXVI) in the lunette above the main portal of the hall, two fragments of the scenes of *Battling Knights* (Plate XXVII) on the east and west sides of the north wall, *The Contemplative Man* (Plate XXVIII) in the southeast spandrel of the eighth arch, *The Man with the Rearing Horse* (Plate XXIX) on the northwest side of the eighth arch, *The Knight in Prayer* (Plate XXX) in the southwest spandrel of the eighth arch, *The Soldiers Crossing a Bridge* (Plate XXXI) on the northwest face of the seventh arch, *The Knight Battling a Dragon* (Plate XXXII) on the southwest side of the seventh arch, *The Woman Riding a Horse* (Plate XXXIII) on the northwest side of the fifth arch, and *The Bull and Boar* beneath the window between the sixth and seventh arches.

Before attempting to explicate the subjects and themes, it should be pointed out that the style of the works is once more related to general principles and approaches established in the Biblical representations. The quality of the works now under consideration is somewhat more uneven than in the preceding groupings, but there is a consistency of composition and of orientation to suggest again that the works, although executed by several artists of varying abilities, were nonetheless shaped by a unifying concept.[3]

There appears to have been little in the way of a fixed tradition in the depiction of the planets and their influences during the thirteenth and early fourteenth centuries in Italy. This is as we might expect, for in addition to the fact that there existed a large and varied number of literary sources for the astrological knowledge of the time, both ancient and contemporary, as well as a remarkably diverse range of applications to which this knowledge was put, there were few if any comparable earlier works upon which the Perugia scheme might have been based.[4] The astrological culture of the time was simply not a very settled one. Arabic and classical practices and thought vied with new principles introduced by scholastic applications. By the fourteenth century the status, nature, and value of astrology would be more firmly established as these various elements converged to form a uniform body of belief and philosophy, but at the moment—the late thirteenth century— astrological perceptions were in flux.[5] Fortunately the more extensive and better preserved astrological works that replaced Giotto's in Padua beginning in about 1340 are quite close to the Perugia cycle both in terms of general design and specific motifs and scenes.[6] For this reason the Padua murals will be of great importance in the interpretation of the Perugia frescoes.

The cycle begins with the lunette-shaped representation of *January and February* (Plate XXVI). January is personified by a man holding two containers aloft and seated before a table laden with food. The single anomalous feature in this otherwise traditional interpretation is the upraised arms of the figure, a posture that is perhaps to be explained by the ever-present desire of the artists to make the details of the murals easily visible to the viewer.[7] The personification of February as a monk warming himself before a fire also follows an established formula.[8]

The problem of accounting for the representation of the particular months in a civic palace can be resolved in two ways. On the primary level of interpretation, the works illustrate the role of the commune as provider for the citizens through the most difficult months of the year. After the justification of the commune as protector of the citizens and as the maintainer of order and concord, perhaps the second most often cited justification for government in the Middle Ages was that it helped to provide food for the citizens.[9] Indeed, the obligation to maintain peace and order was important in large measure precisely because these were the only conditions under which food could be produced and distributed. The peace of the food-producing *contado* was thus a leading end for government.[10] During the second half of the thirteenth century Perugia ceased using the surrounding countryside as a source of revenue and began using the *contado* for its grain supplies. The preservation of order in the countryside was even more essential than earlier.[11] One can easily understand why after the appearance of new cathedrals and town halls, the building of new and expanded town graineries, as in Perugia, was among the most common features in the urban development of the thirteenth century. Hans Baron and his theory of medieval wealth notwithstanding, it would seem to be increasingly true that the justification of civic and private wealth in fifteenth century Italy derives in no small part from the experiences of the thirteenth-century commune.[12] *January and February* thus stand as reminders of how the town provides for the bodily needs of its citizens.

But this explanation does not proceed far enough. A second aspect of the meaning of the scenes is suggested when we examine the murals that follow the months. The succeeding frescoes, I believe, represent inclinations of Jupiter and Saturn, the planets associated with, respectively, January and February.[13] The representation of these particular months can now be explained more completely.

The spheres of influence of Jupiter and Saturn are of the greatest political consequence among all the planets. Jupiter has always been the special planet of rulers. More specifically, the planet's province is dignity and dominion, the leading attributes of rule. The association of Jupiter with the protection of religious and secular leaders, warriors, religion, laws, and the public good, brings the planet into even closer relationship with political questions.[14]

Saturn, the planet of February, complements Jupiter in that its sphere governs public works and welfare, the ends and goals of the ideal leader and of government.[15] Saturn is believed to be the protector of agriculture and the *arte meccaniche*. Also, while Jupiter is associated with action and war, Saturn is linked with contemplation.[16]

Only during the late thirteenth century did Saturn take on once more these positive attributes, ones that the planet had held in the ancient world, although few philosophers would change their negative outlooks before the middle of the fourteenth century. The translation of Aristotle's *Problemata physica* between 1258 and 1266 was the most important influence in the early stages of the revival of the general link of the planet with genius and rule and the purging of its medieval association with lowliness, evil, and sorrow.[17] One of the few leading figures in the intellectual life of the age who early championed the revivified classical conception was Pietro d'Abano, the philosopher whose views are most important for the astrological scenes at both Perugia and Padua.[18]

Embodied in the isolation of the two planets are the twin foundations of good rule: an aggressive and active form of leadership that is grounded in the careful and thoughtful consideration and mapping out of policies. January and February are closely allied, then, to a major subject in the other elements of the decorations at Perugia. A notion of leadership derived from the celebration of military genius and the careful consideration of the practical and moral consequences of policy is the ideal proposed in the murals, an ideal drawn from the Old Testament and from Aesop. Now this ideal is placed within its planetary context and assigned a planetary guardianship. Moral, Biblical, practical, and astrological imperatives coalesce in the enunciation of political wisdom.

The use of personifications of the months to orient a scheme of astrological decorations is not unusual. The most immediate successor of the plan of decorations at Perugia was that of the Palazzo della Ragione in the mid-fourteenth century.[19] At least two other later, important arrangements of astrological embellishments, those at Trent, (c. 1410)[20] and Ferrara (c. 1470),[21] followed this same organization. Reference to these similar designs serves largely, however, to affirm the unique character of the Perugia murals. Only at Perugia were two months and their associated planets singled out. The specific, political implications of Jupiter and Saturn appear even more significant when the special character of the Sala dei Notari murals is considered. The choice of January and February was carefully determined to stress and to complement the meaning of the Biblical and allegorical scenes.

The two scenes that oppose the months on the north side of the eighth arch dramatically highlight the distinction between Jupiter and Saturn as the twin protectors of the city. Facing the personification of February is *The Contemplative Man* (Plate XXVIII), a figure seated in a summarily noted landscape with his left hand raised to his forehead in the classic posture of thought. The mural opposite the month of January is *The Man with the Rearing Horse* (Plate XXIX), a straining figure barely able to control the struggling animal. The configuration of this latter scene follows that of the *Dioscuri;* the meaning of the work is determined in part by this borrowing. The two frescoes define the fundamental contrast between the planets: the contemplative inclination of those individuals inspired and guarded by Saturn is expressed by the "thinker" while the horseman may be considered a personification of strength. The union of opposites, of thought and action, is expressed, and the major foundation of the decorations is thus distilled in a simple confrontation of scenes.

The images are not entirely without reflection in the contemporary art. Among the illustrations of Saturn's inclinations at Padua is a contemplative figure in very much the same posture as that at Perugia.[22] Among the murals grouped around the planet Jupiter in the Palazzo della Ragione there is a rearing horse that also appears to echo the related scene at Perugia. The horse at Padua, without the tamer, stands for the unstable individual. In conjunction with the also related representation of *The Man Riding a Camel,* which has been interpreted as a symbol of strength, the implication is analogous to that at Perugia.[23] Now a beneficent influence of the planet is the control of instability through strength and, while the meaning of the Sala dei Notari mural is somewhat more precise, we may safely interpret instability to be synonymous with civil disorder. Once more the meaning of the cycle reflects the concern of the political theorists and theologians alike with the role of government as the enforcer of order, concord, and harmony.

The union of opposites, of strength and contemplation, at both Perugia and Padua, also illustrates ideal traits of the ruler. From the chivalric idealization of the hero to the definition of the duties of the *podestà,* which were described first in the literature of the North Italian communes of the twelfth century and later in the Perugian statutes themselves,[24] the "Big Man," as the anthropologists would call him,[25] was at once an informed and intelligent individual as well as one able to perform as a warrior when occasion so demanded. Although the precise intentions of the scenes of *The Battling Knights* cannot be determined, the works do offer at least a further generalized indication of the importance of the theme of the leader as warrior and of the primacy of military strength as a bulwark of the commune.

The similarity of the Padua and Perugia schemes suggests a common source. But the problem of a common source can be put aside for the moment in order to deal first with the meaning of each of the scenes. Comparison with the Padua decorations serves to point out the originality of the *Dioscuri* configuration with the planet Jupiter. Quite apart from the remarkable archaelogical accuracy of the scene, there is an added element of meaning that the work assumes through this derivation. In the most popular of the pilgrim guides of Rome during the period, the essentially twelfth-century compilation of fact and legend known as the *Mirabilia,* the *Dioscuri* are given a political meaning entirely consistent with the Perugia program. The rearing horse was said to be a symbol of tyranny being stamped from the face of the earth.[26] Perhaps, then, the choice of the ancient grouping in the astrological decorations included some allusion to the popular symbolism ascribed to the monument. The astrological definition of the scene in fact complements that found in the *Mirabilia.* Both express the importance of fortitude in the defense of moral political ends.

The scenes that follow *The Man with the Rearing Horse* on the west side of the hall illustrate other inclinations and aspects of the planet Jupiter. The fact that only a single mural corresponds to the planet Saturn intimates the far greater importance granted to values associated with Jupiter. The activist, martial emphasis in the astrological series is consistent with the rest of the frescoes.

Following *The Man with the Rearing Horse* is *The Knight in Prayer* (Plate XXX). This work relates to Jupiter in several ways. We have already observed that the protection of religion fell within the sovereignty of Jupiter. So too did the protection of warriors. The subject unites within itself then, two of the chief influences of the planet. Prayer was a highly institutionalized ritual among soldiers of that period. so the scene honors a current practice as well.[27] As for the artistic setting for the theme, representations of knights in prayer were common manuscript border illustrations. The image appears to have been especially widespread in crusader-related manuscripts.[28] The influence of the contemporary crusading drive is perhaps again evident at Perugia. The conviction that the mission of the commune was a holy one, and that the heroic feats of such sacred individuals as Gideon, Moses, and Saint George were meant to be emulated by the leaders and citizens—this pattern of ideals is reflected in *The Knight in Prayer.*[29]

Comparison with the astrological designs at Padua is again instructive. Several representations of figures in prayer and of figures offering or receiving blessings are found among the inclinations of Jupiter.[30] The prominence of martial values at Perugia is now even more obvious, for none of the related Padua murals represents warriors engaged in such actions.

The following mural, *The Soldiers Crossing a Bridge* (Plate XXXI), gives additional support to the knightly motif. The aspect of Jupiter to which the scene relates, I believe, is the planet's role as overseer of public welfare. The woman who obstructs the soldiers by standing in their path appears as the spirit of a moral order that reigns in the city not simply because of the force that the city has at its disposal—we have already seen ample illustration of this source of civic coercion—but because she is the embodiment of a just principle followed by the city's upright, chivalric knights. Water was considered a symbol of instability, so that a bridge over water would represent another token of order.[31]

There are, once more, several analogous scenes at Padua following a standard formula of a bridge spanning a turbulent body of water. Barzon has interpreted these scenes in much the same way suggested for the mural at Perugia: symbols of the stability that comes with the domination of the planet Jupiter.[32] At Perugia the idea does not remain static; one beholds a narrative illustration of the principle. Apart from offering fresh evidence of the desire to make political principles as accessible and as clear as possible, the subject is brought into the orbit of chivalric and crusader imagery of the type also exemplified by the preceding scene of *The Knight in Prayer.*

The specific order of theme that relates to *The Soldiers Crossing a Bridge* is epitomized by those works generally described as "courtly," those in which the influence of feminine love overcomes the force of arms.[33] As we saw earlier in the examination of *Saint George and the Dragon*, the work would appear to portray the transmutation of feudal notions regarding love and service and chivalric devotion into strict adherence to the social and political law of the community. Such adaptations should be understood within the setting of the vigorous campaign that the populist political associations of Perugia were then conducting against the special rights of the nobles of the city. The putative chivalric elements of the murals were intended to make clear that the first duty of the *magnati* was to the community and not to the privileges and perogatives formerly attached to their class.[34]

The modification of the tradition of courtly love to conform to the conditions of Italian civic life is in fact one possible way of regarding the whole literary phenomenon of the *Dolce stil nuovo.*[35] But one need not even take into account the feudal aspects of the culture to see how the power of love became a kind of political manifesto. For the Aristotelianism of the age is rooted in traditional Christian thinking in the sense that a special place was reserved for love as the bond of the community.[36] Seen thus, *The Soldiers Crossing a Bridge* is a response to the artistic and literary theme of armed knights defeated by women whose only weapons are flowers.[37] The fact that the soldiers succumb without a struggle at Perugia only adds to the credit of the knights of the city. And that they are Perugian soldiers cannot be doubted: on the shield of the leading figure is the *stemma* of the *podestà* of the city.[38]

One other scene associated with Jupiter at Padua, in addition to those representing a bridge over water, supports this interpretation of the Perugia mural. The subject of the related work is that of a woman aiding an old man.[39] Like the work at Perugia where soldiers are swayed by principle, the scene deals in the most general sense with the nobility of spirit that is an aspect of the reign of Jupiter.

The inclusion of scenes of chivalric and charictable actions at both Padua and Perugia may be associated, finally, with the virtue of Charity herself, who in the hierarchy of political virtues, held a position second only to that of the virtue of Justice.[40] The subject of an old man being helped derives more immediately from Charity-related imagery, but the late medieval conception of the Virtue was sufficiently broad to include the more original depiction of the "charity" of knights as expressed in their relationship with women.[41]

The next mural in the series, *The Knight Battling a Dragon* (Plate XXXII), would seem to make generalized reference to the Jupiter-war relationship. The work is clearly a translation of the image of Saint George's struggle with evil into an expression of the meaning of Jupiter's guardianship over Perugia. In this sense the doubly-charged scene joins the preceding three murals. *The Man with the Rearing Horse* refers to the relation of the planet with strength, *The Knight in Prayer* to the relation of the planet with religion, *The Soldiers Crossing a Bridge* to chivalry as a foundation of the public good, and now the scene of *The Knight Battling a Dragon* to the relation of the planet with war. The dragon, as in the mural of Saint George, is the likeness of that which the city seeks to expunge in its struggles under the joint protection afforded by prayer and by Jupiter. Among all the phases of the planet that we have seen depicted thus far, the most common parallel is with this last inclination, that of war. On many contemporary and later calendar illustrations for the month of January, as well as in other astrological programs with the god Jupiter, there is included either a generalized, symbolic conflict of the sort we have seen at Perugia, or a realistically detailed description of a particular conflict.[42]

The Woman Riding a Horse (Plate XXXIII), the final astrological scene in the spandrels, draws the significance of Jupiter's guardianship away from war and back to a more chivalric-related concept, that of *dignitas*.[43] Dignity, proper bearing and conduct were all inclinations of the planet indicative of the ideal behavior of a leader. The more secure identification of the Padua murals is a basis for this interpretation. Several figures related to Jupiter show individuals comporting themselves in a stately manner, such as the depiction of a man walking at a slow and measured pace.[44] The grave and serious air and the noble bearing of the woman on the horse offer very much the same impression of great composure, dignity, and distinction.

Again, however, the fresco at Perugia includes another possible allusion to martial motifs. The only notable artistic precedent for the depiction of a woman seated on a horse is that of a legendary maiden who was believed to be a protector of knights.[45] Like the significance that the figure of Saint George holds for the program, one possible implication of *The Woman Riding a Horse* is that of a guardian of warriors.

The final part of the astrological program survives only in what I believe to be a fragment of the original design. At the base of the east wall, between the second and third arches, is a mural of a boar and a lion. The work was perhaps part of a cycle of animals of the zodiac that ran the length of the window wall. The function of these animals is made clear through comparison with the similar arrangement to be found at Padua. Barzon and Grossato note that the animals at Padua illustrate judicial sayings. (The image of the lion on the Senator's Palace in Rome functions in much the same way.) Maxims based on popularly perceived aspects of the animals were written beneath them to reveal the specific legalistic implications of each.[46] The animals of the zodiac at Perugia and Padua would seem to have the same practical purpose and content as those of the Aesop fables—they reduce the general principles of the narrative murals to mundane truths or helpful rules of conduct.

The proposed linkage between an astrological scheme and a communal ideology perhaps would appear at first to be unlikely if not wholly antithetical. As most historians have stressed the fatalistic and scholastic implications of the astrology of the late Middle Ages, a system of political beliefs that would employ astrology to justify the pre-eminence of the free commune and free individual seems confused and inconsistent.[47]

The issue can be analyzed in its sharpest outlines in Padua during the first decades of the fourteenth century. As the enunciation of republican principle became more pronounced during the last years of communal freedom, so too, as a possible defensive reaction, did the conviction and faith of the ruling class in the uses of astrology. This concurrent development can be traced most clearly in the evolution of the thought of the leading member of the city's literary and political culture, Albertino Mussato.[48] Mussato's republicanism and astrology would not appear to be unnatural allies. For Mussato's view of history, as made up of cycles that repeated themselves in regular and predictable patterns, implied that history could be brought to the service of the state.[49] History could thus be "scientifically" employed for social and political ends. The past had lessons to teach. Among these lessons was that of vigilance in the preservation of republicanism because the alternative, tyranny, would be abhorrent.[50] Thus, far from locking man into a deterministic or mechanical universe, the particular form of astrology that flourished at the moment made it possible for man to come to grips with the past and to influence, as did the planets, the present and the future.

The conception of astrology in the free cities of the time was much like the contemporary understanding of the meaning of fortune. The caprices and evil effects of fortune, it was then believed, might be remedied or at least made predictable through an active life dedicated to virtue.[51] The public function that astrology assumed in Padua through the decorations by Giotto in the 1320s in the Palazzo Comunale, and through Mussato, and perhaps most importantly through Pietro d'Abano, can now be understood. Far from suggesting fatalistic withdrawal from the world, the decorations proclaim, like the contemporary conception of fortune, the possibility of seizing and shaping one's life.

A final aspect of the astrology of the epoch takes the philosophy even further from the refined and unworldly realm of scholasticism. I refer here to the underlying belief that the city as a human community was subject to natural laws.[52] The task of the astrologer was to interpret these laws and to relate them directly to the life and experience of the city and the citizen.

Mention of the "task" of the astrologer raises another problem in this contextual examination of the planetary inclinations at Perugia. Padua had a long record of astrologers working in the employ of the government and engaged in the business of discovering days propitious for beginning a war or for engaging in a battle.[53] But Padua was not alone in this practice. Almost all the communes employed astrologers if only for a short time or on an irregular basis.[54] The astrological scenes at Perugia and at Padua support the free spirit of the two towns and reflect the practical sense in which the study of the planets was very much a part of policy making.

That the work of the astrologers was concerned chiefly with the conduct of war reveals the appropriateness of murals illustrating the inclinations of Jupiter for the highly militant culture of the city as well as for the martial emphasis throughout the program of decorations in the Sala dei Notari. The direct relationship between war and astrology is apparent in other ways as well at the time. An important bit of artistic evidence is a group of works in the castle of Angera dated about 1300 and a scheme of frescoes from Castelbarco dated 1310.[55] In both, the signs of the zodiac are represented together with important battles in the histories of the towns. Before the last decade of the thirteenth century, it might be noted in contrast, the major astrological schemes in Italian art were for the most part simply representations of the signs of the zodiac either as sculptural embellishments for the facades of the North Italian cathedrals or as mosaic floor decorations of an equally generalized nature.[56]

Also suggestive of the same purposes and interests as the Perugia murals is the fact that the chronicles of the time contained references and citations pointing again and again to the causal relationships between communal successes, especially to military victories, and the proper conjunction of stars and planets.[57] The case of Giovanni Villani would appear to be typical. The deaths of such illustrious men as Philip V of France and Pope John XXII had, according to the chronicler, astral counterparts in preceding eclipses.[58] The prevalence of war in 1325 was explained by the conjunction of Mars and Saturn that occurred in that year.[59] But among the planetary conjunctions, none was more important than that of Jupiter and Saturn. For Villani this periodic association of the planets at Perugia reflects a similar conviction in their special significance.

Villani's enthusiasism for the planets, however, was not without qualification. He often reminds the reader that the planets are simply manifestations of divine will, that they have no meaning or worth outside the divine scheme of things.[60] For example, Villani, like almost all his contemporaries, condoned the punishment meted out to the astrologer Cecco d'Ascoli for his having held that certain events in sacred history were the necessary result of planetary law.[61] A further qualification on Villani's part reminds us that the astrology of the communes was not incompatible with the notion of free will or with the philosophy of the free individual who stood at the center of republican belief. For as the movement of the stars was solely a manifestation of God's will, so virtuous behavior was a means of avoiding the possible evil effects of stellar portents.[62] After all, Villani's chronicle, like all the literature of the age, was instructive in purpose. To have projected an image of man at the whim of the planets and other non-human forces outside himself would have negated the possiblity of rational continuity, of learning from the past.

If Mussato's and Villani's views best summarize the intellectual forces that contributed to the Perugia frescoes, then the Florence Campanile sculptures (c. 1350) offer the clearest indication of the public role astrology assumed in the art. Trachtenberg has shown, rightly I believe, that the unifying element in the Florence decorations is the theme of redemption through work.[63] In this context, and here I take issue with Trachenberg, the representations of the seven planets have little scholastic taint about them. They are part of a program dedicated to an activist role for the citizen in the life of the city.[64] Like Villani's proclamation that when one is virtuous the stars will be favorable, or at least their evil effects can be anticipated and thereby minimized or thwarted, so on the Campanile an analogous dictum is publicly announced. That there is at least one distinctly local emblem glorifying the city among the sculptures—the relief of Hercules—points all the more certainly to the evidence that astrological representations did not imply or preach a fatalistic withdrawal. Rather, the stars were protectors of the city and were reduced to benign and beneficent figures because the citizens led lives devoted to active forms of virtue. At Perugia we have already seen how the same kind of recognition was given to the redemptive value of work.

Without doubt the most important astrological works of the early part of the fourteenth century in Italy are those ascribed to Giotto. As the Giotto scheme apparently included representations of the seven planets with illustrations of their properties, the relation with the Perugia works is clearly quite close.[65] The name of Pietro d'Abano has been associated with the frescoes by Giotto since the beginning of the fourteenth century, as the early sources state that Giotto worked directly with Pietro in designing the program. Because Pietro's most important astrological work was organized around the months, the associated gods, and their inclinations, it would seem possible that some text by this leading astrologer of the day was a source for the Perugia murals.[66] (The relevance of Pietro's notion of Saturn has already been noted above.)

A statement by Pietro might be taken to summarize the function of the astrological murals at Perugia. He wrote that "aside from God, the celestial bodies are the first causes of the happenings in the world."[67] The statement explains in simplest form how the conjunction of Biblical and astrological scenes contributes to the overall meaning of the cycle by underscoring points of emphasis in the sacred narratives, and by uniting (in the spirit of Pietro's pronouncement) with the Biblical subjects in the enunciation of the hallowed mission of the city and of the protection accorded to the city by Old Testament leaders as well as by Jupiter and Saturn.

The Perugia Cycle and Communal Art: A Comparative View, 1100-1300

Monuments related to the Perugia program have been noted throughout this discussion in order to understand better the meaning of the frescoes. That so few directly relevant works have been discovered suggests in itself something of the extraordinary character of the murals. There is now to be considered some of the broader tendencies and developments in the civic-political art of the period of about 1100 to 1300. Although many of the monuments that will be examined here have a quite different import from the works at Perugia, they do nonetheless serve to provide a more precise indication of the special meaning and historical position of the Sala dei Notari frescoes.

However difficult it is to generalize about communal decorations when so much has either been lost or is in a poor state of preservation, a cursory look through the Italian chronicles of the late Middle Ages is sufficient to indicate that the Perugia frescoes would not stand apart quite so sharply if more of the contemporary political works had survived.[1] For whatever reasons, medieval secular art throughout Europe has suffered far more grievously than religious art; the situation in Italy is no exception.

A second difficulty here is that without an exhaustive reading of the chronicles of the time, and without a thorough examination of the art of the time, the study of course cannot claim to be exhaustive. The works to be presented now, however, are fairly representative, for, barring the addition of a monument of a wholly new order, they seem to represent variations on only a limited number of ideas. In this context, the originality of the Perugia frescoes appears to reside more in the number of established motifs that are brought together and in the particular ways in which these themes relate to one another, rather than in the general content of the scheme.

The earliest phase in the development of civic art begins in the first half of the twelfth century in Northern Italy. The political life of this region was perhaps the most highly developed because of the early, strong, and persistent influence of imperial law and thought.[2]

No monument more clearly epitomizes how imperial themes were transformed into communal variations in the North than the group of sculptural decorations on the main façade of *Il Broletto* in Brescia dated about 1200.[3] These works, which have been attributed to the School of Antelami, include a representation of an enthroned judge with a personification of Justice at his side. Even the most cursory comparison reveals essential distinctions between communal and imperial art. On Frederick II's now destroyed triumphal arch at Capua, dated about 1200, a portrait of the emperor was, according to most reconstructions, placed above an enthroned personification of Justice between two judges.[4] There is no ruler portrait on the communal monument; the judges, as interpreters of the legal meaning of justice and as servants of the city, are themselves elevated to embodiments of ideal rule. The scheme thus responds to the communal belief, one perhaps derived from imperial law, that justice should be the cornerstone of government and the principal criterion for assessing the actions of the city's magistrates.[5]

The ideal of justice in itself, apart from any earthly personification in pope or emperor, was of great importance precisely because the commune was free of such traditional foci of rule and thus sought new means for rationalizing its acts.[6] The fact that judges led most civic processions is a convincing indication of how they came to assume the symbolic leadership of the cities.[7]

The primacy of justice in communal thinking was also expressed in other forms in the early political art. The most notable symbol of the ideal was the personification of the commune itself as the Virtue Justice. The fresco said to be by Giotto in the Palazzo del Podestà in Florence, dated about 1305, is the best known example of this genre of civic art.[8] The antecedents for this political image are to be found in the art of the twelfth and thirteenth centuries. The work at Brescia is one such precedent, as is the example of a personification of an enthroned figure of Justice holding a lily in the Palazzo della Ragione at Verona, dated about 1250.[9] The transition from this type of work to the representation of the Commune as Justice seems natural and not at all difficult to anticipate; indeed, it was a necessary preliminary stage.

The importance of justice is apparent in at least one other broad sense in early communal art. I believe that the functions of the altarpieces produced after about the middle of the thirteenth century and into the early part of the fourteenth century in which scenes from the life of a local saint were represented with personified virtues, may be considered political.[10] The life of the saint was intended to stand as that of an exemplary citizen, the virtues making clear the didactic values of the saint's life. That figures of Justice appear to have been the most commonly represented of the virtues on such monuments, either in isolation or as the featured one among a more developed program, can be explained by the special importance of the Virtue.

At Perugia the concern with justice is not evident in a direct or simple fashion. The theme is made manifest through reference to the rule and leadership of Moses and Gideon, through the injustice of the Pharoah and Cain—and the just punishment of these criminals—and finally through reference to the chivalric ideals expressed in several of the astrological scenes and in the representation of *Saint George and the Dragon.* Thus the motif of justice, as we have observed, is in one way or another developed, however obliquely, in several aspects of the Perugia program.

It is now necessary to return to the formative period in North Italy in order to examine three of the most comprehensive of the early civic programs: the sculptures of the cathedral façades in Verona, Borgo San Donnino, and Modena. We are of course considering now what are ostensibly ecclesiastical programs, while almost all other examples of public or political art heretofore discussed decorate civic administratitive structures. An attempt will be made shortly to explain more fully this move into the religious sphere, but for the moment suffice to say only that it has already become evident that no firm boundaries existed between theology and politics. The politics of the time has already been portrayed as arising from, or as justified by, a theological ordering of experience. The fact that there are no clear boundaries between secular and religious settings for the display of civic ideals is in part a consequence of this mixture or overlapping.

The politically-based works on the western façade of San Zeno in Verona are dated about 1140.[11] The two representations drawn from the legend of Theodoric and the relief of Bishop Zeno, patron saint of the city, stand, respectively, as symbols of bad and good government. The literary and artistic transformation that was made in Italy of the German legend of Theodoric is one of the most striking instances of how an ideal in imperial thought and art was changed into one that served the free Italian cities. While Theodoric was conceived as a model ruler and milirary leader by the Germans, for the Italians of the late Middle Ages he was thought of as a sinful and foolish individual, one emblematic of misguided rule.[12]

The reliefs are contrasted with the neighboring scene of Bishop Zeno treading on the most popular symbol of political evil, the dragon. The hand of the Bishop is raised in benediction. To his left is the cavalry of the commune and to his right the infantry. An inscription reads: "The Bishop gives to the people the standard [for] a worthy a defense. Zeno gives the banner with serene heart" (Porter translation).[13] The Bishop as head of the Veronese militia inspires the citizens with Christian zeal in defense of the city, as opposed to the ignoble purposes of Theodoric. The relief clearly represents the meaning of civic Christianity and its transmutation into political and military action.

The relief also incorporates a documentary or historical ambition. The freedom of the commune had been officially recognized only a few years before the sculpture was executed.[14] The sculpture, may therefore stand as a public proclamation and remainder of independence. In addition, the sculpture demonstrates the way in which history was often distorted by the communes in the service of didactic ends. The Bishop had in truth led the city in its unsuccessful defense against Theodoric in the sixth century;[15] but when the commmune finally freed itself from the empire in the twelfth century the event was interpreted as signifying the triumph of the Veronese citizens, with Zeno returned to lead them in a mythical re-making of their struggle against Theodoric. The relief sets the actions of the commune within a pseudo-historical context that confers allegorical significance to contemporary events and helps also to buttress and glorify the dedication of the citizen to the commune. Although independence was finally granted without military action, the commune chose to see the event as final victory in the struggle against Theodoric—the triumph of good government over bad government.

Other aspects of the San Zeno sculptures of about 1140 provide further dimension to the early communal self-image as expressed through art. Alongside the conception of the Bishop as a leader of epic proportion, are, appropriately, heroes drawn from the romances. At the ends of two groups of prophets on either side of the portal are figures that have been identified as Roland and Oliver.[16] They are guardian figures for the church and exemplars of the ideal form of service that can be rendered to the city. Above the figures, following a cycle of scenes drawn from the Old Testament, are two combat reliefs probably also inspired by the genre of Arthurian and Carolingian romance. The maidens for whom the knights do battle are represented in an adjoining relief.

A link between this scheme and the murals at Perugia would seem quite certain. At Perugia we have also found the intercourse of sacred and profane elements in the service and glorification of the state. Although no historic scenes are represented, we have nonetheless seen that the impetus for the decoration of the hall derived in part from a heightened sense of historical self-consciousness and civic pride evident in Perugia by the late Duecento. The fact that military service had become the supreme act of civic devotion at Verona is even more clearly related to the murals at Perugia. The delineation of the character and conduct of the warrior-defenders of the city, in part through chivalric representations, is another common feature.

The façade sculptures on the Cathedral in Borgo San Donnino (Fidenza) are a local variant on the type of program found at Verona. The works that concern us are dated about 1180 and are attributed to Antelami.[17] In them, historical fact and myth conjoin once more to sustain and glorify the commune.

In the tympanum of the northern portal is a representation of an emperor seated on a throne. Above him is the inscription, . . . KARVLVS IPR. The adjoining relief represents Pope Hadrian II investing the archpriest of the city with miter and croisier. As all commentators have noted, the scene commemorates some privilege granted to the city by Charlemagne,[18] who was the legendary granter of freedom to Borgo San Donnino and who had come to assume a sacred role in the town chronicles.[19] Above the relief of the emperor is a figure of King David, an allusion to the transfiguration of Charlemagne into his sacred role as the "new" David.[20]

On one side of the relief of the deity in the middle of the archivolt of the central porch on the west façade is a figure of Moses in the dress of a contemporary warrior and followed by personifications of the Commandments. The conviction of the communes that they were following the example of the Old Testament patriarchs, and the example of Moses in particular, is made strikingly visual in this sculpture. The legions of Borgo San Donnino are matched by the Commandments-as-warriors. Their leader is Moses, thus completing the crusading gloss applied to the military affairs of the city. The metaphor of Moses as an inspiration for the leaders and civic programs of Perugia is more directly stated at Borgo San Donnino.

The sculptures on the southern portal relate in another sense to the legendary importance of Charlemagne in the early history of the city. The reliefs appear to be illustrations of the romance, *Les Enfances Roland,* specifically the long narratives of Bertha and Milo and the story of Orlandino. These stories were invented to "cleanse Roland's mysterious birth of its suspicion of incest."[21] Only when exorcised and purified in this fashion could Roland typify, as he is meant to at Borgo San Donnino, the ideals of the knightly class.

If one of these ideals was a noble and morally upright background, then another was surely strength. Appropriately, a figure of Hercules holding the Nemean lion is found nearby. Beneath this relief is the inscription, FORTIS HERCVLES. A further aspect of the hero is suggested in the neighboring sculptures of the Virgin and Child and the prophets. The story of Bertha and Milo includes several miraculous appearances of the Virgin, so there is a narrative accounting for the sacred scenes. There is also a more general, typological significance to these scenes: the perfect warrior as a devout individual. All the elements seen here that treat the nature and meaning of military service are also presented at Perugia, as noted earlier, although the manner of transmitting the ideals is quite different.

Finally, one other major cathedral program in North Italy, involving to an important extent the pronouncement of civic principles, are the sculptures of the Cathedral and Campanile in Modena, dated about 1150.[22]

The presence and possible meaning of the allegory of good and bad judges in the Campanile has already been touched upon. The other political references are of a type which we now expect to find. An exterior capital at the east end of the Cathedral is decorated with a representation of a combat between knights, behind each of whom stands a woman, emblematic of the ideals for which they struggle. A more complete display of how the conflicts described in the epics and romances are meant to act as a source of inspiration for the commune is seen in the already mentioned Arthurian cycle in the archivolt of the Porta della Pescheria (*c.* 1140). This relief is the earliest such monument in Europe.[23] Other reliefs drawn from the lives of Roland and Arthur are found in the Campanile together with depictions of King David, a reminder of the fact that Arthur, like Charlemagne, was frequently designated the "new" David.[24]

Throughout the twelfth and early thirteenth centuries the themes introduced at Verona, Borgo San Donnino, and Modena established the basic pattern of civic embellishment of both ecclesiastical and secular structures. Scenes of combats, both generalized and historical, constitute without question the leading motif of these schemes.[25] The use of guardian figures and stories borrowed from the romances are widespread as well throughout this period.[26]

Variations on these themes are, of course, to be found. Perhaps the most important among these are illustrations of how the city is ruled by a kind of council of sacred and secular individuals. The idea was expressed in many ways. The simplest and most popular was the representation of the conclave of heavenly rulers themselves. Among the more original examples of the motif is the scene of the women of Parma offering gifts to the Virgin, patroness of the city.[27] The depiction is perhaps related to the more conventional glorification of the city adjacent to the relief, a scene of knights engaged in combat, with other knights in attendance. The works decorate the Parma Cathedral and are dated about 1150.

One other notable type of embellishment is the representation of a single historical communal leader or hero. Included within this rather small group of works are the various depictions of Vergil that were erected in public settings in Mantua during the thirteenth century. Of the most famous of these works, that placed in the Palazzo della Ragione in about 1250, a contemporary chronicler wrote that "tutti i giorni i giudici si recevono a fare giustizia." The passage points out most distinctly the saintly importance that such secular personnages assumed. Vergil, a great source of civic pride throughout the Middle Ages in Mantua, became a kind of patron saint of the city, and his writings appear to have taken on a Biblical or sanctified aura.[28] As a wise and thus exemplary citizen, he became in his apotheosis a paragon of ideal citizenship. The interest in Vergil, and the artistic manifestations of this interest during the thirteenth century, illustrate in a more general sense the fascination of the city-states with their histories and with the possible inspirational and propangandistic values of the past.

More frequent than the depiction of composite cultural heroes was the representation of truly historic rulers. An important example is the equestrian statue placed on the Palazzo della Ragione in Milan in about 1240 honoring Oltrado da Tressino. Oltrado was the *podestà* who initiated the construction of the palace. Beneath the statue is the following inscription:

MCCXXXIII DOMINVS OLDRADO DE TREXENO POT. MEDIOLANI ATRIA QVI GRANDIS SOLII REGALIA SCANDIS CIVIS DAVDENTIS FIDEI TVTORIS ET ENSIS PRESIDES NIC MEMORIS OLDRADO SEMPER HONORES QVI SOLIVM STVXIT CATHAROS VT DEBVIT VXIT.[29]

The inscription gives public expression, in imperious language and tone, to the manner in which an individual served the city and thus proved himself virtuous and worthy of being honored. The accomplishment of Oltrado, like that of Vergil for Mantua, proclaims another form of ideal and exemplary citizenship. The historical ethnocentrism of the Milanese, their sense of the present importance and external worth of their own acts, is another indication of how directly and self-consciously the commune's image of itself was transferred into art.[30]

A second example of the idealized portrait in civic art might at first appear to fall outside our survey: the figure of Emperor Otto IX on the eastern façade of the Palazzo della Ragione in Padua, dated about 1220.[31] The Emperor was a supporter of the hated tyrant Ezzelino. Despite such support, however, Otto had been sympathetic to the cause of Paduan imperialism in the region and had granted several towns to the consul who led the successful war of independence against the Imperial Vicar of Frederick I.[32] This was an instance, perhaps, of the good outweighing the bad in the decision to allow the statue to remain standing during the republican epoch. It might be added that the custom of commemorating rulers with honorary portraits appears to have begun in the Lombard communes when they were under imperial control.[33]

Although no particular individual is honored in the Sala dei Notari at Perugia—indeed, one should recall here the specific injunction made against the display of family *stemmi* in the hall as an indication of the communal spirit of the decorations—the obvious interest of the designers of the scheme in defining ideal leadership and rule is a sign of the ideological kinship of the murals with the works in Mantua and Padua. The Perugia frescoes are therefore again seen to be unique not so much because of their subject matter but rather because of the special way in which a fairly established subject matter is presented.

The more immediate and direct antecedents of the Perugia frescoes are a rather varied group of about a half dozen town hall decorations of the thirteenth century. The murals appear to have been executed at a moment when several other cities decorated their administrative centers with similarly ambitious programs. Generally, the history of town palace embellishment follows, as we might expect, the history of town palace construction. Just as the role of the churches as meeting places for the city assemblies and administrators was gradually usurped by the new civic structures, so the focal point for the display of political art moved from ecclesiastical to civic buildings.[34]

The first of these major civic undertakings is that found in the Palazzo della Ragione in Mantua. The fragments of a fresco cycle dated about 1200 are on the north wall of the council hall.[35] The remains consist of battle scenes, a cycle of the labors of the months, and a Madonna and Child with saints and angels. Of special interest for us, aside from the fact that the works are at least of a sufficiently ambitious and variegated nature to remind us of the Perugia program, is the representation of the months, a most direct parallel with the Sala dei Notari frescoes. As the twelve months are represented at Mantua the special aura and emphasis of the Perugia scheme are of course different. The Mantua decorations follow more closely the typical associations and range of ecclesiastical art; however, it is possible that the fact that the works have been appropriated for display in a public structure might in itself give them something of the social and political significance they have at Perugia. That is, the months may be said to introduce the notion that honest labor is the means for guaranteeing heavenly as well as for earthly reward, and to imply that both types of reward are measured according to the manner in which the citizen contributes to the successful functioning of the state.[36] The incorporation of the sacred assemblage is therefore perhaps an indirect reference to the theme of heavenly salvation, while the battles might stand for the quintessential way in which the individual's contribution to the public welfare is judged.

Continuing in chronological sequence, the next important surviving town hall embellishments are those at Todi, dated about 1290. Fragments of two cycles of decorations are found in the council halls of the first and second floors and comprise the following scenes: a tourney and a seated male figure, perhaps a ruler, on the first story; an Annunciation, Saint Michael holding a spear and scale, a head of Christ, and again, a representation , on the second story, of a man who might have been a leader of the commune.[37] The works are in too poor a state to permit any generalizations regarding the overall meaning of the scheme, and there are indications that the original grouping was more extensive. Important in a general way is that these Umbrian murals are the first contemporary examples comparable in scope to the Perugia frescoes. (I have already drawn attention to the relation between the Perugia works and the Todi decorations in the context of the Umbrian political situation at the time.[38])

Two points should be made about the content of the Todi frescoes. First, the inclusion of a tourney or joust suggests again the intermingling of vestiges of the feudal world and of republican ideals in town hall decorations. The joust does not simply glorify a dying aristocratic virtue or pursuit; in its setting it signifies, as did the chivalric allusions at Perugia, a general civic dedication to noble ideas. An available symbol was simply appropriated by the city-states and transformed into a referent of a rather new order.

The second point about the Todi frescoes is that the inclusion of the representation of Saint Michael with the scale is another persuasive bit of evidence for the belief that communal governments had come to conceive of themselves as presiding over a kind of secular salvation. The emphasis on the labor of Adam and Eve at Perugia seems to offer in different form the expression of a similar idea.

Another decorative arrangement, the sculpted and painted embellishments in the Palazzo Pubblico in Novara of 1290, is equally important in its unification of diverse themes in the enunciation of political principle and as a preparation for what we have already found at Perugia just a short time later.[39] The decorations consist of the following elements: a painted frieze on the main façade showing a man fighting against a lion with his lady by his side, two knights battling one another, and a rustic scene set before a castle. Contemporary sculptural decorations are also found on the façade representing figures of Christ, God, two males in dress *all'antica,* and two males in contemporary dress with a portrait-like specificity in their facial features.

We have seen such subjects as these in other cycles; for example, the union of the town's heavenly and earthly rulers—I believe, with Baroni, that the second group of males are local rulers[40]—and the borrowing of literary and chivalric motifs. The two figures in antique dress are perhaps the only novel devices here and they might be representations of ancient personages involved in the foundation of the city. Perhaps the figures are Romulus and Remus, as one historian has suggested, as these mythological characters appear in the Novarese chronicles.[41] It is difficult, however, to agree to so specific an identification. If the works do indeed refer to the ancient past of the city, then they resemble only one other civic decoration of which I am aware: in the Cathedral at Bergamo there is a scene, aptly titled by Toesca, *Buona antica vita della comune,* representing figures in ancient dress engaged in various kinds of labor.[42] Like the two classical figures at Novara, perhaps nothing more is intended than the recognition of the formative importance of the city's ancient past or a symbolic statement of how the city uses the past as an inspiration and guide for its policies.[43]

The council hall in the Palazzo Comunale in San Gimignano was frescoed in 1295. Payments made to a Maestro Azzo in that year are believed by Ridolfi to be for the frescoes.[44] The mural scheme is the most extensive and the most important example of political art in the period aside from the Perugia frescoes. The following scenes are represented, together with many coats-of-arms of contemporary leaders in the city: a nobleman or ruler seated on a throne while his attendants prepare dogs and falcons for the chase, a combat between two knights or a tourney, hunting scenes, struggles between animals, and a centaur shooting an arrow at a dragon.

√The single new motif here is the hunt. Several explanations might account for such scenes. As the commune was chief provider for the citizen, the hunt might be an emblematic notation of this role, or at least a reminder that the *contado* must be pacified by the commune in order to make hunting possible. The representation of a hunt beneath the personification of Giotto's Commune as Justice in the Arena Chapel, Padua, of about 1305, underscores the relationship between just rule and the ability of the citizen to procure food. But the greater significance of the scenes relates to yet another communal transformation of an imperial theme in art. For while the hunt in Byzantine and Carolingian art symbolized the virtue and nobility of the leader as an embodiment of his people, in a communal context the scene connotes first the virtue of the people and only secondarily that of their leader.[45] Just as we have noted how personified Justice was changed into a kind of community symbol from that of a simple emblem of the greatness of the emperor, so too is the traditional symbolism of the hunt reversed in its communal context.

The relevance of transmutations such as these for the Perugia program is readily evident. The portrayal of Moses and Gideon as expressions of the aspirations of a people rather than solely of their leaders represents a similar shift in focus in a traditional imperial motif. Further, the use of an imagery derived from feudal or aristocratic elements in society in the pronouncement of communal beliefs, such as the tourney at San Gimignano and the scene of the knights crossing a bridge at Perugia, is another feature common to both cycles.

The final elaborate program of the thirteenth century appears to have been executed just a few years later than the Sala dei Notari frescoes—the murals on the east wall of the main council hall in *Il Broletto* in Brescia, dated 1300.[46] The following scenes are represented: a *Maestà*, a bishop and a saint in gestures of blessing, a *Madonna and Child*, the *Flight into Egypt*, the *Entry into Jerusalem*, and the *Peace between the Guelphs and Ghibellines in 1298* (identified by Panazza).[47]

The prominent position of Mary and the Christ-Child in the grouping is an early example of how Mary as the Queen of Heaven was cited as a model for earthly rule, or was actually declared a ruler in her own right.[48] The first known occurrence of this latter innovation was in Verona in 1222, a transformation that was commemorated by a frescoed image of the Virgin.[49] Of greater immediate interest for us, however, are the Biblical scenes. They symbolize the "flight" from tyranny and the honor later accorded to Christ by the city then regarded as a paradigm of earthly order.[50]

The depiction of the *Peace Between the Guelphs and the Ghibellines in 1298* is a rare instance, if the identification is correct, of the illustration of a contemporary historical scene in the civic art of the age. The choice of this particular event serves to stress the priority given to order and civic peace that we have already seen as an intention of the Perugia frescoes. Once more at Brescia, as in all the other civic programs that have been discussed, sacred and secular truths co-mingle in the pronouncement of a similar and rather limited set of political principles.

Among the surviving civic decorations of the twelfth and thirteenth centuries, the Perugia frescoes are the most varied and encompassing in terms of themes and sources. Only the cycles in Brescia and Novara begin to approach the breadth of the Perugia program. Neither of these schemes, however, is the product of a sustained undertaking but rather both are the cumulative consequence of two campaigns of work. The special importance of the Sala dei Notari becomes even clearer when one recognizes that several of the features of the decorations are unique: the particular grouping of Old Testament scenes, the inclusion of representations of Aesop, and, finally, the earliest appearance of an astrological scheme. As remarked more than once, the political principles enunciated at Perugia are fairly commonplace; what is extraordinary is the far more elaborated form in which they are treated and developed and the particular devices employed for the expression of political ideals.

The framework afforded by the general examination of the civic art of the late Middle Ages in Italy enables us to understand and also to appreciate more profoundly the scope and diversity of the subjects of the Perugia murals, and also to account for the commissioning of the frescoes during the 1290s.

Political or civic art originates and begins to develop in the communes during the first half of the twelfth century. The initial diffusion of civic motifs was for the most part limited to North Italian cathedral decorations. The subjects of these early decorations were adopted and the nature and type of literary sources widened by the decorators of the first civic palaces in North Italy. Not until the last third of the thirteenth century do these themes begin to flourish in Central Italy. Umbria seems to have been especially receptive to such influences. Many of the subjects of civic art appear first in France before they move to Northern Italy and then to Central Italy. (There is a parallel phenomenon evident in the dispersion of sacred themes.[51]) The direct source for the richer and more varied iconography of the art of Central Italy, however, is to be found in Northern Italy rather than in France, contrary to the view held by most historians.[52]

We have seen that there were few differences of any consequence between the adornments of civic palaces and those of cathedrals. The reason for this is simply that the early civic programs borrowed much from ecclesiastical art. The first civic palaces probably date from the middle of the eleventh century, or some two centuries after the beginnings of the era of the free city-state.[53] The churches were for a long period, then, the only monuments available for the display of political art. It is perhaps revealing of the kind of cultural traditions from which such borrowing derived that in the seemingly exhaustive catalogue of architectural pursuits and genres to be found in the encyclopedias of the age there is no separate category for profane decoration.[54] So undeveloped and poorly defined as a distinct classification were the subjects of the adornments of the first public structures that the embellishment of private palaces was for the most part indistinguishable from that of public palaces.[55] Thus, the earliest civic artists (or their patrons) were in a real sense the initiators of a new tradition in art and, although of necessity dependent on earlier art, were free to combine diverse and original motifs.

Although the Perugia murals are not touched directly by the romances, epics, and legends that appear to have been important sources for political themes in the formative period of civic art, the concern with establishing the nature of knightly obligation and the central importance of warfare in the Perugia frescoes establishes a kinship between the murals and the distinguishing features of the literature. Similarities also occur in the effort to create communal heroes, whether they are Moses and Gideon at Perugia, or Roland at Borgo San Donnino. The nature and special achievements of the heroic tales are, in short, keys to an understanding of the general purposes and meaning of the civic art between about 1150 and 1200. This problem merits some further discussion.

There is possibly some truth in the common if romantic view that the troubadors introduced the romances into Italy in public performances on the city *piazze*.[56] An almost natural follow-up is that the same tales and heroes should appear next on the cathedrals and civic palaces situated on these same squares. Indeed, the importation of manuscripts seems to have had no direct influence on the early decorations. The manuscripts were collected in areas where a feudal court life thrived, and few found their way into the communes.[57] But stronger evidence of the special importance of the troubadors is that the earliest known illustration of an Arthurian romance in Italy— in fact in Europe—is found in the free city of Modena, about a century before any related French or Italian literary source is known to have existed in Italy.[58] The point is an important one because it suggests that the popularity of the tales derived from something less sophisticated than a shift of interest in the refined and isolated literary culture of the age. The legends are re-created on the building façades because they were intended to appeal to the same wide public that was entertained by the troubadors.

Why, then, were the romances popular in the city-republics as early as about 1100? A partial answer is perhaps that there was no "national" epic tradition in Italy and thus the city-states had to look elsewhere at a moment when they might be expected to draw on such a tradition to illustrate and to celebrate their virtues and achievements, real and imagined. The period during which the tales of England and France became popular coincides with the beginning of the communal era and thus with the period when the epic mode was available and could prove most useful. Expressed in somewhat different terms, the communes is about the year 1100 were, as Levi-Strauss might characterize them, "societies with no history," because, with often only the exception of records of the local manifestations of divine personages, they possessed no real corpus of glorified tradition about their own past.[59] This being so, the cities had to invent a past. The very nature of the free commune, cut off as it was from the empire and the papacy, demanded an effort toward self-justification partly through the search for a "usable past."[60] The effort to seek popular heroes was satisfied, in part, by imported romance, and a kind of "instant" past was conjured up for the communes. The early chronicles and their marvelous stories of the foundation of cities, involving inevitably Arthur or one of his knights, or Roland and his family, are testimony enough to the need for a cast of epic characters to provide a defense and justification through history for the freedom of the commune.[61] The broad nature of such a need is even more evident in the fact that by the early 1200s war cries borrowed from the romances were common, as was the adoption of Arthurian names by rulers.[62] In this sense the heroes found on the churches and palaces are responses to the fortress-obsessed or defensive mentality of the insecure early commune. The emphasis on war and on martial virtues in the stories and civic decorations should not be wondered at in an age when the state was itself defined in military terms.[63]

Lionel Trilling has shown how our contemporary definition of "hero" as one "who commits an approved act of unusual courage" represents only one facet of the more traditional conception. In the earlier view the hero was also one who was favored by God, or gods, and contained within himself certain divine traits that were called forth in word and in action.[64] In the largest sense, then, epic as well as Biblical heroes served several ends: they were *exempla* of courage and other martial virtues, they were "proof" of the divine favor with which the city was regarded, and they were ingredients in the communal search for a supportive and glorious past.

There is a final element to be considered in the evident preoccupation of the commune with war and with the divinely-motivated hero. Many of the cities took part in the crusades, if only by expressing their support in word and in art for the Christian cause.[65] The holy quests and wars that unfold in the epics and tales offered romanticized parallels to the crusades; *The Story of Roland* deals directly with the crusades. The crusades were perhaps an important influence in the shaping of the profane decorative schemes of the churches. It is no mere coincidence, therefore, that the most significant precedent for the representation of battles as ecclesiastical decoration is found in the crusader churches of France and Spain.[66]

We have seen how the interest in romance was related to a need for historical justification. The pursuit of history, as typified by the early chronicles, was not a disinterested search for real or true fact; it was rather a creative act, offering a kind of poetic truth that was often discovered in the divine principles revealed in the working out of history. The historian's craft, as it was to remain at least until Guicciardini, was to "offer moral guidance" and the historian was thus "permitted to select and to stylize the events of the past."[67] History was meant to serve as a guide to human action and had little independent or objective significance. The Bible and literary myth were equally a part of history. When artifacts were dug up, the reality they might have disclosed was neatly stylized or distorted to conform with the preconception of the city's mythical foundation. The unearthing of a body presumed to be that of Antenor of Padua is a notable example of this practice.[68]

The fact that one moves easily in the chronicles from sacred stories to romance and sometimes to objective history reflects precisely the same interests and proclivities and "discoveries" that we have observed in the communal decorations of the age. The very diversity of the Perugia program and the related works of the twelfth and thirteenth centuries reveals this uncritical passion most sharply and suggests the opportunism and inventiveness of the artists of the time as they strove to construct from a wide range of earlier materials the ingredients of an idealized and poeticized communal past.

Appendix

History of Previous Research

Recognizing the fact that the frescoes in the Sala dei Notari have never before been examined within the context of the communal art of the late Middle Ages, the scant reference in the literature to other aspects of their significance is not unexpected. For it must be admitted that the most important interest that the frescoes hold are their civic implications. This, of course, is not to suggest that the works are without aesthetic or stylistic importance. On the contrary, the secure attribution of the scenes of the Old Testament within the orbit of Pietro Cavallini, perhaps by the master himself, assures a firm place for the murals in the evolution of the Roman School of the late Duecento.[1]

The absence of early sources in the literature is, in great part, a consequence of very meager documentary evidence, along with a complete absence of reference in the early chronicles.[2] In addition, the frescoes were covered over from the sixteenth century through the late eighteenth century and were not rediscovered until the 1860s—a situation that would certainly account for an almost total lacuna in the *fortuna critica* of some 300 years.

Pellini's brief but accurate rehearsal of the early history of the Palazzo dei Priori has already been discussed.[3] Of the Sala dei Notari itself Pellini has little to say except to note that its appearance no longer reflects the original intentions of its designers.[4] In his description of the history of the hall, and most importantly in his failure to mention the fresco decorations, Pellini appears to follow the form of Crispolti's general guide of the city that appeared in 1648. Crispolti wrote that the hall

> Gia era Sala Papale chiamata per esser iui nella volte varij Pontifici al naturale dipinti; Hora chiamati Sala dei Notarij, chi vi stano a seriuere gli Atti in banchi ben disposti, e acconci, per benefitio de Alessandro Riario Cardinale, gia nostro Legato, il quale ristauro, e orno detta Sala, nel modo, che oggi si vede, collocado nel capo di seei il belli, e magnifici Seggi, oue i Guidici Ciuili rendono ragione.[5]

The literature of the nineteenth century echoes, with one notable exception, these early cursory accounts. Orsini, for example, in his guide of 1784, remarks only that "la Sala dei Notari e ora richotta moderna."[6] In 1806, however, Mariotto made an important addition to the literature. He paraphrased, as follows, a document that has remained the secure foundation for the date for the frescoes, 1297:

> Il di 25 Giugno del 1297 fu ordinato dal General Consiglio, che si scancellearasere tutte le armi, e tutti i ritratti de' Potesta, e Capitani dipinti nel Palazzo del Commune o dentro, or fuori, e che per l'avvenire non vi si dipingeresso mai pier.[7]

It was not until 1910, however, that the document was finally published by Briganti.[8] Recent writing on the Perugia frescoes—Boskovits (1973)—refers to Briganti's publication of the document as representing the single bit of evidence in support of a date of 1297 apart from the stylistic evidence.[9]

The first history of the palace, that of Rossi-Scotti, was published in 1864 and adds nothing to the earlier literature.[10] The rediscovery of the frescoes during the 1860s did lead, however, to the first comment on the iconography of the cycle in 1879; Tiberi wrote in that year that they represent a "civile argomento."[11] Further evidence of the very slow awakening of interest in the works is the fact that Venturi did not include them in his *Storia dell'arte italiana* of 1907, although he did mention the so-called *Maestà della Volte (c.* 1297) that was placed on an exterior section of the palace at about the same time that the frescoes were executed.[12] It should of course be remembered that the state of Umbrian studies in general was poor at this time, and indeed has remained so until the present.[13]

A major impetus for the introduction of the frescoes into the mainstream of art historical literature was the exhibition of Umbrian art held in Perugia in 1907. Attributing the works to Pietro Cavallini, Gnoli remarked in his catalogue that the subjects included scenes drawn from the Old Testament and "apologhi e favole allegoriche."[14] In the same year, 1907, Cristofani refined this first effort to attribute the frescoes by arguing that only the best scenes in the cycle, those drawn from the Old Testament, were by Cavallini.[15]

The cycle remained for the moment within the orbit of local studies. Bombe's history of Perugian art (1912) included the first extensive examination of the works.[16] Bombe's primary interest was with the identification of the subjects of the scenes. No effort was made to relate the paintings to the contemporary art in the city, apart from noting a general iconographic affinity with the Fontana Maggiore; and as for the general meaning of the works, Bombe asserted only that they represent a glorification of profane ideals. Eight of the scenes, those I have included among the astrological representations, were not identified. The works, however, finally were recognized as one of the most important and impressive civic monuments of the Duecento.

Another early landmark in the rise of modern Perugian studies was the work of a second German scholar, Jacobson, who, in his history of Umbrian art published in 1914, stated that the works were not by Cavallini, but rather by an imitator.[17] But the secure place of the decorations within the field of Cavallini studies were established shortly after, in 1918, by Lothrop.[18] Lothrop wrote that the condition of the restored frescoes was too problematical to permit a positive attribution to Cavallini. The frescoes were nevertheless clearly related to Cavallini, as he remarks, and especially to the artist's works at Sta. Cecilia.[19] Lothrop's identification of the subjects of the frescoes follows Bombe's.

The introduction of the frescoes into the Cavallini literature at this time coincided with the contemporary effort to define with greater precision the evolution of the Roman School. Wilpert, *Die romischen Mosaiken und Malerein der Kirchlichen Bauten vom IV bis XIII Jahrhunderts* of 1917, made the first serious effort to place the Perugia frescoes within a Roman stylistic context, although he emphasized the iconographic parallels of the works with the Old Testament cycle in S. Paolo.[20]

With a fairly clear view of the stylistic place of the frescoes established, and major aspects of the meaning of the program at least superficially worked out, the way was prepared for the inclusion of the frescoes for the first time in a general survey of Italian art: Van Marle, 1923.[21] Van Marle sets the frescoes within the Roman school and suggests an attribution to the School of Cavallini. "The figures," he notes, ". . . are somewhat more animated and more expressive than those of Cavallini." On the iconography, Van Marle repeats the earlier commentators in their belief that "no leading idea can be discerned in the choice of subjects."

The debate over the precise position of the frescoes within the art of Cavallini and of his followers dominated the literature for the following few years. In 1923, Hermanin returned to the problem that he had earlier examined in 1902 in light of the work of Lothrop and of Wilpert and concluded that the follower of Cavallini who executed the Old Testament scenes was one of the artists who had worked at Sta. Cecilia in Trastevere with Cavallini.[22] Busuioceaunu reached the same conclusion in 1925 in a study that offered the first summary of the rapidly growing bibliography of related works.[23] At the same time work went forward on the problem of determining the relation of the Old Testament frescoes to other Italian cycles. Notable among these early efforts is Cockerell's, a part of a general investigation of Biblical iconography published in 1927.[24] Two later studies of Demus, one of 1935 in which the frescoes were related to the mosaics of San Marco,[25] and one of 1950 in which the works were compared to the Norman mosaic cycles of Sicily,[26] remain the most important forays in this area.

The developing sense of the importance of the works is reflected in the fact that in the first modern guide of Perugia, that of Magnini-Briganti published in 1925, the frescoes are described in some detail from archival, iconographic, and stylistic points of view.[27] Study of the relation of the decorations to their Perugian setting was first seriously broached by Thaon di Revel in 1932.[28] In Guardabassi's history of the city, published during these same years, 1933-1935, the frescoes are for the first time said to be a reflection of a specific moment in the development of the city. Further, following Bombe's lead, the relation of the meaning of the paintings to the iconography of the Fontana Maggiore is suggested as well.[29] Tarchi's detailed architectural description of the Sala dei Notari in 1938, and of the location of the frescoes within it, was the last important addition to the literature at this time.[30]

During the early 1950s there occurred the next major spate of writing on the frescoes. Perhaps stimulated in part by the art restorations undertaken shortly after the war, a number of guides, local histories, and architectural studies of the Palazzo dei Priori were produced. The major works are by Lupatelli (1950),[31] Santi (1950),[32] Rapone (1950),[33] Johnstone (1952),[34] Schneider (1952),[35] and Gurrieri (1962).[36] There is no single fresh contribution here, however, to the study of the frescoes.

Sindona's study of Cavallini (1958) marks the beginning of the modern phase of research on the attribution of the cycle.[37] Sindona follows the lead of Cristofani in stating that the best scenes in the cycle were indeed close to the style of Cavallini. Shortly after, Andriola (1959), returned to Busuioceanu's contention that the style of the works is closest to a Cavallini assistant at Santa Cecilia in Trastevere.[38] The most recent views of the problem, that of Boskovits (1973), restates this position.[39] But the continuing uncertainty in this area is perhaps nowhere more evident than in the fact that Longhi (1953-54) takes no stand on the issue and states only that the works might be by Cavallini or, at the very least, that they represent one of several instances in the art of the late Duecento in Perugia in which Cavallini's influence is apparent.[40] Two recent archival studies—a general one by Nessi (1967) on Umbrian art[41] and another by Martini (1968) on the early development of the palace[42]—add nothing to the documentary history of the decorations. As for the iconographical interpretation of the frescoes, the field is even more barren. A single exception is Hoffmann-Curtius's re-statement of the observation that the program appears similar to that of the Perugia fountain.[43]

Notes

Chapter 1

1. Peter Gay, *Art and Act: On Causes in History—Manet, Gropius, Mondrian,* New York, 1976, p. 7.

2. The term "political culture" is used here, and throughout the paper, as it has been defined by Gabriel A. Almond and Sidney Verba, *The Civic Culture,* Princeton, 1963, pp. 5ff.

3. Ernst Kantorowicz, *The King's Two Bodies: A Study in Mediaeval Political Theology,* Princeton, 1957, p. 78.

4. The most significant study in this field is Edna C. Southard, *The Frescoes in Siena's Palazzo Pubblico, 1285-1539.* New York, 1979, where the general political and cultural environment have only an ancillary importance.

5. See also, Eugenio Battisti, *Cimabue,* University Park, 1967, pp. 5 ff., who offers only vague generalities to suggest that the art of Cimabue was the direct outgrowth of a kind of democratization of arts that occurred during the communal epoch. Federick Antal, *Florentine Painting and Its Social Background,* London, 1947, pp. 110 ff., also sees a connection between artistic style and the towns. (For critiques of these two works see, a review by Carlo Volpe in *Paragone* 12 (1964) 61 ff., and, for Antal, a review by Millard Meiss in *Art Bulletin* 31 (1949): 143 ff.)

6. Studies undertaken early in this century remain the basic synthetic treatments. Note, for example, Paolo d'Ancona, *L'uomo e le sue opere nelle figurazione italiane del medioevo,* Florence, 1923.

7. Carlo Martini, "Il Palazzo dei Priori a Perugia," *Palladio* 20 (1970): 43.

8. A. Mariotti, *Saggio di memorie istoriche perugine,* Perugia, 1806, p. 54.

9. See above, p. 92.

10. Jonathan B. Riess, "Uno studio iconografico della decorazione ad affresco del 1297 nel Palazzo dei Priori a Perugia," *Bollettino d'arte,* 9 (1981)-forthcoming.

11. Item stanciatum et reformatum fuit quod superstites palacii novi populi teneantur figuram capitanei preteriti destrui facere de dicto palacio in quo picta est, et omina insigna et arma potestatum et capitaneorum picta in palacio comunis vel populi, intus vel extra neutrum dictorum palaciorum, similiter raddi faciant et cancelari. Nec ulterius figura alicuius potestatis vel capitanei in aliquo dictorum, palaciorum, vel arma seu insigna eorumdem vel alterius eorum modo aliquo depingantur. Perugia, June 25, 1297, Archivio di Stato di

Perugia, A.S.P., *Consigli e riformanze, 12, c. 60 recto.* Dr. Gino Corti transcribed the document for me.

12.   Dr. Gino Corti has searched thoroughly for any new documents relating to the frescoes, and was unable to find any.

Chapter 2

1.   See pp. 77 ff., for a general discussion of the relation of the themes of the Perugia frescoes to other important decorative cycles. Helene Wieruszowski's general comments on the rise of the communes and civic art, while superficial —a problem with any brief synthesis—are nevertheless a good place to begin the study of the common origins of the civic decorations ("Art and the Commune in the Time of Dante," *Speculum 19,* 1944, 14-33). Unfortunately, the better studies of individual schemes, such as Nicolai Rubinstein, "Political Ideas in Sienese Art: The Frescoes of Ambrogio Lorenzetti and Taddeo di Bartolo in the Palazzo Pubblico," *Journal of the Warburg and Courtauld Institutes* 21 (1958): 179-208, leave the matter of sources in the political life of the city untouched.

2.   Johannes Wilde, "The Hall of the Great Council in Florence," *The Journal of the Warburg and Courtauld Institutes* 7 (1944): 65-81.

3.   The palace is known by several names; I will refer to it as the Palazzo dei Priori throughout the book. The building is now generally designated the Palazzo Comunale or the Palazzo dei Priori. The former name appears in most guides, while the latter is used generally in scholarly treatments. The Palazzo del Popolo was a first name for the building; it was not until after 1355 that the building was called the Palazzo dei Priori (Carlo Martini, "Il Palazzo dei Priori a Perugia," *Palladio* 20, 1970:40).

4.   For the history of the site and of the *piazza* see: Mary A. Johnstone, *Perugia and Her People,* 1956, pp. 13 ff.; Ettore Ricci, "La Piazza del comune e le logge di Braccio Fortebraccio," in *Il Tempio di San Francesco al Prato a Perugia,* 1927, pp. 55 ff.; G. Fasola, *La fontana di Perugia,* Rome, 1951, p. 14.

5.   See pp. 23 ff., for the early history and bibliography.

6.   There are two reliable, modern studies of the portal: M. Guardabassi and F. Santi, *Il Portale maggiore del Palazzo dei Priori,* Perugia, 1953, and Annarosa Garzelli, *Sculture toscane nel Dugento e nel Trecento,* Florence, 1969, pp. 76 ff. Neither examination includes much material relating to icongraphic problems.

7.   An early bibliography of regional studies is T. Reinhardt, *Umbrische Studien,* Berlin, 1914, and a summary bibliography of the important histories of the art of the area is found in Miklos Boskovits, *Pittura umbra e marchigiana fra medioevo e rinascimento* Florence, 1973, p. 28, n. 1. In an interesting study B. Toscano has attempted to account for the relative lack of interest in Umbrian art: "La fortuna della pittura umbra e il silenzio sui primitivi," *Paragone,* 193 (1966), 3-32. I should add that two recent exceptions to the generally poor state of historical research are works by Daniel Waley: *Medieval Orvieto: The Political History of an Italian Town, 1157-1334,* Cambridge, 1952, and *The Papal State in the Thirteenth Century,* London 1951.

8.   Pompeo Pellini, *Dell'Historia di Perugia,* 3 vols., Venice, 1664, and William Heywood, *A History of Perugia,* ed., R. Langston Douglas, London, 1910. In another sense, however, the student of the Perugian *Deucento* is especially hampered by the fact that there are no surviving accounts of the period written by contemporaries. Ariodente Fabretti, *Cronache e*

storie inedite della città di Perugia, 5 vols., Torino, 1887, is the basic source for Perugian chronicles. The earliest eyewitness accounts begin with the years 1305 and 1308. For a general commentary on the evolution of the early chronicles see Francesco A. Ugolino, *Annali e cronaca di Perugia dal 1191 al 1336,* Perugia, 1962.

9.   Sarah Rubin Blanshei, *Perugia, 1260-1340: Conflict and Change in a Medieval Italian Urban Society, Translations of the American Philosophical Society,* vol. 66, part 2, 1976. To a remarkable degree the work of Pellini is substantiated in this rigorous archival and demographic study.

10.   By this I mean that the institutional and economic development of the city parallels that of the other communes. I shall have occasion above to refer to specific points of correspondence. For the present, it might be noted that an excellent survey of the political evolution of the towns during the Duecento, as well as a brief look at economic developments, is J. K. Hyde, *Society and Politics in Medieval Italy: the Evolution of the Civic Life, 1000-1350,* London and Basingstoke, 1972, pp. 94 ff.

11.   For a list of the dates of the construction of the palaces, see J. Paul, *Die Mittelalterlichen Kommunalpäläste in Italien,* Dresden, 1963, pp. 123 ff., and F. Rodolico and G. Marchini, *I palazzi del popolo nei comuni toscani del medievo,* Florence, 1962, pp. 63 ff. (In the course of the discussion of the history of palace construction in Perugia, specific correspondences with other cities will be pointed out.)

12.   *Commentary on Codex, Tres Libri,* Turin, 1577, C.X. 31.61, p. 61, Heywood, *op. cit.,* p. 100, and C.N.S. Woolf, *Bartolus of Sassoferrato,* Cambridge, 1913, p. 116, also quote this passage. The connection between Perugia's legal position vis à vis the emperor and pope and Bartolus's theory is explored by G. Scalvanti, "Un opinione del Bartolo sulla libertà Perugina," *Bollettino della Deputazione di Storia Patria per l'umbria,* 2 (1887), pp. 59 ff., and by Daniele Segolino, "Bartolo da Sassoferrato e la Civilitas Perusiana," in *Bartolo da Sassoferrato: Studi e documenti per il VI centenario,* 2, Perugia, 1962, pp. 513 ff.

13.   Garrett Mattingly, *Renaissance Diplomacy,* Oxford, 1955, p. 24. Woolf, *op. cit.,* pp. 116 ff., and Scalvanti, *op. cit.,* pp. 59 ff., briefly treat how the independent way in which Perugia acted in regard to the emperor and pope during the century was a source for Bartolus's thought. A. Gewirth has suggested analogous sources in the political experience of the Duecento for the theory of Marsilius: *Marsilius of Padua,* New York, 1951, pp. xxv ff. Walter Ullmann's assertion that the "factual situation was ready" in the late thirteenth century for Marsilius "but not for the doctrine," might apply also to the case of the relation between Bartolus and Perugia *(Principles of Government in the Middle Ages,* New York, 1961, p. 230).

14.   The aid that Perugia contributed throughout the century is recorded by Daniel Waley in *The Papal State in the Thirteenth Century* (London, 1951), pp. 242-280. Waley notes that Perugia was one of very few cities that responded throughout the Duecento to "calls for help" (p. 181). On the conclaves, notably that of 1292, see T.S.R. Boase, *Boniface VIII,* London, 1933, pp. 33 ff.

15.   Pellini, *op. cit.,* 1, pp. 172, 283 and 295. For example, in 1273 the city was fined and excommunicated because of its claim to the *contado* of Gubbio (283). Perugia answered with protest demonstrations, refusals to pay the fine and assertions of its liberty (Waley, p. 249). For the city's anti-church legislation, see Luigi Bonazzi, *Storia di Perugia,* I, Città di Castello, 1959, pp. 257 ff. The war against Foligno during the 1280s and 90s, for example, was conducted despite papal disapproval, and the diplomatic and legislative proceedings related to the war are filled with statements about the freedom of the city and of its citizens

(Pellini, pp. 290 ff.). Waley, p. 206, and Giovanni Cecchini, "Fra Bevignate e la guerra contro Foligno," *Storia e arte in umbria nell'età comunale: Atti del VI Convegno di studi umbri,* 2, pp. 353 ff. One effect of the excommunication was, as in Florence, to increase the sense of civic loyalty (Gene Bruckner, *Renaissance Florence,* New York, 1969, p. 14).

16.   Bartolus drew many parallels between the policies of the ideal free city and those of the emperor (Woolf, *op. cit.*, pp. 113 ff.). Bartolus appears to have had the same mixed feelings about the emperor as Dante. He expressed great contempt for him, but also used the emperor in his model for the organization of the ideal state. For a discussion of Dante's and Bartolus's attitudes toward the emperor, see A.P. d'Entrèves, *Dante as a Political Thinker,* Oxford, 1952.

17.   One example of her activity as peace-maker was the part the city played in helping to end the civil war of 1293 in Todi (Heywood, p. 88).

18.   Ferdinand Gregorovius, *Geschichte der Stadt Rom in Mittelalter,* vol. 2, Wurtemburg, 1926, p. 180.

19.   The population of Perugia during the late thirteenth century is estimated by Waley to have been about 30,000 (p. 85). Blanshei (*op. cit.*, pp. 21-31) offers detailed demographic studies to support this estimate. Such a population, Blanshei remarks, placed Perugia in the "middle ranks" of the Northern and Central Italian cities, about one-third the size of the great population centers, such as Florence, and about twice the size of neighboring Assisi.

20.   Giustiniano degli Azzi, "Lo statuto del 1342 del comune di Perugia," *Corpus Statutorum Italicorum,* 1, Perugia, 1961, Lib. IV. Rubr. I. The statute is mentioned by Wolfgang Braunfels, *Mittelalterliche Stadt-Baukunst in der Toskana,* Berlin, 1953, p. 184.

21.   A complete elucidation of this theme is found in Kathrin Hoffmann-Curtius, *Das Program der Fontana Maggiore in Perugia,* Dusseldorf, 1968, pp. 27-74. Hoffmann-Curtius does not discuss how the iconography relates directly to Perugian politics and diplomacy, but stresses the links between the fountain sculptures and representations of the Fountain of Life. John White's reconstruction of the fountain, although the foundation for a somewhat different interpretation of the monument, does not in itself necessitate a rejection of Hoffmann-Curtius's point of view ("The Reconstruction of Nicola Pisano's Perugia Fountain," *Journal of the Warburg and Courtauld Institutes,* 33, 1970, pp. 70 ff.). White believes that the fountain is based on the organization of the medieval encyclopedia (*Art and Architecture in Italy: 1250-1400,* Baltimore, 1966, pp. 50 ff.) I should add that the originality of aspects of the subjects of the sculptures has perhaps been exaggerated. The wide scope of the secular subjects is anticipated in the decorations of the North Italian cathedrals of the twelfth century.

22.   The relevant statutes are found in degli Azzi, *op. cit.,* Lib. II Rubr. I. Such actions were typical of the stronger communes of the period, but this fact should not influence our understanding of the meaning of this policy within the local context. The systematization of the statutes in 1279 is in itself indicative both of the increasing complexity of the government and of the general ordering of the appearance and of the institutions of the city that was occurring at the same moment.

23.   There are only three general discussions of the urban evolution of Perugia of which I am aware: M. Belard, *Il nucleo storico di Perugia e le zone per il rinascimento,* Gubbio, 1960; G. Cecchini, *Contributo alla raccolta di fonti per la storia dello sviluppo urbanistico di Perugia,* Perugia, 1965; Luisa Chiumenti, "Perugia," *Dizionario enciclopedico di architettura e urbanistica,* 4, Rome, 1969, p. 421.

24. Ugolino Nicolini, "Le mura medievali di Perugia," *Storia e arte in Umbria nell'età comunale,* 2, Perugia, 1969, pp. 605 ff., is the basic source for the history of the medieval walls. For the Etruscan circuit of walls, see V. Campelli, *La cinta muraria di Perugia,* Perugia, 1935. Heywood's summary history of the medieval city is most useful (pp. 336 ff.). Pellini notes that some major reconstruction took place in 1276 (p. 286). Such activity before about 1320, however, would appear to be the exception.

25. Nicolini, *op. cit.,* p. 367.

26. Belardi, *op. cit.,* pp. 5-7; Heywood, p. 340.

27. Heywood, p. 340.

28. Blanshei, *op. cit.,* pp. 44 ff. Of some significance here as well is that the wealth of the city was still concentrated in the *città vecchia.*

29. Blanshei, p. 52.

30. See above, p. 14.

31. Blanshei has described the political history of the period in the following words: "new political institutions were established which broadened the base of the government's representation and gradually transformed the commune into a guild republic" (p. 7).

32. In 1130 the inhabitants of *Isola Pavese* made a submission "in the presence of the whole Perugian people in the *Piazza of S. Lorenzo* and in the hands of the consuls" (Heywood, p. 23; Pellini, pp. 176 ff.). F. Briganti has studied the early growth of the city as an "imperialist" power in the region (*Città dominanti e comuni minori nel medio evo con speciale riguardo alla republica perugina,* Perugia, 1906); and C. Volpe has written of the institutional significance of the first submissions (*Il medioevo,* Rome, 1926, pp. 294 ff.).

33. Pellini, p. 286. There is in fact some dispute about the exact year. A document of 1174 is simply the first surviving one in which the *podestà* is mentioned. Giovanni Cecchini has dealt fully with this problem as a part of the finest institutional history of the city: *Archivio storico di Perugia; Inventario,* Rome, 1956, pp. v-viii.

34. Heywood, pp. 30-31; Vincenzo Ansidei, *Prefazione al Volume Primo del Rigestum Reformationum Communis perusii ab anno MCCLVI ad annum MCC,* Perugia, 1935, p. 22. The consuls were chosen on the basis of two for each of the five administrative districts of the city (Blanshei, pp. 53 ff.).

35. Hyde portrays Paduan patriotism as representing a reaction against the tyranny of Ezzelino *(Padua in the Age of Dante,* Manchester, 1966, pp. 1-4). Lest the impression be given that crisis was unimportant for the formulation of republican theory and defense, Florentine political writings of the period, notably Remigio de'Girolami's still vastly under-appreciated *Tractatus de bono communis,* has also been convincingly explained as deriving from a period of crisis in the political life (C.T. Davis, "An Early Florentine Political Theorist: Fra Remigio de' Girolami," *Proceedings of the American Philosophical Society,* 104, (1960), 662-676. The "Baron thesis" is a further indication of how present scholarship tends to view republican ideals as arising during periods of crisis (Hans Baron, *The Crisis of the Early Italian Renaissance,* rev. ed., Princeton, 1966). Although Baron's belief that the Milanese threat to Florence in the late fourteenth and early fifteenth centuries was the primary reason for a return to ancient Roman republican political ideals has come under some question— see Jerrold E. Siegel, " 'Civic Humanism' or Ciceronian Rhetoric," *Past and Present,* No. 34, July 1966, pp. 3 ff.—the thesis remains the starting point for any examination of the political thought of the Renaissance.

36. The relevant statutes are found in Giovanni Belelli, *L'istituto del podestà in Perugia nel secolo XIII,* Bologna, 1936, pp. 34-43.

37. W.M. Bowsky, "The *'Buon Governo'* of Siena (1287-1355): A Medieval Italian Oligarchy," *Speculum,* 37 (1962), 368 ff. The comparison with Perugia is my own.

38. Ansidei, *op. cit.,* pp. 15-16.

39. L. Zdekauer, *La vita pubblica dei senesi nel dugento,* Siena, 1897, p. 13.

40. Cecchini, *op. cit.,* p. viii. As in the case of the *podestà* there is some question abut the date (A. Belucci, "Un singolare errore sulla creazione della Capitano del Popolo in Perugia," *Bollettino della Deputazione di Storia Patria per l'Umbria,* 16, 1910, 895 ff.).

41. J.K. Hyde, *Society and Politics . . . ,* p. 117. The basic source for the institutional history of the city during the second half of the century is A. Briganti, *Le corporazione della arti nel comune di Perugia,* Perugia, 1910. Blanshei, pp. 54 ff., has also outlined the powers of the captain. She notes that at first many administrative duties were shared by the *podestà* and the captain, and that not until the 1280's did the captain fully emerge as a free agent and force in the city.

42. Briganti, pp. 33 ff. In Perugia, as elsewhere, the *podestà* was representative of the older, propertied class of the city (Blanshei, pp. 51 ff.).

43. Heywood, p. 37.

44. This evolution of communal power has been most thoroughly examined in two case studies, both of which deal with Florence: Nicola Ottakar, *Il comune di Firenze al fine del Dugento,* Torino, 1962, pp. 3-32, and Robert Davidsohn, *Storia di Firenze,* IV, i, Florence, 1973, pp. 169-182. The Perugian situation, as characterized by Briganti, is similar. The document referred to in the text is cited by Briganti, *op.cit.,* p. 51. See also Blanshei, pp. 55 ff.

45. Blanshei, p. 56.

46. Ibid., pp. 59 ff.

47. Briganti, p. 101. Several of the statutes note that this is a power that the *podestà* shared with the captain. This fact might point to the beginning of the gradual transition of such tasks to the priors.

48. Hofmann-Curtius has summarized the documentary record *(op. cit.,* pp. 8-10).

49. The basic sources for the coinage of the Perugian commune are: Franco Panvini Rosati, "La Monetazione delle città umbre nell'età dei Comuni," *Storia e arte in Umbria nell'età Comunale* Vol. 2, 1969, 239-252; G.B. Vermiglioli, *Della zecca e della monete perugine,* Perugia, 1816.

50, For a note on the role of a city's patron saint in the inducement of partiotic devotion, see E. Kantorowicz, " *'Pro Patria mori,'* in Medieval Political Thought," *Selected Studies.* Locust Valley, 1967, pp. 308 ff.

51. Azzi, *op. cit.,* pp. 86 ff.

52. Blanshei, pp. 54 ff.

53. See above, pp. 14-15.

54. Braunfels discusses the general significance of communal wall decorations of the second half of the Duecento *(op. cit.,* pp. 50-51). The themes of the Perugian decorations are discussed by Nicolini, *op. cit.,* p. 40.

55.   For the names of the eleven churches founded during this period, see "Perugia," *Enciclopedia italiana,* 10, Milan, 1935, p. 905. Ettore Ricci, *La Chiesa di San Prospero e i Pittori del Duecento in Perugia,* Perugia, 1929, and U. Tarchi, *L'arte medievale dell'Umbria e della Sabina,* 2, Milan, 1938, offer general histories of the church building during the time. One reason for the unprecedented magnitude of this church-building campaign, even when compared to that of leading Tuscan cities, was the wave of popular religiosity that rose in the city during the last third of the Duecento. Etienne Delaruelle, "La piété populaire en Ombrie au siècle des Communes," *Storia e arte in Umbria nell'età Comunale,* 2, 397-413, is the most recent treatment of the flagellent movement in Umbria, a movement that began in Perugia in about 1260.

56.   I have been able to discover no analogous example of official priority given to local studies. For the early history of the university in Perugia, see Pellini, pp. 290-291; Giuseppe Ermini, "Fattori di successo dello studio perugino delle origini," *Storia e arte in Umbria nelle età comunale,* and G. Ermini, *Storia della Università di Perugia,* Bologna, 1947, pp. 3-10.

57.   For comparative studies on what appears to represent the more normal course of development of the communal universities, see H. Wieruszowski, "Arezzo as a Center of Learning and Letters in the Thirteenth Century," *Tradition,* 9 (1953), 321-391; and Hastings Rashdall on the university in Bologna, *The Universities of Europe in the Middle Ages,* 1, Oxford, 1936, 63-257. One fairly analogous situation of direct government involvement in the early stages of a developing university is that of Bologna, as it is described by J.K. Hyde, "Commune, University and Society in Early Medieval Bologna," *Universities in Politics,* eds. J.W. Baldwin and R.A. Goldthwaite, Baltimore, 1972.

58.   Bellini, pp. 301 ff.; Waley, pp. 76 ff. For Perugia, relations with Foligno are the main source of conflict.

59.   Ermini, *Storia* . . . , pp. 9-11.

60.   Pellini, p. 3. See above, p. 33 ff., for an explanation of the poem and its specific relevance for the frescoes in the Sala dei Notari.

61.   Heywood, p. 346.

62.   Ibid.

63.   Ibid.; A. Bellucci, "La Chiesa di Sant'Ercolano di Perugia," *Augusta Perugia* 2 (1907): 11-19.

64.   Blanshei, p. 55.

65.   Ibid., pp. 59 ff.

66.   Ibid., p. 1 f.

Chapter 3

1.   Chiumenti, *op.cit.,* p. 242, has dealt most thoroughly with the later evolution of the square and with its relation to the establishment of new centers of political and economic activity within the city.

2.   Paul, *Die Mittelalterlichen Kommunalpaläste,* p. 192. The square was also called the *platea communis.*

3.   For a useful survey of the communal squares and palaces of Umbria, see U. Tarchi, *op. cit.,* 2, pp. 14 ff., and M.C. Faina, *I palazzi comunali umbri,* Milan, 1954, pp. 32, 39, 52, 63 and 72.

4.   O. Gurrieri, *Il Palazzo dei Priori à Perugia: Guida Illustrata,* Perugia, 1962, p. 23; M.M. Rapone, *Peruse: Le Palais des "Priori,"* Paris, 1950, p. 21. Such utilization of the loggia of a civic palace was not unusual for the palaces of Umbria.

5.   The church was "appropriated" in the initial expansion of the fabric in 1307. Martini believes that such an enlargement was not planned from the outset (*op. cit.,* p. 42), while Francesco Santi maintains that the church was from the start considered a part of the palace ("Note sul Palazzo dei Priori à Perugia," *Bollettino della Deputazione di Storia Patria per l'Umbria,* 69, 1972, 49-53). The original fabric was, however, a coherent and complete design. I fail to see how the enlargement could have been conceived when the first plans of the palace were discussed.

6.   M. Guardabassi, *Indice-Guida dei monumenti pagani e cristiani dell'Umbria,* Perugia, 1972, p. 63; Heywood, *op. cit.,* pp. 350-351.

7.   G.B.S. Rossi, *Il Palazzo del Popolo,* Perugia, 1864, p. 6.

8.   Martini, pp. 50 ff.

9.   On the original appearance of the stair ramps of the two palaces, see A. Bellucci, *Osservazioni sulla scala esterna del Palazzo del Popolo,* Perugia, 1899.

10.   Martini, p. 43; Heywood, pp. 352-353.

11.   E. Ricci, *La Piazza del Comune e le logge di Braccio Fortebracci,* Perugia, 1927.

12.   Heywood, p. 353.

13.   The square is often cited as an excellent example of how the unexpectedly great degree of control exercised over the growth of the medieval towns anticipated aspects of Renaissance urban planning. A most important recent expression of this notion is Martini, p. 43. Two early visual representations of the piazza help give us some idea of its appearance: Follower of Meo da Siena, *S. Ercolano, c.* 1328 (see *Galleria Nazionale dell'Umbria: dipinti, sculture, e oggetti d'arte di età romanica e gotica,* Rome, 1969, p. 62, for a description of the city as it appears in the painting); and B. Bonfigli, *Seconda traslazione, del Corpo di S. Ercolano,* 1454-1464 (Perugia, *Capella dei Priori, Palazzo dei Priori*). See Martini, p. 42, for a discussion of the use of this fresco in attempts to reconstruct the early appearance of the piazza.

14.   Paul stresses, perhaps too greatly, the importance of geographical factors in Umbrian civic architecture (p. 83). The Palazzo del Comune in Cortona is a second important example of how a topographical setting similar to Perugia's helps to account for a design not unlike that of the Palazzo dei Priori.

15.   Chiumenti, *op. cit.,* p. 421. Writing generally on the site of the city, she notes that "Il luogo, situato al centro della peninsula, egualemente distante dai due mare e in facile communicazione con i vicini popoli dell'Italia centrale, fu considerato dagli Etruschi particularmente adatto alla fondazione di una città" (p. 421).

16.   This attempt to relate the form of Umbrian towns to political and religious considerations has been made by O. Gurrieri, *Agnelo da Orvieto, Matteo Gattapone e i palazzi pubblichi di Gubbio e Città di Castello,* Perugia, 1962, pp. 4-5.

17.   The fountains of Viterbo and of Narni are two notable predecessors of the Fontana Maggiore. The case of Siena, however, might be given special emphasis here as there is a clear history of centrally-placed fountains sponsored by government involvement and patronage going back to the period before that of Roman colonization (Ann Coffin Hanson,

Jacopo della Quercia's 'Fonte Gaia', Oxford, 1965, pp. 4 ff.). The inclusion of two fountains close to the form of the Fontana Maggiore in the idealized *Civic View* in the Palazzo Ducale, Urbino, suggests how the communal squares of the Middle Ages became an inspiration for the urban thinking of the Renaissance.

18.   Hanson, p. 4. The often mythic connotations that accrued to this supremely important role of the government as it was symbolized by the fountain is suggested in many ways, among which is the fact that Dante mentions the celebrated *Fonte Branda* and an associated myth in the *Inferno* (XXX, 78). Hoffmann-Curtius's identification of the Fontana Maggiore as representative of a Fountain of Life and as an embodiment of baptismal functions might be generally descriptive of the medieval civic fountain (pp. 78 ff.). The implication is that not only is the communal piazza and fountain the living center of the city but that it also symbolizes less tangible sustenative forces of the *polis*.

19.   Ricci, *op. cit.*, p. 57, has also written of the stylistic parallels between the two structures. This part of the Cathedral was under construction beginning in about 1300, or shortly after the completion of the first section of the Palazzo dei Priori (Gurrieri, *La cattedrale . . .*, p. 7). Professor James Beck has suggested to me that such prominence for a side portal that had an important role in civic and religious ceremonies is not unusual (a notable related example is the Porta della Mandorla in Florence); unusual, however, is the formal correspondence between the design of the Perugia portal and the neighboring structures.

20.   Richard Krautheimer, "Introduction to an 'Iconography of Medieval Architecture,' " *Studies in Early Christian, Medieval, and Renaissance Art,* New York, 1969, 115-150, is the most well-known study in this field. Like most other such research in the realm of ecclesiastical architecture, the examination proceeds from the conviction that the form of a building derives from liturgical considerations. The leading studies of iconography in the field of civic architecture are concerned with the self-conscious revival of ancient Roman political structures. The most successful of these studies is H.P. l'Orange, *Art Forms and the Civic Life in the Late Roman Empire,* Princeton, 1975. In a more specialized study, David Rosand has recently shown how in Venice the Palace of the Doges was conceived of as a palace of justice and was "deliberately associated" with the Temple of Solomon ("Titian's *Presentation of the Virgin in the Temple* and the Scuola della Carità," *Art Bulletin* 58 (1976): 76 ff.).

21.   Martini, pp. 42-43.

22.   G. Cristofani, "Ritmi veneziani nel Palazzo dei Priori di Perugia," *Atti del Secondo Convegno nazionale di Storia dell'Architettura,* Assisi, October 1-4, 1939, pp. 221-222.

23.   Paul (p. 83) and Martini (p. 56) assert that the design of the Todi palace was a formative ingredient for the Perugia palace. The Todi palace was started in 1292, which is either one year before or several years after the work began in Perugia (P.N. Cavalli, *Profilo storico-artistico della città di Todi,* Todi, 1937).

24.   For the political relations between the cities, see G. Ceci, *Todi nel medioevo,* Todi, 1897, pp. 18 ff.

25.   On the localism of Umbrian architecture and art, see Paul, p. 82, and Tarchi, p. 3.

26.   For a reconstruction of the Senator's Palace, see Gregorovius, 2, 219 ff., and C. Pietrangeli, *Le Prime fase architettoniche del Palazzo del Senatorio,* Rome, 1959.

27.   Boniface's political program for the Papal State has been discussed by, among others, Gregorovius, 5, p. 234, and by Peter Partner, *The Lands of St. Peter: the Papal State in the*

Middle Ages and the Early Renaissance, Berkeley and Los Angeles, 1972, pp. 286 ff. For art under Boniface, see A. Muñoz, *L'arte à Roma nel tempo di Dante,* Milan, 1926, pp. 30 ff., and Robert Brentano, *Rome Before Avignon: A Social History of Thirteenth Century Rome,* New York, 1974, pp. 300 ff., who includes a complete bibliography.

28.   See p. 47, for a discussion of social disorder in Perugia.

29.   Marvin Becker, *Florence in Transition 2,* Baltimore, 1967, 11 ff. Becker himself writes briefly of the role of art in the enunciation of the communal *paideia.* For example, he discusses the program of decorations for the Cathedral complex in Florence as one important example of such a role (pp. 31-32).

30.   Martini, p. 56. The palace appears in one sense to be little more than two large assembly halls, or naves, supported by the formerly open loggia. This simple, reductive interior is typical of the civic architecture of the region.

31.   For the history of the bronzes, see A. Briganti, "Notizie sui primordi delle arti in Perugia," *Rassegna d'arte umbra,* 1 (1910): 87-88, and Clara Zaggerini Cutini,"Sulla datazione del grifo perugino," *Bollettino della Deputazione di Storia Patria per l'Umbria* 69 (1972): 53-61.

32.   Bonazzi, *Storia . . . ,* 1, p. 282; Ansidei, *op.cit.,* p. 10. This was the common course of the communes. For the better researched and documented case of Florence, see Davidsohn, *op. cit.,* 5, 104 ff.

33.   Paul, p. 83.

34.   Braunfels believes that the closeness of church-state connections at this time was responsible for such a choice of meeting place (p. 56.).

35.   Martini, p. 40.

36.   Paul, p. 242.

37.   Martini, p. 52; Nessi, "Documenti sull'arte umbra," *Commentari* 18-19 (1967): 76.

38.   W. Bombe (*Perugia,* Leipzig, 1914, p. 10) suggests 1271. P. Toesca (*Il Trecento,* Turin, 1951, p. 133) supports a date of 1282. Pellini's 1293 is the most widely accepted (p. 310).

39.   The documents have been published by Martini, pp. 67 ff.

40.   Nessi, *op. cit.,* p. 59.

Chapter 4

1.   John Milton, *Paradise Lost,* Book XII, pp. 220 ff.

2.   Ibid., Book I, p. 342.

3.   Ibid., Book XII, p. 265.

4.   Douglas Bush, *John Milton, a Sketch of His Life and Writings,* London, 1965, p. 146.

5.   The inscriptions for the four scenes survive. They are, in the order in which the works are listed above: *GEDEON. SIGVM. VIDIT. AQVAE. I. VELERE., MOISES. AUTE. PASSCEBAT. OVES. RETRO. CONGNA. APPARVIT QM. EI. DNS. I FLAMA IGNIS DE MEDIO RUBI, MOISES. ET. AARON. DIXERVT. FARAONI. HEC DICIT DNUS DEVS ISRAEL DIMITE POPVLVM MEVM., CVQUE. EXTEDISSET. MOYSES MAVM. COTRA. MARE REVERSV EST AD PRIORE LOCUM.*

6.   As nature was created by God's will, so it must contain a religious mission or duty for man. The Biblical accounts of the Fall through the atoning death and resurrection of Christ marked the beginning and final goal of human history (Karl Vossler, *An Introduction to Dante and His Times,* 1, London, 1929, p. 283). The bibliography on medieval political theory is vast. I will not attempt to list the major works here. A still useful and reliable handbook is Otto Gierke, *Political Theories of the Middle Ages,* Cambridge, 1900. It is remarkable, however, that there appears to be no systematic interpretation of the relation between the Bible and political theory. To be sure the theme is treated in such fundamental works as Ernst Kantorowicz, *The King's Two Bodies: a Study in Medieval Political Theology,* Princeton, 1957, and in Michael Wilks, *The Problem of Sovereignty in the Later Middle Ages: the Papal Monarchy with Augustinius Triumphus and the Publicists,* Cambridge, 1964. But references to the Bible occur in an almost incidental fashion, and no coherent sense emerges of the general importance of the Scriptures in medieval political thought. See also Quentin Skinner, *The Foundations of Modern Political Thought, I: The Renaissance,* London, New York, and Melbourne, 1978, pp. 3 ff.

7.   For a discussion of the distinctions between natural and divine law, see Heiko A. Oberman, *The Harvest of Medieval Theology; Gabriel Biel and Late Medieval Nominalism,* Cambridge, 1963, pp. 90 ff. Herbert A. Deane has dealt with general questions of the various types of law discussed by early Christian philosophers and the relation of these discussions to political thought: *The Political and Social Ideas of St. Augustine,* New York and London, 1963, p. 197.

8.   An interesting discussion of the relation of Biblical sources to late medieval historiography in Italy is found in Louis Green, *Chronicle into History: An Essay on the Interpretation of History in Florentine Fourteenth Century Chronicles,* Cambridge, 1972, p. 21. So far as I am aware, no study of the political theory of the encyclopedists has been undertaken. Henry Osborn Taylor, *The Medieval Mind,* 1, New York, 1919, pp. 345 ff., includes an excellent general characterization of the political beliefs of Vincent of Beauvais. Maurice de Wulf has dealt with the beliefs of Isidore of Seville: *Philosophy and Civilization in the Middle Ages,* New York, 1953, pp. 115 ff. In this context I should note that all types of political documents of the late Middle Ages were also filled with Biblical references—from the *Liber Augustalis* of Frederick (*"The Liber Augustalis," or Constitutions of Melfi Promulgated by the Emperor Frederick II for the Kingdom of Sicily in 1231,* translated and introduced by James M. Powell, Syracuse, 1971, pp. 4 ff.) to the texts of civic statutes (Peter Riesenberg, "Civicism and Roman Law in Fourteenth Century Italian Society," *Society and Government in Medieval Italy: Essays in Honor of Robert L. Reynolds.* ed., David Herlihy, Kent, 1969, pp. 237-254).

9.   Cited by Deane, *op. cit.,* p. 87.

10.   Staale Sinding-Larsen, *Christ in the Council Hall; Studies in the Religious Iconography of the Venetian Republic,* with a contribution by A. Kuhn, Institutum Romnum Norvegiae, Acta ad Archaeologian et Artivm Historiam, 5, Rome, 1975, stresses the importance of placement of decorations in relation to the celebration of political and religious liturgy in the Palazzo Ducale and in San Marco.

11.   For a treatment of the importance of placement for the iconography of a contemporary cycle of decorations, see Michael Alpatoff, "The Parallelism of Giotto's Paduan Frescoes," *The Art Bulletin,* 29 (1947), 149 ff. Alpatoff has noted thematic and stylistic links between pairs of corresponding murals.

12.   For a general discussion of the iconography and diffusion of the scene, see the following: Günter Bandmann et al., *Lexikon der Christlichen Ikonographie,* 3, Rome-Freiburg-Basel-

Vienna, 1971, 282 ff.; Louis Réau, *Iconographie de l'Art Chrétien,* 2, Paris, 1956, pp. 185 ff.;
Joseph Wilpert, *Die Römischen Mosaiken und Malerein der Kirchlichen Bauten vom IV-
XIII Jahrhundert,* 1, Freiburg, 1917, 446 ff.; Otto Demus, *Die Mosaiken von San Marco in
Venedig, 1100-1300,* Vienna, 1935, p. 98, n. 42; Joseph Garber, *Wirkungen der Frühchristlichen Gemaldezyklen der Alten Peters-und-Pauls-Basilken in Rom,* Berlin and Vienna,
1918; J.J. Tikkanen, *Die Genesismosaiken von S. Marco in Venedig,* Helsinki, 1889, pp. 80
ff.

13.　The representation of this event is, so far as I can determine, most unusual in Italy, but not
uncommon in France after the twelfth century (Bandmann, *op. cit.,* 2, 126; E. Mâle, *The
Gothic Image, Religious Art in France of the Thirteenth Century,* New York, 1958, p. 157;
Adelheid Heimann, "The Capital Freize and Pilasters of the *Portail Royal:* Chartres,"
Journal of the Warburg and Courtauld Institutes, 31 (1968), 95 ff.; Rosalie B. Green, " 'Ex
Ungue Leonum,' " "De Artibus Opuscula xl," *Essays in Honor of Erwin Panofsky,* New
York, 1961, 157 ff.). Mâle discusses Gideon as a prefiguration of Christ, while Heimann and
Green show how the miracle of the fleece was a common type for the virginity of Mary. It is
interesting to note, although the scheme has no bearing on the Sala dei Notari, that *Moses
before the Burning Bush* has also been seen as a symbol of Mary's virginity, and the two
scenes—that of Gideon and of Moses—when found together in earlier art appear to share
this symbolism (Georg Swarzenski, "The Song of the Three Worthies," *Bulletin, Museum of
Fine Arts,* Boston, 56, 1958, 30 ff.). The theme was widespread in the twelfth century
(Swarzenski, p. 44). For a general discussion of this aspect of the symbolism of the Virgin,
see Yrjö Hirn, *The Sacred Shrine: a Study of the Poetry and Art of the Catholic Church,*
London, 1958, pp. 144 ff.

14.　Of the several ways in which Moses and Gideon are represented in art, their role as warriors
is the least frequent. For Gideon, see Heimann, *op. cit.,* p. 95; and for Moses see Léjeune and
Stiennon, *The Legend of Roland . . .,* pp. 153 ff.

15.　A general bibliography on Moses in art is offered above, n. 12. On the diffusion and
traditional iconography of this scene, see Réau, *op. cit.,* p. 188. On the role of Aaron in the
scene, see Charles L. Souvay, "Aaron," *The New Catholic Encyclopedia,* 1, London, 1907,
3. If Moses can be considered a typification of the ideal leader, then Aaron is the perfect
minister in the part that he acts out in the meetings with the Pharoah.

16.　L.D. Ettlinger has stressed the same point in his discussion of the murals from the life of
Moses in the Sistine Chapel (*The Sistine Chapel before Michelangelo: Religious Imagery
and Papal Primacy,* Oxford, 1965, p. 65). Ettlinger has also drawn attention to earlier
examples of the pairing of the scenes of *Moses and Aaron before the Pharaoh* and the
Pursuit of the Israelites (p. 65, n. 1).

17.　See Réau, p. 192, for general notes on the representation of the scene in medieval art. For
comments on the ways in which the scene was depicted in Early Christian art, see Kurt
Weitzmann, *Illustrations in Roll and Codex,* Princeton, 1947, p. 33.

18.　Augustine, *Corpus Scriptorum Ecclesiasticorum Latinorum* XXIV (2) pp. 50 ff. The
passage is cited by Deane, *op. cit.,* p. 197. Augustine concludes the section by writing that
"always both the bad have persecuted the good, and the good have persecuted the bad: the
former doing harm by their uprightness, the latter seeking to do good by the administration
of discipline; the former with cruelty, the latter with moderation; the former impelled by
lust, the latter under the constraint of love" (Deane, p. 250).

19.　Augustine, *The City of God,* 5, translated by Eva Matthews Sanford and William McAllen
Green, Cambridge and London, 1955, Book XVI, 197.

20. Ibid., 7, Book XXII, X, p. 255. Augustine's attitude toward the Roman Empire, and the relation of this attitude to the views of his contemporaries, is examined by Theodor E. Mommeson, "St. Augustine and the Christian Idea of Progress: the Background of *The City of God,*" *Medieval and Renaissance Studies,* ed. Eugene F. Rice, Jr., Ithaca, 1966, pp. 265 ff. The debate over the placement of the Altar of Victory is a fascinating aspect of the early Christian attitude toward pagan images (Ibid., pp. 288 ff.). That Augustine himself believed that images carried extraordinary powers is clear in, among other places, his reference to a passage in Terence in which a man becomes aroused because of the sight of a painting (*Confessions,* translated by R.S. Pine-Coffin, Harmondsworth, 1961, p. 37).

21. The general picture drawn of Augustine's rejection of the earthly city is often somewhat overstated, it might be remarked here. If the ruler is virtuous, then the state functions not as a kind of legalized robber, but rather as a compassionate educator (Ernst Troeltsch, *The Social Teaching of the Christian Churches,* 1, London and New York, 1956, pp. 230, 239, 244, and 259; Deane, *op. cit.,* pp. 116 ff.) The title of Deane's chapter on the question aptly summarizes this element of Augustine's thought: "The State: The Return of Order upon Disorder."

22. The work has been dated on the basis of internal evidence between 439 and 455 (Salvian, *On the Government of God,* translated by Eva M. Sanford, New York, 1930, pp. 18 ff.). The central theme of the book, as it has been summarized by Sanford, must be cited in order that the references to Moses and to the Pharoah be understood properly: "the decline of the Roman power actually demonstrated God's government and judgment of human actions, since the sins of the Romans were such as had always, since the fall of Adam, been visited with instant punishment" (p. 4). The statement is made at the conclusion of a paraphrase of the Biblical account of the story of Moses. "I think you must recognize," Salvian writes, "that in all these cases God shows equally his care for human affairs and his judgment of them" (p. 50).

23. Ibid., p. 57.

24. Ibid., p. 56.

25. For the importance of this notion in early Christian historiography, see Mommeson, *op. cit.* The theme is placed within a far more general historiographical context by Randolph Starn, "Meaning-Levels in the Theme of Historical Decline," *History and Theory: Studies in the Philosophy of History,* 14, n. 1, 1975, 1 ff. That the ancillary notion was true, i.e., that good governments and virtue are synonymous with progress, emerges most clearly in the late medieval revival of the stoic notion of fortune.

26. Salvian, pp. 198 ff. Gideon's triumph is contrasted with the defeat of the Romans by the barbarians.

27. The issue is discussed by Aquinas in the *De Regimine Principum* (translated by G.B. Phelan, Toronto, 1932, pp. 42 ff.). The implications of the theory have been treated by Ullmann (*Principles . . . ,* pp. 215 ff.).

28. Aquinas, *Selected Political Writings,* ed. A.P. d'Entrèves, Oxford, 1948, pp. 23 ff.

29. On the "political science" of Aquinas, see Ullmann, pp. 210 ff.

30. d'Entrèves, p. 75.

31. Otto, Bishop of Freising, *The Two Cities: A Chronicle of Universal History to the Year 1146, A.D.,* translated by Charles Christopher Mierow, New York, 1928. On the representation of Biblical narrative in the universal histories see Rosalie B. Green, "The

Adam and Eve Cycle in the *Hortus Deliciarum,"* *Late Classical and Medieval Studies in Honor of Albert Mathias Friend,* ed. Kurt Weitzmann, Princeton, 1955; Buchtahl, *op. cit.,* pp. 68 ff.; Paul Meyer, "Les Premières compilations francaises d'histoire ancienne," *Romania,* 14 (1885): 1 ff. and 36 ff.; M. Budinger, "Die Universal histoire in Mittelalter," *Denkschriften d. Kaiserl. Akademie d. Wiss., phil-hist.,* 46, 1900, 13 ff. Otto's effort to correlate the chronology of the Old Testament with ancient writings and contemporary romances is typical of all universal histories.

32.   See pp. 137 ff. Five authorities are listed as corroborators of the Biblical account. I do not mean to suggest that the Bible was not always considered "history," but wish only to point out that the endeavor to find supporting voices suggests a more modern and critical historical spirit. On the general question of the relation of Bible and history during the late Middle Ages, see Beryl Smalley, *The Study of the Bible in the Middle Ages,* Oxford, 1952, especially pp. 37 ff. and 214 ff. and *A History of Historical Writing,* New York, 1942, I, pp. 103 and 268 ff.

33.   I. Berlin, "The Originality of Machiavelli," *Studies on Machiavelli,* ed. Myron P. Gilmore, Florence, 1972, pp. 150-206.

34.   A favorite device of the chroniclers, through at least the first half of the fourteenth century, was the relating of contemporary events to Biblical parallels or precedents. This point is important in Green's study of Florentine historiography (*Chronicle into History . . .*). Myron P. Gilmore, among many others, has also dealt with the matter as a part of his examination of the sources for the writing of history during the Renaissance: "The Renaissance Conception of the Lessons of History," *Humanists and Jurists: Six Studies in the Renaissance,* Cambridge, 1938, pp. 1 ff.

35.   Basic sources for study of this motif in imperial art and thought of the West and the East are: Kantorowicz, *The King's Two Bodies: A Study in Medieval Political Theology . . . ,* pp. 206 ff.; Ernst H. Kantorowicz, *"Laudes Regiae": A Study in Liturgical Acclamations and Medieval Ruler Worship,* Berkeley and Los Angeles, 1946, pp. 42 ff.; Walter Ullmann, *The Carolingian Renaissance and the Idea of Kingship,* Birkbeck Lectures, 1968-1969, London, 1969, pp. 71 ff.; André Grabar, *L'Empereur dans l'Art Byzantin,* Publications de la Faculté des Lettres de l'Université de Strasbourg, 75, Paris 1936, pp. 94 ff.; Michael Wilks, *The Problem of Sovereignty in the Later Middle Ages . . . ,* p. 92; and Christopher Walter, "Papal Imagery in the Medieval Lateran Palace," *Cahiers Archéologiques,* 20 (1970), 155 ff. and 21 (1971), 109 ff. The connection between this subject and the art of the communes has not been previously drawn. The fundamental study of the theme and its relation to late medieval art is Adolf Katzenellenbogen, *The Sculptural Programs of Chartres Cathedral: Christ, Mary, Ecclesia,* New York, 1959, pp. 27 ff.

36.   C. Ligota, "Constantiniana," *Journal of the Warburg and Courtauld Institutes* 26 (1963): 178 ff.

37.   Kantorowicz, *"Laudes" . . . ,* p. 56. The fact that this conception was still essential for the notion of the ruler in the late fourteenth century is demonstrated by Joseph R. Strayer, "France, the Holy Land, the Chosen People, and the Most Christian King," *Action and Conviction in Early Modern Europe: Essays in Memory of E.H. Harbison,* ed. Theodore Raab and Jerrold E. Seigel, Princeton, 1969, pp. 3 ff. Rhetoric such as this was of course shaped largely by occasion or function; reference to Rome rather than to Israel is just as common.

38.   Ibid., p. 56.

39.   Helen Rosenau, *The Ideal City in Its Architectural Evolution*, London 1959, pp. 22 ff. Rubinstein's analysis of the question in relation to the murals of Ambrogio Lorenzetti at Siena points to a later translation of the theme into art ("Political Ideas in Sienese Art . . .," pp. 205 ff.).

40.   E. Kantorowicz, *The King's Two Bodies . . .* , pp. 61 ff.: Percy E. Schram, "Das Herrscherbild in der Kunst des Mittelalters," *Vortrage der Bibliothek Warburg* 1 (1924): 195 ff.

41.   Grabar, *op. cit.*, pp. 96 ff.

42.   Adolf Katzenellenbogen, *Allegories of the Virtues and Vices in Mediaeval Art*, London, 1939, p. 12; Kantorowicz, *The King's Two Bodies . . .*, pp. 112-113. On the so-called political and social virtues and their representation in art, see Herbert Bloch, "Monte Cassino, Byzantium, and the West in the Earlier Middle Ages," *Dumbarton Oaks Papers* 3 (1946): 177 ff.

43.   Gregory describes tyranny in general terms as follows: "everyone of a proud spirit practices tyranny after his own fashion . . . [most probably] through his own inner malice, regarding not God in his inmost thought. . . . He is a tyrant at heart, being governed within by iniquity" (Ephraim Emerton, *Humanism and Tyranny: Studies in the Italian Trecento*, Cambridge, 1925, p. 127).
      Augustine, Ambrose, and Isidore all maintained that the leading criterion for determining if a state of tyranny existed was to ascertain if the laws were informed by Christian principles. This point of view may be taken as a precedent for the legalistic definition (Gierke, *Political Theories* . . . , pp. 33 ff.; R.W. Carlyle and A.J. Carlyle, *A History of Medieval Political Theory in the West*, 1, New York, 1936, p. 164). On the question of the religious foundation of the medieval notion of rule, see A.D. d'Entrèves, *The Medieval Contribution to Political Thought: Thomas Aquinas, Marsilius of Padua, Richard Hooker*, Oxford, pp. 8-9.

44.   For a general examination of legalistic definitions of tyranny during the Trecento and of Bartolus's place within this context, see Carlyle, 6, p. 16 and Emerton, *op. cit.*, pp. 119 ff.

45.   Carlyle, 1, p. 105. The view was shared by all the Fathers. For example, in the commentary of the so-called "Ambrosiaster" on St. Paul's Epistle to the Romans, Mosaic Law is seen as a supplement and confirmation of the natural law (p. 104), while Jerome notes, in what is largely a simple restatement of Ambrose, that the Mosaic Law was necessary because natural law had been destroyed (p. 105).

46.   Kantorowicz, *The King's Two Bodies . . .* , pp. 101 ff.

47.   F. Herter, *Die Podestàliteratur Italiens im 12. und 13. Jahrhunderts*, Diss. phil., Leipzig, 1910, pp. 43 ff.; Hyde, *Politics and Society . . .* , pp. 38-39, Skinner, *op. cit.*, I, pp. 33 ff., and 40 ff.

48.   Belelli, *op. cit.*, pp. 12-17. Sinding-Larsen has shown how a similar conception was rooted in the statutes of Venice (*op. cit.*, pp. 141, 146, 151 ff., 258 ff.).

49.   Woolf, *Bartolus . . .* , p. 116.

50.   At the beginning of the statutes of 1279, there is a section dealing with the ideal attributes of civic leaders. Only the most Christian attributes, such as evidence of the ruler's piety, are given emphasis (Giustiniano degli Azzi, *op. cit.*, Lib. II, Rubr. I). The scope of these statutes is thus very much like the earlier "Mirror Of Princes," where stress is laid on the temperance and magnanimity of the ruler (Ernest Barker, *Social and Political Thought in Byzantium*, Oxford, 1957, pp. 20 ff., 54 ff., 151 ff.).

51. It should be recalled here that there are problems associated with the original placement of the figures (see above, p. 98, n. 22).

52. The same observation is made by Hoffman-Curtius, *op. cit.*, pp. 33 ff. For a definition of the more common medieval typology of Moses as the forerunner of Christ, see Bandmann et al., *Lexikon . . .* , pp. 282 ff.

53. This explanation or accounting for what is surely one of the most fundamental themes in communal political thought is also made by Kantorowicz, *The King's Two Bodies . . .* , pp. 142 ff.

54. See Ettlinger, *The Sistine Chapel before Michaelangelo . . .* , p. 65. for discussion of these scenes as prototypes for the actions of rulers.

55. For the "Nine Worthies," see J. Huizinga, *The Waning of the Middle Ages*, New York, 1954, pp. 72 ff.; Roger Sherman Loomis, "The Heraldry of Hector, or Confusion Worse Confounded," *Speculum* 42 (1967): 32 ff.; David J.A. Ross, *Alexander Historiatus*, London, 1963, p. 105. This popular type of palace decoration developed in the early fourteenth century. The scheme was composed of three groups of three heroes, each of whom fought for his religion. The relation of such cycles to the "Famous Men" programs of the fifteenth century has been examined by C.W. Westfall, *In This Most Perfect Paradise: Alberti, Nicholas V, and the Invention of Conscious Urban Planning in Rome, 1447-55*, University Park and London, 1974, p. 158.

56. Kantorowicz, *The King's Two Bodies . . .* , p. 198.

57. The ideology of this school received its first major exposition by C.B. Fischer, "The Pisan Clergy and Its Awakening of Historical Interest in a Medieval Commune," *Studies in Medieval and Renaissance History*, ed. William M. Bowsky, Lincoln, 1966, pp. 141 ff. This discussion has recently been supplemented by E. Cristiani, "Aspetti di una coscienza cittadina nella storia pisana dei secoli XII e XIII," *La coscienza cittadina nei comuni italiani del Duecento, 11-14 ottobre 1970, Convegni del centro di studi sulla spiritualità medievale*, 9, Todi, 1972, 345 ff. The victories of the city over the infidel in the crusades were attributed by the historians to their alliance with God. Fischer's belief that this tendency in Pisan historiography is owed largely to the growing power of the clergy during the same period, however, seems to limit too strictly the importance of the movement. Religious links with the developing civic chauvinism are basic general elements in the movement throughout Europe during the later Middle Ages (E. Kantorowicz. " *'Pro Patria Mori'* in Medieval Political Thought," *Selected Studies*, Locust Valley, pp. 308 ff., and Gaines Post, "Two Notes on Nationalism in the Middle Ages," *Traditio*, 9. 1953, 281 ff.)

58. For the later evolution of this theme in the chronicles of the Trecento, beginning with Giovanni Villani, see Green, *Chronicle . . .* , pp. 91 ff. One problem with Green's work, in the light of Fischer's study, is that too little attention is paid to the early communal historiography. The providential element in Villani is in large measure a traditional historiographic motif.

59. Fischer, p. 160.

60. Fischer, pp. 192 ff. I quote the following passage from the *Gesta Triumpha*, composed largely in 1119, to give a more precise idea of the tone and style of this literature: "First I praise the most powerful hand of the Redeemer, by which the Pisan nation destroyed a race most impious. This is completely similar to the miracle of Gideon" (p. 193).

61. On the papal politization of the crusades, see Walter Ullmann, *A Short History of Political Theory*, London, 1965, p. 263. "The crusading idea escalated [during the thirteenth

century]," Ullmann writes, "but suffered a debasement." On the more widespread "debasement," see Hyde, *Society and Politics* . . . , p. 263; while for Boniface VIII and the crusades, see T.S.R. Boase, *Boniface VIII,* London, 1933, pp. 131 ff. and 222 ff.

62.   Aziz Suryal Atiya, *The Crusade in the Later Middle Ages,* London, 1938, pp. 97 ff. R. Scholz has shown how the crusade propaganda of Boniface related to the general political publicity of his reign: *Die Publizistik zur Zeit Philipps des Schonen und Bonifaz VIII,* Stuttgart, 1908. For an examination of the various "crusades" of the time, see Gregorovious, *op. cit.,* 5, pt. II, pp. 546 ff.; Boase, *op. cit.,* p. 214; Steven Runciman, *A History of the Crusades: The Kingdom of Acre and the Later Crusades,* 3, Cambridge, 1954, pp. 398 ff.

63.   Information regarding the involvement of Perugia in the political crusades of the late thirteenth and fourteenth centuries is scattered, and the nature of evidence is most diverse. A possible indication of the contribution of the city to the pamphleteering aspect of the campaign against the Moslems in the first decades of the fourteenth century is the following manuscript composed during the 1290's in Perugia: *Tractatus domini Johannis de Turrvremata card. sancti Sixti ord. pre. contra principales errores Mahumetti* (Biblioteca Comunale, Perugia: 1002-M. 25). For mention of the nature of Perugia's share in the campaigns, see Atiya, pp. 97 ff., 251, n. 3, 252, and 307; Boase, 152 ff.; Runciman, 3, pp. 409, 427 ff.; Pellini, 1, p. 564; Heywood, p. 181.

64.   Atiya, p. 97.

65.   Reprinted in *Cronache e storie inedite della città di Perugia, dal MCL al MDLXIII; Archivio storico italiano,* 16, 1895, pt. 1, pp. 3 ff.

Chapter 5

1.   The words *XPS* and *ADAM* identify the two figures. For the representation of *The Creation of Adam* in Umbria, including iconographic types and location, see: Garrison, *Studies in the History of Medieval Italian Painting* 1 (1953-54): 10 ff.; 3 (1957): 33 ff., 89 ff., 105 ff., 169 ff., 183 ff., 4 (1960-62), 117 ff., 201 ff. The iconography of the Perugia God-Father seated on a representaion of the universe and blowing the breath of life through a reed is common in Umbria from the early twelfth through the late thirteenth centuries and occurs in Perugia in a series of so-called "giant" Bibles. Anthony, *Romanesque Frescoes,* (p. 75), discusses the relation between the Umbrian Bible type and mural painting. In addition to the above references, Buchthal has treated the Perugia Bible type and has drawn attention to the evolution of this Biblical form and the art of the Crusader Kingdom: *Miniature Painting in the Latin Kingdom of Jerusalem,* Oxford, 1957 pp. 48 ff. A general word on the derivation of this kind of Creation scene is offered by Weitzmann, *Illustrations in Roll and Codex,* Princeton, 1947, pp. 176 ff., and by Olga Raggio, "The Myth of Prometheus, Its Survival and Metamorphoses up to the Eighteenth Century," *Journal of the Warburg and Courtauld Institutes* 21 (1958): 44 ff.

2.   The figures are inscribed *ADAM* and *EVE*. The representation follows the standard regional pattern of the period. For a general treatment of the iconography, distribution and bibliography, see H. Schade, "Adam and Eva," *Lexikon* . . . , 1, 42 ff. The most common meaning of the scene was the creation of Eve as representative of the creation of the church. In such manner, for example, the scene was interpreted in the *Bible moralisée* (L. Bréhier, *L'Art chrétien: Son developpement iconographique des origines à nos jours,* Paris, 1918, pp. 96 ff.).

3.   The figures are again identified by name. Wolfgang Braunfels has examined the group of images to which the Perugia scene belongs and has noted how the works deviated from

comparable French examples: "Giotto's Campanile," *Das Münster* 1 (1948): 206 ff. See also Katzenellenbogen, *The Sculptural Programs of Chartres Cathedral: Christ, Mary, Ecclesia,* New York, 1959 p. 74, and P. Brandt, *Schaffende Arbeit und bildende Kunst im Alterum und Mittlelalter,* Leipzig, 1927, pp. 213 ff. and 254 ff. Finally, Schade, *op. cit.,* pp. 42 ff., presents a lengthy bibliography related to all aspects of the scene as well as notable examples of the representation.

4. See p. 36.

5. The façade was altered in 1647 and several of the reliefs are now in the Pinacoteca Comunale. There is no certainty that these works represent the complete grouping of decorations (*Marche,* TCI, Rome, 1962, p. 61; Paul, *Die Mittelalterlichen Kommunal-paläste in Italien . . . ,* p. 196; G. Marchini, *La Pinacoteca Comunale di Ancona,* Ancona, 1960, pp. 10 ff.). For the re-designing of the façade see *Elenco degli edifici monumentali provincia di Ancona,* Rome, 1932, p. 63. The stylistic context for the reliefs has been described by L. Venturi, "Opere di sculture nelle Marche," *L'Arte* 19 (1916): 25-50.

6. The role of Solomon as an exemplar of the Just Judge or ruler in the thirteenth century is discussed by Brentano in his examination of the postition of Innocent III in Roman politics: *Rome Before Avignon . . . ,* pp.' 147 ff. See also for the general conception of Solomon in medieval political theory: Gierke, *Political Theories of the Middle Ages,* pp. 101 ff. The iconography of the Cain and Abel scenes is discussed above.

7. Dating and stylistic questions are discussed by John Pope-Hennessy, *Italian Gothic Sculpture,* London, 1955, pp. 222 ff. and W. Wolters, *La Scultura Veneziana gotica (1300-1460).* Venice, 1976, pp. 91 ff. The *Judgment of Solomon* is generally dated somewhat earlier. This chronology, however, is not in itself evidence that the works should be considered unrelated to one another. A similar grouping of Solomon with *The Fall* is found on one other town hall as well: the exterior sculptures of Saint Antonin (c. 1180) (R. Hamoan-Maclean, "Das Ikonographische Problem der 'Friedberger Jungfrau,' " *Marburger Jahr für Kunstwissenschaft,* 10, 1937, p. 65.)

8. This point is also made by M. Trachtenberg, *The Campanile of Florence Cathedral: "Giotto's Tower,"* New York, 1971, pp. 92 ff. Trachtenberg notes the major examples of the traditional form of the Italian Genesis cycle.

9. F. Antal, *Florentine Painting and Its Social Background,* London, 1947, p. 232, perhaps goes too far in drawing a relation between changing social and political phenomena and cycles of redemption, and in suggesting that the popularity of such schemes was due to the growing secular power of the Church. Redemptive themes were prominent in art before the twelfth century. The positive point of view advanced here concerning the role of Adam and Eve contrasts with Debra Pincus, *The Arco Foscari: The Building of a Triumphal Gateway in Fifteenth-Century Venice,* New York and London, 1976, p. 213, n. 7.

10. This aspect of the Campanile sculptures has been emphasized by Trachtenberg, pp. 93 ff., Antal, p. 234, and Becker, *Florence in Transition,* 1, p. 33.

11. Uta Felges-Henning, "The Picture Program of the *Sala della Pace:* A New Interpretation," *Journal of the Warburg and Courtauld Institutes* 35 (1972): 145-163.

12. Otto Demus, *The Church of San Marco in Venice: History, Architecture, Sculpture,* Washington, D.C., 1960, pp. 151 ff. I believe that a problem with Demus's examination of the sculptures, in light of the works discussed here, is that he grants a uniqueness to this expression of Venetian civic salvation that appears unjustified.

13. Trachtenberg, *op. cit.*, p. 93.

14. Carlyle, *A History of Medieval Political Theory in the West . . ., 5, p. 5*. Paul's interpretation is shared by all the Fathers from St. Ireneus in the second century to St. Gregory the Great in the sixth.

15. Ibid., p. 6. Although the political order is termed "unnatural," the proto-political order that is described as having existed before the Fall is similar to Aristotle's and Aquinas's view of the primeval order.

16. Deane, *The Political and Social Ideas of St. Augustine*, pp. 16 ff.

17. Ibid., pp. 116 ff.

18. Ibid., p. 17.

19. Ibid., p. 17.

20. Ibid., p. 21.

21. Ibid., p. 117.

22. A like interpretation of a possible political meaning of the Fall has been suggested by Sinding-Larsen for the figures of Adam and Eve on the Piazzetta corner of the Palazzo Ducale: "In this group it is God himself who enforces justice through his angel. Since God . . . had created man a 'social animal' . . . the first human being represented the origin of the state. God's administration must therefore be viewed in a political perspective" (*Christ in the Council Hall . . .*, p. 168).

23. S.D. Wingate, *The Medieval Versions of the Aristotelian Scientific Corpus*, London, 1931, p. 6.

24. Deane, pp. 79-80.

25. The recovery of Aristotle's *Politics* in the second half of the thirteenth century brought about an immediate and profound change in the political outlook of the age. The fact that members of Aquinas's circle were directly involved in this revival helps to explain why his work in particular brought Aristotle into widespread circulation. For a brief discussion of the impact of the text among the jurists and theologians of the late thirteenth century, see E. Kantorowicz. For a general discussion of the impact of Aristotelian thought on the art of the time see J. Riess, "French Influences on the Early Development of Civic Art in Italy," *Annals of the New York Academy of Sciences*, 314 (1978), 285-311. For the medieval anticipations of the *Politics* see G. Post, *Studies in Medieval Legal Thought; Public Law and the State, 1100-1322*. Princeton, 1957, 97-143.

26. Aquinas, *Selected Political Writings*, p. 5.

27. Ibid. On the date of the tract, see Saint Thomas Aquinas, *On the Governance of Rulers*, trans. G.B. Phelan, London and New York, 1938, pp. 8 ff.

28. Examples are given in Chapter 6.

29. Scholz, *Die Publizistik . . .*, pp. 32 ff.

30. Carlyle, vol. 5, pp. 8 ff.; Ugo Mariana, "Egidius Colonna," *Enciclopedia Italiana*, vol 13, pp. 534 ff. Egidius's adaptation of Thomistic ideas was especially important in the struggle with Philip the Fair. To indicate some measure of the impact of Egidius's writings, I need only note Mariana's opinion that they constituted a major foundation for the *Unam Sanctum*.

31. A recent treatment of the imperial ideal is Francis A. Yates, *Astraea: The Imperial Theme in the Sixteenth Century,* London and Boston, 1975, pp. 5 ff.

32. Ibid., p. 8. For a complete examination of this subject see E. Kantorowicz, *Frederick II,* New York, 1954, 258 ff. The relevant passages in the Constitution Melfi are found in the opening section: *The "Liber Augustalis"* . . . , pp. 5 ff.

33. Yates, *op. cit.,* p. 8.

34. Kantorowicz, *The King's Two Bodies* . . . , pp. 200 ff. and 468 ff. This ideal of "all in one," as Wilks has expressed it, was generallly associated with the defense of monarchic government and of papal supremacy (*The Problem of Sovereignty in the Later Middle Ages,* pp. 38 ff.). My interest here is to describe the conception of Adam in various political ideologies. The fact that "Adam mysticism" was generally anti-communal in meaning offers no serious problem; we have already seen how in other ways communal political beliefs represent variations of imperial and papal ideas.

35. Wilks, 539 ff.

36. For the relations between the two universities, see Ermini, *Storia della Università di Perugia,* 67 ff. For the early history of the study of law in Bologna and its connections with the early communal ethos, see Hyde, "Commune, University and Society . . . ," 17 ff.

37. Yates, *Astraea* . . . , pp. 6 ff.

38. The place of Adam and Eve in the chronicles and world histories has been studied by Green, "The Adam and Eve Cycle in the *Hortus Deliciarum.*"

39. The general conception of original sin during the late thirteenth century has been discussed by Heiko Augustinus Oberman, *The Harvest of Medieval Theology: Gabriel Biel and Late Medieval Nominalism,* Cambridge, 1963, 120 ff. Briefly, the idea that sin is inherent in man's nature was rejected, and emphasis was placed instead on the notion of free choice. It is just such an idea that would seem to be the implicit foundation of a political theology that maintained that original sin did not necessarily make the state a coercive instrument; that man could choose to be virtuous without the threat of force.

40. Ullmann, *Principles* . . . , pp. 243 ff. Ulmann's summary of the essence of Thomas's views follows: "What Thomas did was to create a synthesis of disparate and irreconcilable elements—Christian, stoic, neo-platonic, Aristotelian . . .a synthesis that deprived Aristotelianism of those ingredients which, from the theoretic point of view, were justifiably considered harmful" (p. 243). For an analysis of Thomas's conception of the political and heavenly virtues, see Rose E. Brennan, *The Intellectual Virtues According to the Philosophy of St. Thomas,* Washington, D.C., 1941, pp. 43 ff.
     One artistic change that reveals this conception is the new representation of the personification of Charity at the beginning of the fourteenth century, a change that brought to the forefront the social implications of charitable behavior. See R. Freyhan, "The Evolution of the 'Caritas' Figure in the 13th and 14th Centuries," *Journal of the Warburg and Courtauld Institutes* 11 (1948): 68 ff.

41. Ullmann, *Principles* . . . , pp. 243 ff.; Antal, *Florentine Painting* . . . , pp. 38 ff. Antal asserts that Aquinas's modern view of the market is the formative factor in his acceptance of the idea of secular salvation. Rubinstein has shown how the Thomistic idea of the common good is an important subject in Ambrogio Lorgnzetti's frescoes of *Good and Bad Government:* "Political Ideas in Sienese Art . . . ," pp. 145 ff.

42. Aquinas, Qu. 92., in *Selected Political Writings,* p. 45.

43.   Herlihy, *Medieval and Renaissance Pistoia: The Social History of an Italian Town*, New Haven and London, 1967, pp. 246 ff. Herlihy cites the administration of the *Opera di San Jacopo* in Pistoia as a model where loyalty to the commune was expressed through traditional manifestations of Christian piety. Another important examination of this facet of communal citizenship is Riesenberg, "Civicism and Roman Law . . .," pp. 237 ff. For a complete and current bibliography on medieval citizenship, see Hyde, *Society and Politics . . . ,* pp. 202, 209 ff.

44.   The fundamental treatments of his theory are: Kantorowicz, *The King's Two Bodies . . .* , pp. 487-480; Richard Egenter, "Gemeinnutz vor Eigennutz: Die soziale Leitidee im Tractatus de bono communi des Fr. Remigus von Florenz," *Scholastik* 9 (1934): 79 ff.; Davis, "An Early Florentine Political Theorist . . . ." The portrayal of Remigio's thesis is my own, although Kantorowicz, p. 479, also touches on this issue. Egenter's introduction to the *Tractatus . . .* appears to overdraw the uniqueness of Remigio's position. It can be said that the Florentine is only the first philosopher-apologist for the communes, for in the contemporary statutes and chronicles a like attempt is made to establish the legitimacy of the republics. See Ronald Witt, "The Rebirth of the Concept of Republican Liberty in Italy," *Renaissance Studies in Honor of Hans Baron,* ed. Anthony Molho and John Tedeschi, Florence, 1971, pp. 173 ff.

45.   Egenter, p. 84, n. 11; also quoted and translated by Kantorowicz, p. 479.

Chapter 6

1.   The scene is inscribed, *ABEL, CAIN*. It is the only one of the three murals in the series still to bear an inscription.

2.   The group of scenes comes closest to the so-called Cotton Genesis. The absence of The Temptation at Perugia and the non-Biblical order of the scenes are departures from such a mode. For the Cotton Genesis and its fortunes in Umbria, see the studies by Garrison cited above, p. 88, n. 1; Tikkanen, *Die Genesismosaiken von S. Marco*, pp. 81 ff. remains the most complete general examination of the type. Finally, Weitzmann, *Illustrations in Roll and Codex . . .* , pp. 130, 140 ff., 176 ff., 189, 194, summarizes all the problems connected with the recension. The fact that the Perugia frescoes cannot be set within any established Biblical type proves nothing in itself of course, but it does indicate the apparent willingness of the designer of the decorations to alter ecclesiastical programs for the special purposes of a civic palace.

3.   As for the figure style, it is characterized by the same broad conception of form and simplified treatment of drapery. In the *Offering of Cain and Abel* a few bits of vegetation enliven the standard barren landscape setting of the other scenes. The figures in the *Offering* are also somewhat more active than in the previous scenes, although the formula of confronting figures remains the same. The static oppositions of the preceding murals and the comparatively unvaried description of gesture and movement have been supplanted by a far more developed sense of movement and of contrast.

4.   Otto Demus has described most succinctly the various types of interpretation that can be made of Biblical scenes. Demus cites the historical meaning as the initial level of interpretation (*The Mosaics of Norman Sicily,* New York, 1950, p. 245).

5.   Meyer Schapiro, *Words and Pictures: On the Literal and the Symbolic in the Illustration of a Text,* The Hague-Paris, 1973, p. 34.

6.   For the communal sense of history and its possible propagandistic application, see pp. 88 ff.

7. For a basic treatment of the standard theological interpretations of the story of Cain and Abel, see G. Henderson, "Abel und Kain," *Lexikon* . . . , 1, 6 ff. An important expression of this meaning in art is that the *Murder of Abel* is found in conjunction with the *Crucifixion* in the *Bible moralisée* (A. de Laborde, *La Bible moralisée*, 1, Paris, 1911. Plate 8).

8. See above, p. 36.

9. A. Grabar, *Wirkungen der Frühchristlichen Gemadezyklen*, pp. 20 ff. Elisabeth Dhanens's examination of the relation between the representations of Cain and Abel and Adam and Eve in the Ghent Altarpiece is a useful, brief statement of this conception: *Van Eyck: "The Ghent Altarpiece,"* London, 1973, p. 94.

10. Mention of the story of Cain and Abel is found in two places in the *Summa* and in both instances the story is cited as proof of divine understanding (I, 52; IV, 67).

11. The relevance of the Biblical conception for medieval historiography is briefly treated in *The Two Cities* by Otto, Bishop of Friesing, p. 65.

12. Ibid., vol. 4, 495 ff., 511 ff., 532 ff.

13. Wilks, *op. cit.*, p. 538, n. 3; pp. 539 ff.; Kantorowicz, *The King's Two Bodies* . . . , p. 45.

14. Ibid., p. 540.

15. Augustine, vol. 4, p. 414.

16. For the possible political ramifications of the story of Cain and Abel note also Sinding-Larsen's hypothesis that the representation of the *Sacrifice of Cain and Abel* in San Marco is connected with the political liturgy of the state. This meaning is a local one and had no relevance, I believe, for the Perugia frescoes. The significance of the scene of the *Offering* at Perugia is the straightforward Biblical one and is thus simply the necessary impetus for the unfolding of the story.

17. The state as an enforcer of justice, as the maintainer of order, is a leading justification for the existence of government throughout the Middle Ages, no less than it is at present (Carlyle, 5, pp. 93 ff.). For the special relevance of the matter in the communes, see Zdekauer, "Iustitia: immagine e idea," *Bollettino senese di storia patria* 20 (1913): 384 ff.; W.M. Bowsky, "The Medieval Commune and Internal Violence: Police Power and Public Safety in Siena, 1287-1355," L. Martines, ed., *Violence and Civil Disorder in Italian Cities, 1200-1500*, Berkeley and Los Angeles, 1972. Rubinstein's discussion of Ambrogio Lorenzetti's Siena *Allegories* rests on an analysis of the sources and meaning of the communal conception of concord. The immediate source for the interlocked view of concord and order and law, Rubinstein believes, is Aquinas's political theory ("Political Ideas in Sienese Art . . . ," pp. 180 ff.). The relation between artistic patronage and the effort of the commune to stamp out internal divisions has been treated in a most general way by H. Peyer, *Stadt und Stadtpatron im mittelalterlichen Italien*, Zurich, 1955, pp. 45 ff., and John Larner, *Culture and Society in Italy, 1250-1420*, New York, 1971 pp. 62 ff.

18. Among those sources cited most frequently was the fact that the highways were unsafe for trade and travel (Daniel Waley, *The Italian City-Republics*, New York and Toronto, 1969, pp. 218 ff.).

19. Mention of the importance of order and of the ending of individual jealousies and envies appears most frequently in connection with Perugia's efforts to pacify and to subjugate neighboring cities (Waley, *The Papal State* . . . , pp. 242 ff.).

20.   Blanshei, *op. cit.*, pp. 59 ff. In truth, little of the disorder that was to be found in the city was of the conventional variety of noble families engaged in violent conflict with each other. More typical was such a class-motivated "crime" as a noble insulting a worker. The legislation was directed largely against such crimes as this.

21.   Kantorowicz, *The King's Two Bodies . . .*, pp. 207 ff. The section is entitled "Corpus republicae misticum," which in itself reveals much of Kantorowicz's view of this problem.

22.   See G. Masi, *La "pittura infamante" nella legislazione e nella vita del comune fiorentino*, Rome, 1931, and Gherardo Ortalli, *La pittura infomante nei secoli XIII-XVI*, Rome, 1978, for the meaning and history of this popular genre in the secular art of Italy during the thirteenth and fourteenth centuries.

23.   Arthur K. Porter, *Lombard Architecture*, New Haven-London, 1917, vol. 3, pp. 2 ff.; Roger Sherman Loomis, *Arthurian Legends in Medieval Art*, London-New York, 1938, pp. 32 ff.; Arturo Carlo Quintivalle, *La Cattedrale di Modenna; Problemi di romanico emiliano*, 2 vols., Modena, 1971 (most complete collection of photographs). A list of the important Italian examples of the representation of the *Murder of Cain*—fewer than a half dozen—is found in Porter, vol. 1, pp. 388 ff. E. Mâle, *The Gothic Image: Religious Art in France of the Thirteenth Century*, New York, 1956, pp. 202 ff., explores the problem of the origin of the apocryphal tale and the various forms that it assumed. Demus, *The Mosaics of Norman Sicily*, discusses the origins of the representation of the scene in Italy and proposes a Byzantine source (p. 245).

24.   For a discussion of the Modena sculptures see pp. 82 ff.

25.   Carlyle, vol. 5, pp. 93 ff.

26.   The overthrow of unjustly held power, expressed as the glorification of those responsible for rescuing the state from tyranny, is a motif found in later Italian political imagery. Two disparate and notable examples are the following: the representations of the expulsion of the Duke of Athens from Florence found in the Palazzo del Podestà and in the Stinche Vecchie, both dated about 1343, in which the people of the city who rose up against the Duke are personified by an avenging angel (Antal, *Florentine Painting . . .*, p. 262; S. Morpurgo, "Bruto, 'il buon giudice,' nell' Udienza dell' Arte della Lana in Firenze," in *Miscellanea di Storia dell' Arte in onore di I.B. Supino*, Florence, 1930, pp. 89 ff.); Michelangelo's bust of Brutus (1539-1540), a work believed to represent the anti-Medici sentiments of the artist and of the Florentine exiles living in Rome (Charles de Tolnay, *Michelangelo: The Tomb of Julius II*, Princeton, 1944, 4, pp. 76 ff., 131 ff).

27.   O.F. Emerson, "Legends of Cain, especially in Old and Middle English," *Publications of the Modern Language Association of America*, 21 (1906), pp. 839 ff.; J.A. Selbie, "Lamech," *Dictionary of the Bible*, Boston, 1903, vol. 3, pp. 19 ff.

Chapter 7

1.   There are three excellent summaries of the early dissemination of texts and the major patterns of illustrations in the Middle Ages: A. Thiele, *Der illustrierte Lateinische Aesop*, Leyden, 1905, pp. 91 ff.; A. Goldschmidt, *An Early Manuscript of Aesop Fables of Avianus and Related Manuscripts*, Princeton, 1947, pp. 12 ff.; Kurt Weitzmann, *Ancient Book Illumination*, Cambridge, 1959, pp. 40 ff. Although the illustrations are relatively scarce, it is nevertheless true, as Weitzmann has remarked, that Aesop is one of the few classical authors for whom there is a tradition of illustrated texts going back to the Antique (*Roll and Codex . . .*, p. 33). For a general statement about this tradition, see E. P. Evans, *Animal Symbolism*

in Ecclesiastical Architecture, London, 1896, pp. 52 ff. and 80 ff., and F. Klingender, *Animals in Art and Thought,* London, 1971, pp. 229 ff. The most important earlier example of a monumental program of murals illustrating the fables was a lost one in the refectory of the monastery of Fleury in *St. Benoît sur Loire* dating from the beginning of the eleventh century. The works are also important in that, like the fables at Perugia, they were represented together with Biblical scenes and thus were part of a general program (Goldschmidt, pp. 32 ff.; Georges Chenessaux, *L'Abbaye de Fleury à St. Benoît sur Loire,* Paris, 1931). The programs of the French cathedrals are discussed below. For the considerable bibliography on Aesop, see Goldschmidt, pp. 96 ff.

2.   Goldschmidt, pp. 20 ff.

3.   Ibid. On French Aesop illustrations during this time, and on their influence in Italy, see R.W. Scheller, *A Survey of Medieval Model Books,* Harlem, 1963, pp. 53 ff. Goldschmidt, p. 22, notes also that these illustrations were intended to serve as "practical applications of moral precepts" and, further, that "such cases in classical art were exceptionally scanty."

4.   See Milton S. Gower, "Symbolic Animals at Perugia and Spoleto," *Burlington Magazine* 32 (1918): 152 ff. The most famous local example are the fables on the fountain. Hoffmann-Curtius's comment that the fables on the Fontana Maggiore are a moral foundation for the much-abbreviated representation of human history also on the fountain (*op. cit.,* p. 29), is, as I hope to show, not the correct interpretation.

5.   See Gower, pp. 152 ff., for a discussion of these influences. Gower does not stress sufficiently the influence of North Italian Romanesque art where the fables make their earliest appearance in monumental Italian art.

6.   Thiele, *op. cit.,* pp. 101 ff., offers the most succinct treatment of this aspect of the fortunes of Aesop during the Middle Ages, although the emphasis is, again, with the late antique and early medieval period.

7.   On the wide distribution and popularity of texts, see Weitzmann, *op. cit.,* pp. 47 ff., and Goldschmidt, *op. cit.,* pp. 53 ff. Ernst Robert Curtius, *European Literature and the Latin Middle Ages,* New York, 1963, pp. 49 ff., discusses the reasons for this popularity, relating it largely to the importance of the text in the medieval curriculum, a matter that will be treated shortly.

8.   Lloyd W. Daly, *Aesop without Morals,* New York-London, 1961.

9.   Ibid., p. 158.

10.   Ibid., p. 285.

11.   Ibid., p. 150. The scene is inscribed: *E. POTANE. PANE. IN. ORE.*

12.   Ibid., p. 282.

13.   Ibid., p. 159. The scene is inscribed: *D LVPO E GRUE.*

14.   Ibid., p. 285.

15.   Ibid., p. 146.

16.   Ibid., p. 281.

17.   Ibid., p. 100. The scene is inscribed *NONDV MATURA EST.*

18.   Ibid., p. 268.

19.   Ibid., p. 153.

20. Ibid., p. 283.

21. Ibid., pp. 213-214.

22. Ibid., p. 299.

23. Ibid., p. 224-225.

24. Ibid., p. 302.

25. Ibid., p. 110-111.

26. Ibid., p. 271.

27. Ibid., p. 93.

28. Ibid., p. 267.

29. Ibid., p. 186.

30. Ibid., p. 293.

31. Ibid., p. 186.

32. Ibid., p. 293.

33. Ibid., p. 143.

34. Ibid., p. 226.

35. Almost without exception the scenes are, like the Biblical representations, framed or composed in such a way that the outer part of the composition is the more weighted. This helps to lend to the scenes a sense of enclosure and definition. The animals and the architecture or landscape elements are directed inward toward the central part of the arch.

36. This naturalistic element has long been recognized as one of the most remarkable aspects of the decorations. See, for example, Raimond Van Marle, *The Development of the Italian Schools of Painting,* The Hague, 1923-1938, vol. 1, p. 530.

37. Thiele, *op. cit.,* pp. 91 ff.

38. The role of the text in the medieval curriculum has been described by Charles Homer Haskins, *The Renaissance of the Twelfth Century,* New York, 1959, pp. 95 ff.; Curtius, *op. cit.,* pp. 49 ff.; Goldschmidt, pp. 50 ff.

39. A famous example of such criticism is that of Albert Magnus. Magnus separated the fictions of the beast lore from the "truth" of the story of the Virgin and the Unicorn (Evans, *Animal Symbolism . . .,* p. 78).

40. I am convinced that John White's interpretation of the fountain as an image of the medieval encyclopedia is correct (*Art and Architecture . . .,* pp. 51 ff.) and as such Aesop properly should be considered one source of wisdom, like the Liberal Arts (Taylor, *The Medieval Mind,* vol. 2, pp. 343 ff.)

41. Goldschmidt, *op. cit.,* p. 16, makes essentially the same point in writing of the general implications of illustrations of Aesop as opposed to texts of Aesop.

42. Klingender, in his Marxist-based discussion of the role of animals in medieval thought and art, persuasively states this idea in the course of a discussion dealing with the class appeal of different kinds of animal symbolism (*Animals in Art and Thought,* pp. 82 ff.). Much the same reasoning characterizes the approach of Antal (*Florentine Painting . . . ,* pp. 236 ff.).

43.   Klingender, p. 82. However, the lack of real, rather than legendary, biographical data, as well as the problem of assessing early textual revisions, makes it difficult to accept the view that the author of Aesop's fables was actually involved in efforts to displace the entrenched power of the aristocracy (Daly, *Aesop without Morals,* pp. 15 ff.).

44.   Gregorovius, *Geshiechte . . .,* 2, p. 679; Pietrangeli, *Le prime fase archittetoniche del Palazzo Senatorio,* Rome, 1959, p. 22. Westfall, *In This Most Perfect Paradise . . .,* pp. 60 ff., includes a discussion of the relation of these works with the papal art of the Quattrocento.

45.   Gregorovius, 2, p. 679.

46.   Sinding-Larsen, as noted earlier (p. 105, n. 10), has gone the furthest in postulating a relationship between the politics and the ceremonial liturgy of the medieval Italian cities and towns. The point of view derives from his study of Venice. The especially close ties that existed in Venice between religion and politics (Paolo Prodi, "The Structure and Organization of the Church in Renaissance Venice: Suggestions for Research," *Renaissance Venice,* ed. J.R. Hale, Totowa, 1973, pp. 409 ff.) would seem to preclude a general application of the Venetian situation. As the Senate of Rome had no real independence from the pope during the late thirteenth century (Brentano, *Rome Before Avignon . . .,* pp. 91 ff.), so Rome also forms an exception to the more general rule.

47.   The façade has been altered and it is possible that the sculptures are no longer in their original position (*Umbria,* TCI, p. 148; Mario Bigotti, *Narni,* Rome, 1973, p. 353; Gelinda Geroni, *Narni,* Spoleto, 1942, pp. 34 ff.). Geroni notes that the façade was originally adorned with the *stemmi* of the *podestà* as well.

48.   H.W. Janson, *The Sculpture of Donatello,* Princeton, 1957, 2, pp. 198 ff.; Edgar Wind, "Donatello's Judith: A Symbol of 'Sanctimonia,' " *Journal of the Warburg Institute* I (1937-1938): 62 ff.

49.   Antal, *Florentine Painting . . .,* pp. 236 ff., has written on this matter as well.

50.   For a brief introduction to the social and economic context for the era of cathedral building, see Henri Pirenne, "Northern Towns and their Commerce," *The Cambridge Medieval History,* 6, pp. 505 ff.

51.   Evans, *Animal Symbolism . . .,* p. 23. The most important and intelligent discussion of Bernard's attitude toward the general question of profane ornamentation remains Meyer Schapiro, "On the Aesthetic Attitude in Romanesque Art," in *Art and Thought:* Issued in honor of Dr. Ananda K. Coomerswamy on the occasion of his 70th birthday, London, 1947, pp. 133 ff.

52.   Randall, *op. cit.,* p. 40.

53.   Thiele, *op. cit.,* p. cxxxi.

54.   Randall, p. 40.

55.   For a treatment of the animal fables in the Chapel decorations, see Aldo Bertini, "Per la conoscenza die medaglioni che accompagno le storie della vita di Gésu nella Cappella degli Scrovegni," *Giotto e il suo tempo,* Atti del Congresso Internazionale per la celabrazione del VII Centenario della nascità di Giotto, 25 settembre - 1 ottobre 1967, Rome, 1971, pp. 143 ff.

56.   For a discussion limited largely to the motif in Dante, see R.T. Holbrook, *Dante and the Animal Kingdom,* New York, 1902. Related to this is the fact that animal similes were often used to draw out the morals to be learned from events described in the chronicles (E.H. Wilkins, *A History of Italian Literature,* London, 1954, p. 39).

57. Aquinas, for example, sees the clear order and functioning of a colony of bees as a demonstration of the necessity of order in human affairs (*Selected Political Writings* . . ., p. 129).

58. Ibid., p. 58. For a general discussion of this most enlightened aspect of Aquinas's thinking, see Ullmann, *Principles of Government* . . ., pp. 248 ff.

59. Evans, *Animal Symbolism* . . ., pp. 92 ff.; Marin de Boylesve, *Les animaux et leurs applications symboliques à l'ordre spirituel,* Paris, 1881, pp. 14 ff.

60. Ibid., p. 93. The passage derives from Thomasin von Zinclare, *Welscher Gast,* written in the late twelfth century, and which, in addition to containing materials derived from more conventional collections of animal lore, includes a detailed description of court life in Italy and sets down general rules for the conduct of princes.

61. Ibid.

62. Karl Vossler, *op. cit.,* 2, pp. 293 ff. Dante's dream of the rebirth of imperial glory is based on the allegory (Holbrook, *op. cit.,* p. 42). All variations of the story likely derive from a prophecy of Vergil (Vossler, p. 293).

63. Klingender, *Animals in Art* . . ., pp. 456 ff.

64. Ibid., p. 62.

65. Frank Merry Stenton has dealth with the Bayeux fables as part of a general study of the tapestry: *The Bayeux Tapestry: A Comprehensive Survey,* London, 1957, pp. 27 ff. A more specialized study is H. Chefneux, "Les fables dans la Tapiserie de Bayeux," *Romania* 60 (1934): 39-69. The following fables are depicted in the borders: The Raven and the Fox; The Wolf and the Lamb; The Pregnant Bitch and Her Helpmate; The Crane and the Wolf; The Wolf Reigning; The Mouse and the Frog; The Wolf and the Goat; The Cow, Sheep, and Goat Go Hunting with the Lion.

66. Previous studies of the tapestry have ignored the function of the Aesop fables. Chefneux, *op. cit.,* pp. 39 ff., for example examines only the sources for the particular grouping of stories.

67. See above, n. 10.

68. The role of chivalric ideals in the culture of the communes is discussed above, pp. 69-72.

69. This aspect of the role of the Saint has been treated most thoroughly by Paul Deschamps, "La Légende de Saint Georges et les combats croisés dans les peintures murales au Moyen âge," *Monuments Piot* 46 (1950): 109-123. Deschamps deals largely with how the chivalric and martial conception of Saint George was translated into art. During the thirteenth century, perhaps the most obvious expression of the notion of the Saint as ideal soldier is to be found in the several accounts of his life written at the time. See for example the account given by Jacobus de Voragine, *The Golden Legend,* translated by Granger Ryan and Helmut Rippenger, New York, 1969, pp. 232-238.

70. Léjeune and Stiennon, *op. cit.,* p. 366. Deschamps has also touched on the frequent concurrence of Roland and Saint George in the romances and epics of the age as part of a study of the Arthurian legend in the late Middle Ages: "La légende arthurienne à la cattedrale de Modena," *Monuments Piot* 48 (1928): 19-27.

71. The relevance of the chivalric code for the conduct of war by the communes has been studied by G. Golena, "La cultura volgare e l'umanesimo cavalleresco,' " *Umanesimo europeo, umanesimo veneziano,* Florence, 1963, pp. 141-158. A briefer examination of the motif is

found in Davidsohn, *op. cit.*, 5, 375 ff. Finally, some mention of the theme is found in D.P. Waley, "The Army of the Florentine Republic from the Twelfth to the Fourteenth Century," *Florentine Studies: Politics and Society in Renaissance Florence,* ed. Nicolai Rubinstein, London, 1968, pp. 70-97.

72. The role is especially prominent in the *chansons de geste* and in crusader stories (Deschamps, "La Légende . . .," p. 109).

73. Ibid., pp. 111 ff.

74. Ibid.

75. For the S. Giorgio mural, see Van Marle, *op. cit.,* 1, pp. 519-520. The work was apparently commissioned by Cardinal Stefaneschi. The *Codice di San Giorgio* (Archivio di San Pietro, Rome) was executed in about 1305 (Muñoz, *op. cit., pp.* 19-21).

76. The only direct evidence of the Perugian interest in Saint George at the time, aside from the mural in the Sala dei Notari, is the foundation of a monastery dedicated to the Saint in 1300 (Pellini, *op. cit.,* vol. 2, p. 336).

77. Christopher Walter has dealt thoroughly with papal symbolism in art: "Papal Imagery in the Medieval Lateran Palace," *Cahiers Archéologiques* 20 (1970): 155-176; 21 (1971): 109-136.

78. Erich Auerbach, "Adam and Eve," *Mimesis: The Representation of Reality in Western Literature,* New York, 1971, p. 135.

79. Ibid., p. 140.

Chapter 8

1. There is no doubt expressed in the modern scholarship on the subject that the frescoes existed and that Giotto executed them. Alastair Smart notes (*The Assisi Problem and the Art of Giotto,* Oxford, 1971, p. 64) that the lost cycle was one of the most important works of the artist's career. There is, however, remarkably scant literature on the works. The major study, one that includes a summary of all the primary sources, is still G.F. Hartlaub, "Giotto's Zweite Hauptwerke in Padua," *Zeitschrift für Kunstwissenschaft* 21 (1950): 23ff. Lucio Grossato's study is the only other extensive one dealing with the murals, although he has little to add to Hartlaub's apart from discussing the relation of Giotto's decorations to the present ones in the hall: "La decorazione pittorica del Salone," *Il Palazzo della Ragione di Padova,* ed. Carlo Guido Mor, Venice, 1964, pp. 47 ff. The astrological works that presently decorate the Palazzo della Ragione (1420-1440) are generally assumed to be fairly accurate reflections of Giotto's murals (Grossato, 52-53). The original Trecento astrological embellishments included works produced between about 1370 and 1380 (Sergio Bettini, *Giusto de Menabuoi e l'arte del trecento,* Padua, 1944, pp. 118-120).

2. For a summary of the appearance of astrological decorations from the late Middle Ages through the Renaissance, see Paolo d'Ancona, *L'uomo e le sue opere nelle figurazione italiane del medioevo,* Florence, 1923, pp. 133 ff. For the earlier representation of the planets as ecclesiastical embellishments, see J.C. Webster, *The Labors of the Months in Antique Medieval Art,* Princeton, 1938, pp. 41 ff. The fundamental general examinations of the astrological theme in medieval and Renaissance art are: Jean Seznec, *The Survival of the Pagan Gods: The Mythological Tradition and Its Place in Renaissance Humanism and Art,* New York, 1953, pp. 37 ff.; Fritz Saxl, "The Revival of Late Antique Astrology," in *Lectures,* 1, 73 ff.; Saxl, "The Belief in Stars in the Twelfth Century," in *Lectures,* 1, 85 ff. Of somewhat more limited scope, but nonetheless indispensible, is Raymond Klibansky, Erwin

Panofsky, and Fritz Saxl, *Saturn and Melancholy: Studies in the History of Natural Philosophy, Religion and Art,* London, 1964.

3.　The fairly wide range of styles, although always held within bounds by the consistent orientation of the scenes toward the middle of the hall and by the simple and reductive disposition of figures and incidental details, is most apparent in a comparison between *January and February* and *The Man with the Rearing Horse.* In the former scene, the figures are flat and there is little sense of a spatial ambient, while in the latter work forms and space are ample.

4.　The earlier works were ecclesiastical decorations that include almost without exception only the symbols of the zodiac.

5.　Seznec, *op. cit.,* pp. 42 ff.

6.　The most reliable studies of the Padua frescoes are: A. Barzon, *I cieli e loro influenza negli affreschi del salone in Padova,* Padua, 1924, and the studies by Grossato, *op. cit.,* and Nicola Ivanoff, "Il problema iconologico degli affreschi," in Mor, *op. cit.,* pp. 71 ff.; W. Burges, "La Ragione de Padoue," *Annales archéologiques,* 18 (1858): 331 ff., 19 (1859) 241 ff., 26 (1860) 250 ff.

7.　The fundamental source for the study of the representation of the months in Italian art is Webster, *op. cit.,* pp. 7 ff. For the representation of January, see pp. 39 ff.

8.　Ibid., pp. 39 ff.

9.　Carlyle, *op. cit.,* 2, p. 92.

10.　Waley, *The Italian City-Republics,* pp. 36 ff.

11.　This land use policy quickly became one of the most important aspects of the struggle between the *popolani* and the *magnati* (Blanshei, *op. cit.,* pp. 61 ff.).

12.　For the fairly traditional, critical view of the economic outlook of the Church during the thirteenth and fourteenth centuries, see Hans Baron, "Franciscan Poverty and Civic Wealth as Factors in the Rise of Humanistic Thought," *Speculum* 13 (1938):37 ff. Some of the more recent scholarship on the problem of the amassing of wealth, especially on how it relates to the thought of Aquinas during the late Middle Ages, has gone far to eliminate Baron's rather conservative point of view. See, for example, Robert S. Lopez, *The Commercial Revolution of the Middle Ages, 950-1350,* New York, 1971, pp. 130 ff.

13.　A general study on the relation of the months and astrological representations is found in Otto Pächt, "Early Italian Nature Studies," *Journal of the Warburg and Courtauld Institutes* 13 (1950): 13 ff., and in Franz Böll, *Sterdeutung die Geschichte und das Wesen der Astrologie,* Berlin, 1926, pp. 67 ff.

14.　The basic evidence for this aspect of the discussion comes from Barzon, *op. cit.,* and Ivanoff, *op. cit.* Both writers summarize the connections between the planets and the months. Böll, *op. cit.,* pp. 91 ff., also summarizes the planets and their attributes, Barzon (p. 88) describes the protecting properties of Jupiter as follows: "la dignità, la sana sapienza, la nobilità, l'interpretazione dei sogni, le leggi, la religione, i pontefici, i principi or regoli, i condottieri di eserciti, i magistrati, il bene pubblico." The most important depiction of Jupiter during the period is a relief on the Campanile in Florence where the figure was personified as Religion.

15.　The sphere of Saturn is summarized by Barzon, p. 96, as follows: the protection of agriculture, "dei lavori in terra e in acqua, delle Arti manuali o meccaniche, della povertà, dei lunghi viaggi, della prigionia ed esilio, dei ladri, dei vecchi cattivi e stolli, della solitudine, degli inganni e della antiche eredita." The representations of the *arte meccaniche* in Ambrogio Lorenzetti's frescoes of *Good and Bad Government* may include some reference to the reign of the planet (Felges-Henning, *op. cit.,* p. 81).

16. Böll, p. 48; Rudolf and Margot Wittkower, *Born Under Saturn: The Character and Conduct of Artists; A Documented History from Antiquity to the French Revolution,* New York, 1969, pp. 102 ff.; Klibansky et al, *op. cit.,* pp. 67 ff.

17. Klibansky, et al., p. 68.

18. Ibid., pp. 69 ff.

19. See above, p. 122, n. 1.

20. A basic study is by B. Kurth, although the astrological elements in the decorations receive only cursory mention: "Ein Frescenzyklus ins Alterum zu Trient," *Jahr. d. Kunsth. Inst. d. k. Zentralkommission f. Denkmalpflege,* 5 (1911), 9 ff. Some material is to be found in Michael Levey, *Painting at Court,* New York, 1971, pp. 51 ff. Especially useful is Levey's discussion of the general purposes of astrological decorations in the life of the courts.

21. Apart from Aby Warburg's study, "Italienische kunst und internationale Astrologie im Palazzo Schifanoia zu Ferrara," *L'Italia e l'arte straniera. Atti del X congresso internazionale di storia dell'arte,* Rome, 1922, pp. 101 ff.), Paolo d'Ancona, *The Schifanoia Months at Ferrara,* Milan, 1954, is the only noteworthy study of the works. Warburg's examination was never completed, yet it remains the touchstone of all research pursued in this field.

22. The related scenes are described as follows by Barzon: "Un frate siede in una bella cattedra a baldacchino e guarda il cielo in un atteggiamento di tranquilità e meditazione. Un austero anacoreta siede nel cavo di una grotta e sta meditando con un libro aperto sulle ginocchia" (p. 97). This kind of concurrence in astrological imagery at this time is most unusual. For, to repeat a statement made earlier, there was little in the way of a fixed tradition in art regarding the representation of the inclinations of the planets. This point has been made by Fritz Saxl and Hans Meier, *Catalogue of Astrological and Mythological Illuminated Manuscripts of the Latin Middle Ages; Manuscripts in English Libraries,* London, 1953, p. 14. For a general discussion of the representation of Saturn during the thirteenth and fourteenth centuries, see Klibansky et al., pp. 204 ff.

23. The scene is described in the following words by Barzon: " 'Cavallo libero (equus libere currens in agro-instabilis)' . . . corre nel campo" (p. 92). Quoting Barzon again regarding the representation of the camel: " 'Forte': Un soggetto dell'Astrolabio presenta d'uomo forte in un cammello che sta ritto ('Camelus stans - fortis')—Questa inclinazione di natura sara largamente favorita da Giove e dal Sagittario" (p. 93).

24. See above.

25. For the current anthropological perspective on this discussion, see Mary Douglas, *Natural Symbols: Explorations in Cosmology,* New York, 1970, pp. 153 ff.

26. For a general discussion of the pilgrim's guides, see Roberto Weiss, *The Renaissance Discovery of Classical Antiquity,* Oxford, 1969, pp. 6 ff., and Brentano, *Rome Before Avignon . . .,* pp. 75 ff. The relevant passage on the meaning of the *Dioscuri* is to be found in G.M. Rushforth, "Magister Gregorius, *De Mirabilius Urbis Romae:* A New Description of Rome in the Twelfth Century," *Journal of Roman Studies* 9 (1919): 14 ff. For the general examination of the myths, especially those of a political nature that came to be associated with the ancient monuments in Rome during the Middle Ages, see A. Graf, *Roma nella memoria e nelle immaginazioni del medio evo,* Turin, 1923.

27. Schapiro, *Word and Image*, p. 22, notes this point and writes of several such images. See also for a treatment of this problem, John Gage, "La victoire imperiale dans l'Empire Chrétien," *Revue d'Histoire et de Philosophie Religieuse* 13 (1953): 24 ff.

28. L.M.C. Randall "*Exempla* as a Source of Gothic Marginal Decoration," *Art Bulletin* 29 (1957): 97 ff.

29. An alternative meaning of the scene is that it is an illustration of a theme found in the more primitive astrology of the age, such as that outlined in the famous *Picatrix*, in which the rituals for petitioning and honoring the stars are described (Seznec, pp. 53 ff.). Such a motif would be far too "pagan" for the council hall. The cycle is too fully based in theological purpose to allow for the possibility of an open co-mingling with the magical sciences. There was an accepted form of astrology during the time—even Aquinas asserted that the stars helped shape one's character (Klibansky et al., p. 72)—and there was also a more heathen and ritualistic way to express one's faith in the planets, a way that continued to draw stong condemnation from the Church (Lynn Thorndike, *A History of Magic and the Experimental Sciences*, 2, London, 1923, pp. 874 ff.). The Perugia murals conform to the accepted and less extreme approach.

30. Barzon identifies the subjects of scenes 87C and 88C as blessings being offered and acts of charity. Scenes of soldiers before altars were perhaps a more common motif for depictions of the influence of Mars. See for example the representation of Mars in the series of Florentine astrological engravings of the late Quattrocento (*c.* 1465): Arthur M. Hind, *Early Italian Engravings*, 1, London, 1938, 77 ff.

31. Barzon, writing of scene 109 B at Padua, one entitled *Instabilitas* and depicting a deserted bridge over water, notes that "l'acqua significa instabilita nel linguagio astrologico" (p. 92).

32. Barzon, p. 92.

33. J.L. Schrader, *The Waning of the Middle Ages: An Exhibition of French and Netherlandish Art from 1350 to 1500 Commemorating the Fiftieth Anniversary of "The Waning of the Middle Ages" by Johan Huizinga*, The University of Kansas Museum of Art, November 1 - December 1, 1969, p. 67; William D. Wixom, *Treasures from Medieval France*, The Cleveland Museum of Art, 1969, pp. 206 ff. In the sections dealing with secular art there are many objects in different media that enunciate chivalric-related themes much like those at Perugia.

34. See above, p. 70.

35. This description of the origins of the style derives from Hyde, *Society and Politics . . .*, p. 167. For the political implications of chivalric literature, see Robert W. Hanning, "The Social Significance of Twelfth Century Chivalric Romance," *Medievalia et Humanistica*, n. 3, 1972, pp. 3-31.

36. On the social and political implications of Aquinas's conception of love, see Antal, *Florentine Painting . . .*, pp. 38 ff.

37. For a discussion of this subject in art, see Sherman E. Lee, "Two Medieval Ivories in the Seattle Art Museum," *Art Quarterly* 12 (Spring 1912): 192 ff.

38. Stanley Lothrop, "Pietro Cavallini," *Memoirs of the American Academy in Rome*, 2 (1918): 78.

39. Barzon, p. 91, scene 108C: "Donna che sorrege un vecchio—Un povero vecchio, in barba bianca, procede curvo reggenosi malamente ad un bastone. Una giovane donna pietosamente gli pone il braccio sotto il petto ad aiutarlo."

40. The political adaptation of Charity came to special prominence in the Thomistic appropriation of Aristotle (Ullmann, *Principles of Government* . . ., pp. 232 ff.).

41. For a full description of the history of the representation and meaning of Charity during the Middle Ages, see Freyhan, "The Evolution of the 'Caritas' Figure . . .," p. 68 ff.

42. In the scenes of the Labors of the Months at Trent and in the *Très Riches Heures*, for example, representations of warriors and of battles are included with the month of January.

43. Barzon, p. 90.

44. Ibid., p. 84, for a discussion of this image.

45. For a study of this ancient Celtic and Roman goddess, known as Epòna, see S. Reinach, *Epòna*, Paris, 1895, and Lucien Guillot, *Le Cheval dans l'art*, Paris, 1927, pp. 100 ff. There is also a general similarity between the scene and the representations of the *decanni*, such as those to be found at Ferrara.

46. Grossato, *op. cit.*, p. 49.

47. For a traditional statement of the place of astrology in medieval thought, see Thorndike, *op. cit.*, 2, pp. 874 ff., and Theodore Otto Wedel, "The Medieval Attitude Towards Astrology," *Yale Studies in English* 60 (1920): 41 ff.

48. J.K. Hyde, *Padua in the Age of Dante*, Manchester, 1966, pp. 295 ff.; Nicolai Rubinstein, "Some Ideas on Municipal Progress and Decline in the Italy of the Communes," ed. D.J. Gordon, *Fritz Saxl: A Volume of Memorial Essays*, London, 1957, pp. 165 ff. Neither author suggests that there might be a relationship between republican theory and the particular form of astrological thinking that developed at the time.

49. Hyde, *Padua* . . ., p. 303.

50. For Mussato, the record of Ezzelino da Romano's reign during the thirteenth century stood as an historical exemplum of what the rulers of Padua should seek to avoid (Hyde, p. 300). The main source for this aspect of Mussato's thought is the *Ecernis*, the "first secular tragedy written since antiquity" (Weiss, *The Renaissance Discovery of Classical Antiquity*, p. 20). For a general discussion of the didactic conception of history at the time, see Gilmore *op. cit.*, p. 40.

51. For the change in the notion of fortune, see Rudolf Wittkower, "Chance, Time and Virtue," *Journal of the Warburg Institute* 1 (1937-38): 313 ff., and Howard R. Patch, *The Goddess "Fortuna" in Medieval Literature*, Cambridge, 1927, pp. 33 ff.

52. Hyde, p. 303; Rubinstein, "Some Ideas on Municipal Progress . . .," p. 170.

53. Thorndike, *op. cit.*, vol. 2, pp. 874 ff., C.A.J. Armstrong, "Astrology at the Court of Henry VII," *Italian Renaissance Studies*, ed. E.F. Jacob, London, 1960, pp. 433 ff.

54. Green, *Chronicle into History* . . . , pp. 29 ff.

55. L. Beltrami, *Angera e la sua Rocca*, Milan, 1904, pp. 89, 157 ff.

56. See Porter, *op. cit.*, vol. 3, pp. 113 ff., for a brief discussion of the sculptural embellishments. Several notable examples of mosaic decorations are the twelfth century floors from the Monastery at Bobbio, the Cathedral at Otranto, and the Baptistry at Florence: Van Marle, *The Development of the Italian Schools of Painting*, vol. 1, The Hague, 1923-1938. pp. 227 ff.

57. Green *op. cit.*, p. 31.

58. Ibid.

59. Ibid., p. 32.

60. Ibid., p. 32.

61. Ibid.

62. Ibid., p. 33.

63. Trachtenberg, *The Campanile* . . ., pp. 85 ff.; *Florentine Painting* . . ., pp. 233 ff.

64. For the Hercules relief, see Leopold D. Ettlinger, " 'Hercules Florentinus,' " *Mitteilungen des Kunsthistorischen Instituts in Florenz* 16 (1972); 119 ff.

65. See above, p. 66.

66. Thorndike, *op. cit.,* vol. 2, pp. 874 ff.

67. Ibid., p. 891; Burges, *op. cit.,* 26 (1869): 253 ff.

Chapter 9

1. Even the most superficial examination of the chronicles of the age is sufficient to indicate that much has been lost. For example, a Veronese chronicler of the fourteenth century notes that a cycle of history scenes, unspecified by him, decorated the Palazzo Comunale in about 1290 (Paul, *op. cit.,* pp. 60 ff.). Further complicating the problem is the need to determine the accuracy of many early secondary records relating to civic art.

2. Brian Pullan, *A History of Early Renaissance Italy from the Mid-Thirteenth through the Mid-Fifteenth Century,* London, 1957, pp. 157 ff.

3. G. Panazza, *L'arte mediovale nel territorio bresciano,* Bergamo, 1942, pp. 158 ff.; G. Panazza "Affreschi medievali nel Broletto di Brescia," *Commentari dell'Ateneo di Brescia,* 1946/7, pp. 102 ff.; Paul, *op. cit.,* p. 135.

4. Kantorowicz, *Frederick II,* pp. 243 ff.; Thomas Curtis Van Cleve, *The Emperor Frederick II: "Immutator Mundi,"* Oxford, 1972, pp. 133 ff.

5. See above p. 36.

6. This same thesis is offered by Kantorowicz, *The King's Two Bodies* . . ., pp. 110 ff.

7. On the general importance of judges, see Gierke, *Political Theories* . . ., pp. 101 ff., and Kantorowicz, *Frederick II,* pp. 120 ff.

8. Vasari writes that "nella sala grande del Podestà di Firenze dipinse [Giotto] il comune rubato da molti: dove in forma di giudice con lo scettro in mano lo figurò a sedere e sopra la testa gli pose le bilance pari per le giuste ragione ministrate da esso, aiutato da quattro virtù" (*Le Opere,* ed. G. Milanesi, 1, p. 400). Such a subject at this date does not appear to be unlikely. Both Wieruszowski ("Art and the Commune . . .," p. 30) and George Rowley (*Ambrogio Lorenzetti,* Princeton, 1958, 1, p. 489) accept the fact that the fresco existed and attempt to relate it to the contemporary political situation in the communes. Both historians see later reflections of it in the personification of the *Comune* on the tomb of Guido Tarlati and in Ambrogio's *Allegories.* I should add that Giotto's own representation of *Justice* in the Arena Chapel is also similar to the Florence Commune and this might explain Vasari's attribution of the Florence work to Giotto. For a general discussion of these personifications and of the legalistic setting from which they spring, see Zdekauer, *"Iustitia"*. . ., pp. 43 ff, and Riess, "French Influences . . .," pp. 285 ff.

9. Paul, p. 9.

10. The same interpretation is suggested by Antal, *Florentine Painting . . .*, pp. 138 ff., and by J. Schlosser, "Giustos Fresken in Padua," *Jahrb. der Kunsthist. Sammlg. in Wien* 17 (1896): 47 ff. Millard Meiss, without dealing specifically with this type of altar program, implicitly lends support to the thesis in his examination of the didactic purposes of Giotto's virtues at Padua (*Painting in Florence and Siena After the Black Death: The Arts, Religion and Society in the Mid-Fourteenth Century,* New York, 1964, pp. 49 ff.).

11. Porter, *op. cit.,* vol. 3, pp. 330 ff.; Rità Léjeune and Jacques Stiennon, *The Legend of Roland in the Middle Ages,* vol. 1, New York, 1971, pp. 366 ff.; Emile Mâle, "L'Architecte et la sculpture en Lombardie à l'époque romain à propos d'un livre récent," *Gazette des Beaux-Arts* 60 (1981): 41 ff., Michele Catalano, "Le effigie di Orlando e Uliviero sul Duomo di Verona," *Studi medievali,* vol. 3 (1930), 305 ff.; Venturi, vol. 3, pp. 167.

12. The legends associated with Theodoric have been discussed by, among others, Wilhelm Ensslin, *Theodorich der Grosse,* Munich, 1942, pp. 40-53.

13. Porter. *op. cit.,* p. 333; Riess, "French Influences . . .," p. 291.

14. Alice Maude Allen, *A History of Verona,* London, 1910, p. 92.

15. Ibid.

16. Léjeune and Stiennon, p. 64.

17. Porter, vol. 2, pp. 170 ff. and G. de Francovich, *Benedetto Antelami,* vol. 1, Milan-Florence, 1952, pp. 317 ff. The most complete collection of photographs is found in Roberto Tassi, *Il Duomo di Fidenza,* Milan, 1974.

18. Porter, p. 176.

19. Ibid.

20. For a discussion of Charlemagne as the "new" David, see above, pp. 30 ff.

21. Léjeune and Stiennon, p. 170.

22. See above, p. 35.

23. This point has been noted and discussed by the following authors, among others: Leonardo Olschki, *La Cattedrale di Modena e il suo rilievo arturiano,* Florence, 1935, p. 18; E Bertaux, *L'Art dans l'Italie méridionale de la Fine de l'Empire Romain à la conquête de Charles d'Anjou* 1, Paris, 1904, 468 ff.; Léjeune and Stiennon, "La Legende arthurienne dans la sculpture de la   Cathédrale de Modene," *Cahiers de Civilisation* 6 (1963): 281 ff.

24. Roger Sherman Loomis, *The Development of Arthurian Romance,* New York, 1963, pp. 65, 99.

25. Some examples of generalized representations of battles on civic palaces are the following: a series of frescoed scenes of riders and battles on the vaults of the arches in the main council of the Palazzo del Podestà in Fabriano dated 1300 (O. Maroaldi, *Sui palazzi pubblici di Fabriano,* Fabriano, 1870, p. 201); above the portal of the left flank of the Palazzo Pretorio in Arezzo is a relief of a warrior on a horse (Rodolico, *I Palazzi del Popolo . . .,* p. 151; *Toscana,* TCI, 1935, p. 425); above the portal of the Palazzo Comunale in Spello is a relief of battling warriors dated about 1270 (*Umbria,* TCI, p. 169). An example of the representation of a specific battle is the scene of the rebellion of the White Guelphs against the Florentine castle Pulciano in the Palazzo dei Priori in Florence (Wieruszowski, "Art and the Commune

. . .," p. 487, Davidsohn, *Geschichte* . . ., vol. 4, pp. iii, 221; one of the painters was Grifo di Tancredi). The reasons for the representation of the scene are perhaps typical of other works of this type. Pulciano was in posession of Volterra when it was purchased by Florence in 1254 because of its great strategic importance. By the late thirteenth century the castle had become an important center for exiled Ghibellines. In 1303, with the aid of Bologna, the Florentine Guelphs took possession of it. This was a major victory in the Guelph effort to solidify their position in the city (Davidshon, *op. cit.,* vol. 2, pp. ii, 351). The victory and its commemoration in art stood as a warning to other possible transgressors, in much the same sense as the *pittura infamante.*

26.   The most notable examples were found on the west portal of the Cathedral in Ferrara, dated about 1140 by Nicolò. In addition to two figures of guardian warriors, one on either side of the doorway and each carrying a shield adorned with a cross, there were representations of the months, a Christ between two kneeling figures, scenes from the Old Testament and a central representation in the tympanum of Christ standing on the asp and the basilik (Porter, vol. 2, p. 417: Trude Krautheimer-Hess, "The Original *Porta dei Mesi* at Ferrara and the Art of Nicolò," *Art Bulletin* 26 (1944): 152 ff. Krautheimer-Hess notes several related examples of the theme).

27.   Porter, vol. 3, pp. 148-167.

28.   A. Portioli, "Monumenti a Virgilio in Mantova," *Archivio Storico Lombardo* 4 (1877): 536 ff. The passage is also cited by Erwin Panofsky, *Renaissance and Renascences in Western Art,* vol. 1, Uppsala, 1960, p. 101; Paul, pp. 157 ff.; A. Andreani and P. Torelli, *I palazzi del comune di Mantova,* Mantua, 1942, pp. 91 ff. For a general discussion of the context of this work and of the strong local interest in Vergil during this time, see Portioli, pp. 536 ff. and Panofsky, pp. 101 ff.

29.   A. Venturi, *Storia dell'arte italiana,* vol. 3, Milan, 1901-1940, p. 338.; Paul, pp. 149 ff.

30.   The same conception of the instructive values of a monument erected to the fame of a particular individual is found during the fifteenth century; in fact it received a canonic importance in the thought of Alberti (Anthony Blunt, *Artistic Theory in Italy, 1450-1600,* Oxford, 1962, pp. 4 ff.).

31.   Paul p. 168.

32.   Cesare Foligno, *The Story of Padua,* London, 1910, pp. 78 ff.; Hyde, *Padua* . . ., pp. 85 ff.

33.   The point, I believe, is an original one. The general ignorance of these effigies of rulers has led to a distorted picture of the importance of the ruler portraits on the Fontana Maggiore. Hoffmann-Curtius, for example, believes that the Perugia works are without precedent: *op. cit.,* p. 14. The definitive study of ruler portraits is P.E. Schramm, "Das Herrscherbild in der Kunst des Mittelalters," *Vortrage der Bibliothek Warburg* 1 (1924): 198-272.

34.   This fact is also noted by Braunfels, *Mittelalterliche Stadtbaukunst* . . ., pp. 142 ff.

35.   Giovanni Paccagnini, *Il Palazzo Ducale di Mantova,* Torino, 1969; Paul, pp. 152 ff. It is possible that this cycle was of importance for Pisanello's frescoes of related subject that are also found in the palace, although Paccagnini does not mention the early works in his discussion of the sources and iconography of Pisanello's frescoes in *Pisanello e il ciclo cavalleresco di Mantova,* Milan, 1972.

36.   This view of the order of Christian society is not, as I have pointed out earlier, one that originates in the civic philosophy of the fifteenth century. The conception is fully anticipated in the thought of Aquinas.

37. Paul, p. 272; P.W. Cavelli, *Profilo storico-artistico della città di Todi,* Todi, 1946, p. 67; Van Marle, *Italian Schools,* vol. 1 p. 559; Edmondo Briganti, *Todi,* Todi, 1947, pp. 7 ff.; *Umbria,* TCI, pp. 350 ff.

38. See above, p. 21.

39. Pietro Toesca, *La pittura e la miniatura nella Lombardia,* Milan, 1912, p. 155; D'Ancona, *L'uomo e le sue opere . . .,* p. 151 (D'Ancona notes that the works might be a source for the "famous men" cycles of the fourteenth century); C. Baroni, "L'arte in Novara," *Novara e il suo territorio,* Novara, 1952, pp. 557 ff.

40. Baroni, pp. 560 ff.

41. Paul, p. 168.

42. Toesca, *La pittura . . .,* pp. 147 ff.; Anthony, p. 104; the works are cited in a review (unsigned) of Elia Fornoni, *La Cattedrale di Bergamo,* Bergamo, 1903, in *Bollettino della civica biblioteca di Bergamo,* 1907, pp. 37 ff.

43. For an examination of the varying ways in which the communes sought inspiration in the classical past, see: Riesenberg, "Civicism and Roman Law . . .," pp. 237 ff.; N. Rubinstein, "The Beginnings of Political Thought in Florence," *Journal of the Warburg and Courtauld Institutes* 5 (1942): 198 ff. On the interest of the Perugian commune in antiquity, see G. Sacconi, "Un antiquario del secolo XIV," *Giornale di erudizione artistica* 1 (1872): 184-186.

44. Alfredo Ridolfi, "Alcuni documenti e notizie sulla construzione del Palazzo Comunale (1288-1289)," *Rassagna d'arte senese,* 13 (1920) 84; Anthony, *Romanesque Frescoes,* p. 85; Van Marle, *Italian Schools,* vol. 1, p. 370, attributes the works to the school of Guido da Siena; Gotti, *op. cit.,* pp. 382 ff.; Paul, p. 260; Rodolico, p. 187.

45. For the political meaning of the hunt, and in particular its association with a wide range of chivalric notions relating to the skill and virtue of the emperor, see Grabar, *L'Empereur . . .,* pp. 87 ff.; Klingender, *Animals in Art . . .,* pp. 198 ff. For a general examination of the hunt in medieval art, see R. Van Marle, *Iconographie de l'art profane au moyen âge et à la renaissance,* The Hague, 1932, pp. 297 ff. For a general discussion of animal decoration and metaphor in imperial contexts see Ramsay MacMulle, "Some Pictures in Ammianus Marcellinus," *Art Bulletin* 46 (1964): 441 ff.

46. See above, p. 38.

47. *Op. cit.,* p. 49.

48. Rubinstein, "Political Ideas . . .," pp. 179 ff.; Sinding-Larsen, *op. cit.,* pp. 45 ff. The legalistic aspects of the phenomenon have been dealt with by Hermann Kantorowicz, *Studies in the Glossators of the Roman Law,* Cambridge, 1938, pp. 65 ff.

49. Braunfels, p. 47.

50. Braunfels, pp. 48 ff., 133 ff.; Helen Rosenau, *The Ideal City in Its Architectural Evolution,* London, 1959, pp. 22 ff.

51. There is no general study on the spread of iconographic themes during the late Middle Ages in Italy. Porter, *Lombard Architecture,* 3, London, 1917 pp. 25 ff., and Emile Mâle, *L'Art religieux en France au XIIe siècle,* Paris, 1922, pp. 19 ff., elucidate the so-called "pilgrimage roads" view of the introduction of French motifs into Northern Italy. The theory of course does not claim to account for the appearance of similar themes in Southern Italy at the same time, and thus Loomis, "Epic and Romance . . .," is quite unjust when he criticizes Mâle on

precisely this point (p. 92). A more recent overview of the issues raised by Mâle and Porter appears to accept their general view that the diffusion followed the paths of the pilgrims but simply does not use the designation that they give to the theory: M. Weinberger, "Remarks on the Role of French Models within the Evolution of Gothic Tuscan Sculpture," *Acts of the Twentieth International Congress of the History of Art*, 1, Princeton, 1963, pp. 198 ff. As far as the iconography of the Southern monuments is concerned, see Bertaux, *op. cit.*, 1, pp. 181 ff. And for the union of Northern and Southern influences in Central Italy, see E.B. Garrison, *Studies in the History of Medieval Italian Painting*, vol. 2, pp. 5 ff., and E. Panofsky and F. Saxl, "Classical Mythology in Medieval Art," *Metropolitan Museum Studies*, New York 4 (1933): 250 ff.

52. To cite only two examples of this mistaken outlook, Charles Seymour in "Invention and Revival in Nicola Pisano's 'Heroic Style,' " *Acts of the Twentieth International Congress ... of the History of Art, 1, 1963 pp. 207 ff.*, ignores precedents for the programs of the Pisani pulpits in Northern and Southern Italy and hypothesizes a direct link with France, and Trachtenberg in *The Campanile ...*, overlooks the entire field of North Italian sculpture in discussing the themes of the program despite the fact that there are important sources for it in North Italy.

53. Paul, pp. 5 ff., discusses the early history of palace construction in Italy.

54. A. Amelli, *Miniature sacre e profane dell'anno 1023 illustranti l'enciclopedia mediovale di Rabano Mauro*, Montecassino, 1896, pl. VII.

55. The single general study of this problem touches only peripherally on Italian domestic decorations: R. Van Marle, "L'Iconographie dans la décoration profane des demeures premières en France et en Italie aux XIVe et XVe siècles," *Gazette des Beaux-Arts*, 68 (1926), 163 ff.

56. Toesca, *op. cit.*, p. 577, has also written of the possible influence of the troubadors on the profane art of the late Middle Ages in Italy. The view is shared by the literary historians: Edmund G. Gardner, *The Arthurian Legend in Italian Literature*, London-New York, 1930, pp. 30 ff.

57. F. Saxl, "The Troy Romance in French and Italian Art," *Lectures*, vol. 1, London, 1957, pp. 125-138.

58. See above p. 82.

59. For a brief introduction to Levi-Strauss's conception of the relation between epic and history, see Edmund Leach, *Claude Levi-Strauss*, New York, 1970, pp. 53 ff.

60. J.H. Plumb, *Death of the Past*, Boston, 1970, p. 42.

61. Gardner, *op. cit.*, p. 69.

62. Rubinstein, "Early Political Writing . . .," p. 198, and Green, *Chronicle into History*, p. 14 ff.; both include brief discussions of the general significance of the city foundation theories that appear in the chronicles. For a later reflection of the theme of city foundations in art, see Nicolai Rubinstein, "Vasari's Painting of the *Foundation of Florence* in the Palazzo Vecchio," *Essays in the History of Architecture Presented to Rudolf Wittkower*, London, 1967, pp. 97-113. A brief note on the general interest of Perugia in its foundations is G. degli Azzi, "Un Romanzo del Secolo XIV sulla origine poetiche dell'Umbria," *L'Umbria, rivista d'arte e letteratura*, July 1901, pp. 13-23.

63. Nicolai Rubinstein, "Notes on the Word 'Stato' in Florence Before Machiavelli," *"Florilegium Historiale": Essays Presented to Wallace K. Ferguson*, eds. J.G. Rowe and W.H. Stockdale, Toronto, 1971, pp. 313 ff.

64. Lionel Trilling, *Sincerity and Authenticity,* Cambridge, 1971, pp. 84 ff.

65. See above, pp. 34-35.

66. Paul Deschamps, "Combats de Cavalerie et épisodes de croisades dans les peintures murales du XIIe et du XIIIe siècle," *Orientalia Christiana Periodica* 13 (1947) : 454 ff., also deals with this problem and points out several of the ways in which the crusading spirit infused art. Another examination of the specific influences of the crusades on art, again in France, is P. Delaborde and P. Lauer, "Un Project de décoration inspiré du Crédo de Joinville," *Monuments Piot* 16 (1909): 61-81.

67. Felix Gilbert, *Machiavelli and Guicciardini: Politics and History in Sixteenth-Century Florence,* Princeton, 1965, pp. 203 ff.

68. Hyde, *Padua . . .,* pp. 31, 69.

Appendix

1. A general history of the position of the frescoes in Umbrian scholarship is Miklos Boskovits, "Nuovi studi su Giotto e Assisi," *Paragone,* n. 261, 1971, pp. 41 ff. I am in accord with the above-mentioned solution to the problem of attribution. The figures in the Old Testament scenes are of a sculpturesque force comparable to the work of Cavallini or of his finest assistants. There is a decided difference in the style of the succeeding scenes that points to the intervention of local artists, or of lesser members of Cavallini's workshop.

2. For a discussion and bibliography of the Perugian chronicles, see above, p. 77, n. 8.

3. See above, p. 23.

4. Pellini, *op. cit.,* p. 317.

5. Crispolti, *Perugia Augusta descritta,* Perugia, 1648, p. 27.

6. Orsini, *Guida della Città di Perugia,* Perugia, 1787, vol. 1, p. 166.

7. Mariotto, *Saggio di memorie istoriche ed ecclesiastiche della città di Perugia e suo contado,* Perugia, 1806, vol. 1, p. 229.

8. A. Briganti, "Notizie sui primordi delle arti in Perugia," *Rassegna d'arte umbra* 1 (1910): 87-88.

9. M. Boskovits, *Pittura umbra e marchigiana fra medioevo e rinascimento,* Florence, 1973, p. 33, n. 43.

10. Rossi-Scotti, *Il Palazzo del Popolo,* Perugia, 1864.

11. Tiberi, "Il Palazzo Comunale," *Il gironale dell'esposizione provinciale umbra* 1 (1879): 2-4.

12. Venturi, *Storia dell' arte italiana,* 3, Milan, 1901-1940, pp. 39, 386, 838.

13. See U. Toscano, "La fortuna della pittura umbra . . . ," for a history of Umbrian art historical studies.

14. Gnoli, *Catalogo della mostra d'antica arte Umbra a Perugia.* Perugia, 1907, p. 23.

15. Cristofani, "La mostra di antica arte umbra a Perugia," *L'Arte* 1 (1907): 43.

16. Bombe, *Geschichte der peruginer malerei,* pp. 26 ff.

17. Jacobson, *Umbrische Malerei des vierzehnten, funfzehnten, und sechzehnten Jahrhunderts,* Berlin, 1914, pp. 17 ff.

18. Lothrop, "Pietro Cavallini," pp. 77 ff.

19. Ibid., p. 97.

20. Wilpert, *op. cit.*, vol. 2, p. 1032.

21. Van Marle, *op. cit.*, vol. 1, p. 530.

22. Hermanin, "Gli affreschi di Pietro Cavallini in Santa Cecilia in Trastevere," *Le Gallerie Nazionale Italianne*, Rome, 1902, pp. 103 ff.; "Due pitture inedite di Pietro Cavallini," *Rivista di Roma* 11 (1923): 34 ff.

23. Busuioceaunu, "Pietro Cavallini e la pittura romana del Duecento e del Trecento," *Ephemeris Dacormana*, Rome, 1925, pp. 24 ff.

24. Cockerell, *A Book of Old Testament Illustrations of the Thirteenth Century . . .* , p. 41.

25. Demus, *Die Mosaiken von San Marco . . .* , p. 87, n. 45.

26. Demus, *The Mosaics of Norman Sicily,* p. 155.

27. A. Briganti and M. Magnini, *Guida di Perugia,* Perugia, 1925, pp. 95 ff.

28. Thaon di Revel, "Perugia," *Enciclopedia Italiana,* vol. 26, p. 907.

29. Guardabassi, *Storia di Perugia,* vol. 1, p. 92.

30. Tarchi, *L'arte medievale dell'Umbria . . .* , vol. 1, pp. 2 ff.

31. Lupatelli, *Storia di Perugia,* Perugia, 1950, p. 13.

32. Santi, *Perugia: Guida storico-artistica,* pp. 13 ff.

33. Rapone, *Guida di Perugia,* pp. 29 ff.

34. Johnstone, *Perugia . . .* , pp. 76 ff.

35. Schneider, *The Story of Perugia,* London, 1952, pp. 63 ff.

36. Gurrieri, *Il Palazzo dei Priori à Perugia: Guida Illustrata,* pp. 13 ff.

37. Sindona, *Pietro Cavallini,* Florence, 1958, pp. 42 ff.

38. Busuioceunuo, "Maestranze cavalliniane a S. Cecilia in Trastevere," *Studi e contributi dell'Istituto di Archeologia e Storia dell'Arte dell'Università di Bari,* Bari, 1959, pp. 39 ff.

39. Boskovits, *op. cit.*, p. 33, n. 43.

40. Longhi, "La pittura umbra della prima metà del trecento: Lezioni di Roberto Longhi nell'anno academico 1953-1954 attraverso le dispense redatte da Mina Gregori," *Paragone,* Ns. 281-283, 1973, p. 13.

41. Nessi, "Documenti sull'arte umbra . . . ."

42. Martini, *op. cit.*

43. Hoffmann-Curtius, *op. cit.*, p. 14.

Bibliography

Allen, Alice Maud. *A History of Verona*. London, 1910.

Almond, G. and S. Verba, *The Civic Culture*. Princeton, 1963.

Alpatoff, Michael. "The Parallelism of Giotto's Paduan Frescoes," *The Art Bulletin* 29 (1947): 149 ff.

Amelli. A. *Miniature sacre e profane dell'anno 1023 illustranti l'enciclopedia mediovale di Rubano Mauro,* Montecassino, 1896.

d'Ancona, Paola. *The Schifanoia Months at Ferrara.* Milan, 1954.

_____. *L'uomo e le sue opere nelle figurazione italiane del medioevo.* Florence, 1923.

Andreani, A. and Torelli, P. *I palazzi del comune di Mantova.* Mantua, 1942.

Andriola, D. "Maestranze cavalliniane a S. Cecilia in Trastevere," *Studi e contributi del"Istituto di Archeologia e Storia dell'Arte dell'Università di Bari.* Bari, 1959, pp. 39 ff.

Ansidei, Vincenzo. *Prefazione al Volume Primo del Rigestum Reformationum Communis perusii ab anno MCCLVI ad annum MCC.* Perugia, 1935.

Antal, F. *Florentine Painting and Its Social Background.* London, 1947.

Anthony, Edgar Waterman. *Romanesque Frescoes.* Princeton, 1951.

Aquinas, Saint Thomas. *Summa theologiae.* Translated by the English Dominicans, 22 vols. London-New York, 1912-1936.

_____. *The "De Regimine Principum."* Translated by G.B. Phelan, Toronto. 1932.

_____. *Selected Political Writings.* Ed. A.P. D'Entrèves. Oxford, 1948.

Armstrong, C.A.J. "Astrology at the Court of Henry VII," *Italian Renaissance Studies,* ed. E.F. Jacob. London, 1960, pp. 433-452.

Atiya, Aziz Suryal. *The Crusade in the Later Middle Ages.* London, 1938.

Auerbach, Erich. *Mimesis: The Representation of Reality in Western Literature.* New York, 1971.

Augustine. *Confessions.* Translated by R.S. Pine-Coffin, Harmondsworth, 1961.

_____. *The City of God,* 12 vols. Translated by Eva Matthews Sanford and William McAllen Green. Cambridge and London, 1955.

degli Azzi, Giustiniano. "Lo statuto del 1342 del comune di Perugia," *Corpus Statutorum Italicorm* 1, Perguia, 1961.

_____. "Un Romanzo del Secolo XIV sulla origine poetiche dell'Umbria," *L'Umbria, revista d'arte e letteratura,* July 1901, pp. 13-23.

Bandmann, Gunter, et al. *Lexikon der Christlichen Ikonographie,* vol. 3. Rome-Freiburg-Basel-Vienna, 1971.

Barker, Ernest. *Social and Political Thought in Byzantium.* Oxford, 1957.

Baron, Hans. "Franciscan Poverty and Civic Wealth as Factors in the Rise of Humanistic Thought," *Speculum* 13 (1938): 37-63.

_____. *The Crisis of the Early Italian Renaissance,* rev. ed. Princeton, 1966.

Baroni, C. "L'arte in Novara," in *Novara e il suo territorio*. Novara, 1952, pp. 557—569.

Bartolus of Sassoferrato. *Commentary on Codex, Tres Libri*. Turin, 1577.

Barzon, A. *I cieli e loro influenza negli affreschi del salone in Padova*, Padua, 1924.

Becker, Marvin. *Florence in Transition*, 2 vols. Baltimore, 1967.

Belard, M. *Il nucleo storico di Perugia e le zone per il rinascimento*.Gubbio, 1960.

Belelli, Giovanni. *L'istituto del podestà in Perugia nel secolo XIII*. Bologna, 1936.

Bellucci, A. *Osservazioni sulla scala esterna del Palazzo del Popolo*. Perugia, 1899.

_____. "La Chiesa di Sant'Ercolano di Perugia," *Augusta Perugia* 2 (1907): 11-19.

_____. "Un singolare errore sulla creazione della Capitano del Popolo in Perugia," *Bollettino della Deputazione di Storia Patria per l'Umbria* 16 (1910): 895-1102.

Beltrami, L. *Angera e la sua Rocca*. Milan, 1904.

Berlin, I. "The Originality of Machiavelli," *Studies on Machiavelli*, ed. Myron P. Gilmore. Florence, 1972, pp. 150-206.

Bertaux, Emile. *L'Arte dans l'Italie méridionale de la fin de l'Empire Romain a la conquête de Charles d'Anjou*, vol. 1. Paris, 1904.

Bertini, Aldo. "Per la conoscenza dei medaglioni che accompagnano le storie della vita di Gesù nella Cappela degli Scrovegni," *Giotto e il suo tempo*, Atti del Congresso Internazionale per la celebrazione del VII Centenario della nascità di Giotto, 24 settembre - 1 ottobre 1967, Rome, 1971, pp. 143-159.

Bettini, Sergio. *Giusto de Menabuoi e l'arte del trecento*. Padua, 1944.

Bigotti, Mario. *Narni*. Rome, 1973.

Blanshei, Sarah Rubin. *Perugia, 1260-1340: Conflict and Change in a Medieval Italian Urban Society, Transactions of the American Philosophical Society*, vol. 66, part 2, 1976.

Bloch, Herbert. "Monte Cassino, Byzantium, and the West in the Earlier Middle Ages," *Dumbarten Oaks Papers*, 3 (1946): 177 ff.

Blunt, Anthony. *Artistic Theory in Italy, 1450-1600*. Oxford, 1962.

Boase, T.S.R. *Boniface VIII*. London, 1933.

Böll, Franz. *Sterdeutung die Geschichte und das Wesen der Astrologie*. Berlin, 1926.

Bombe, W. *Perugia*. Leipzig, 1914.

_____. *Geschichte der Peruginer Malerei*. Berlin, 1912.

Bonazzi, Luigi. *Storia di Perugia*, 2 vols. Città di Castello, 1959.

Bonifazio da Verona. "Eulistea," *Cronache e storie inedite della città di Perugia dal MCL al MDLXIII*, in *Archivio storico italiano*, vol. 16, pt. 1, 1895, pp. 3-47.

Boskovits, Miklos. "Nuovi studi su Giotto e Assisi," *Paragone*, no. 261, 1971, pp. 41-66.

_____. *Pittura umbra e marchigiana fra medioevo e rinascimento*. Florence, 1973.

Bowsky, W.M. "The 'Buon Governo' of Siena (1287-1355): A Medieval Italian Oligarchy," *Speculum* 37 (1962): 368-392.

_____. "The Medieval Commune and Internal Violence: Police Power and Public Safety in Siena, 1287-1355," *American Historical Review* 83 (1967): 1-17.

Boylesve, Marin de. *Les Animaux et leurs applications symboliques à l'ordre spirituel*. Paris, 1881.

Brandt, P. *Schaffende Arbeit und bildende Kunst in Alterum und Mittelalter*. Leipzig, 1927.

Braunfels, Wolfgang. *Mittelalterliche Stadt-Baukunst in der Toskana*. Berlin, 1953.

_____. "Giotto's Campanile," *Das Münster* 1 (1948): 206-212.

Bréhier, L. *L'Art chrétien: Son développement iconographique des origines à nos jours*. Paris, 1918.

Brennan, Rose, E. *The Intellectual Virtues According to the Philosophy of St. Thomas*. Washington, D.C., 1941.

Brentano, Robert. *Rome Before Avignon: A Social History of Thirteenth-Century Rome*. New York, 1974.

Briganti, A. *Le corporazione delle arti nel comune di Perugia*, Perugia, 1910.

_____. "Notizie sui primordi delle arti in Perugia," *Rassegna d'arte umbra* 1 (1910): 87-88.

Briganti, A., and Magnini, M. *Guida di Perugia*. Perugia, 1925.

Briganti, Edmondo. *Todi*. Todi, 1947.

Briganti, F. *Città dominanti e comuni minori nel medioevo con speciale riguardo alla republica perugina*. Perugia, 1906.

Brucker, Gene. *Renaissance Florence*. New York, 1969.

Buchthal, Hugo. *Miniature Painting in the Latin Kingdom of Jerusalem*. Oxford, 1957.

Budinger, M. "Die Universal histoire in Mittelalter," *Denkschriften d. Kaiserl. Akademie d. Wiss., phil.-hist.* 46 (1900): 13-41.

Burges, W. "La Ragione de Padoue," *Annales archéologiques,* 18, (1858).

Bush, Douglas. *John Milton, a Sketch of His Life and Writings*. London, 1965.

Busuioceaunu, P. "Pietro Cavallini e la pittura romana del Duecento e del Trecento," *Ephemeris Dacormana,* Rome, 1925, pp. 24-85.

_____. "Maestranze Cavalliniane a S. Cecilia in Trastevere," *Studie contributi dell'Instituto di Archeologia e Storia dell'Arte delle Università di Bari*. Bari, 1959.

Campelli, V. *La cinta muraria di Perugia*. Perugia, 1935.

Carlyle, R.W., and Carlyle, A.J. *A History of Medieval Political Theory in the West,* 6 vols. New York, 1936.

Catalano, Michele. "Le effigie di Orlando e Uliviero sul Duomo di Verona," *Studi Medievali* 3 (1930), 305-309.

Cavelli, P.W. *Profilo storico-astistico della città di Todi*. Todi, 1946.

Cecchini, Giovanni. *Archivio storico di Perugia; Inventario*. Rome, 1956.

_____. *Contributo alla raccolta di Fonti per la storia della* Sviluppo urbanistico de Perugia. Perugia, 1965.

_____. Fra Bevignate e la guerra contro Foligno," *Storia e arte in Umbria nell' età comunale: Arti de VI Convegno di arte umbri*. Vol. 2. Perugia, 1969, pp. 493 ff.

Ceci, G. *Todi nel medioevo*. Todi, 1897.

Chefneux, H. "Les Fables dans la Tapiserie de Bayeux," *Romania.* 60 (1934): 39-69.

Chenessaux, George. *L'Abbaye de Fleury à St. Benoît sur Loire*. Paris, 1931.

Chiumenti, Luisa. "Perugia," *Dizionario enciclopedico di archittetura e urbanistica* Vol. 4, Rome, 1969.

Cockerell, Sidney C. *Miniatures: A Medieval Picture Book*. New York, 1969.

Crispolti. *Perugia Augusta descritta*. Perugia, 1648.

Cristofani, G. "La Mostra di Antica arte umbra a Perugia," *L'Arte* 1 (1907): 13-28.

_____. "Ritmi veneziani nel Palazzo dei Priori di Perugia," *Atti del Secondo Covegno nazionale di Storia dell' Architettura*. Assisi, October 1-4, 1939.

Curtius, E.R. *European Literature and the Latin Middle Ages*. New York, Evanston, 1963.

Cutini, Clara Zaggerini. "Sulla datazione del grifo perugino," *Bollettino della Deputazione di Storia Patria per l'Umbria* 69 (1972): 53-61.

Dalaruelle, Etienne. "La Piété populaire en Ombrie au siècle des Communes," *Storia e arte in Umbria nell'eta comunale*. vol. 2. Perugia, 1969, pp. 397-413.

Daly, Lloyd, W. *Aesop without Morals*. New York-London, 1961.

Davidsohn, Robert. *Storia di Firenze,* IV, i. Florence, 1973.

Davis, C.T. "An Early Florentine Political Theorist: Fra Remigio de' Girolami," *Proceedings of the American Philosophical Society* 104 (1960): 662 ff.

Deane, Herbert A. *The Political and Social Ideas of St. Augustine*. New York-London, 1963.

Delaborde, P., and Lauer, P. "Un Projet de decoration inspiré du Crédo de Joinville," *Monuments Piot* 16 (1909): 61-84.

Demus, Otto. *Die Mosaiken von San Marco in Venedig, 1100-1300*. Vienna, 1935.

_____. *The Mosaics of Norman Sicily*. New York, 1950.

————. *The Church of San Marco in Venice: History, Architecture, Sculpture.* Washington, D.C., 1960.

Deschamps, Paul. "La Legende arthurienne à la cathédrale de Modena," *Monuments Piot* 48 (1928): 19-27.

————. "Combats de Cavalerie et episodes de croisades dans les peintures murales du XII et du XIII siècle," *Orientalia Christiana Periodica* 13 (1947): 454-474.

————. "La Legende de Saint Georges et les combats croisés dans les peintures murales au moyen âge," *Monuments Piot* 46 (1950): 109-123.

Dhanens, Elisabeth. *Van Eyck: "The Ghent Altarpiece."* London, 1973.

Douglas, Mary. *Natural Symbols: Explorations in Cosmology.* New York, 1970.

Egenter, Richard. "Gemeinnutz vor Eigennutz: Die soziale Leitidee im Tractatus de bono communi des Fr. Remigus von Florenz," *Scholastik* 9 (1934): 79-92.

Elenco degli edifici monumentali della provincia di Ancona. Rome, 1932.

Emerson, O.F. "Legends of Cain, especially in Old and Middle English," *Publications of the Modern Language Association of America* 21 (1906): 839-851.

Emerton, Ephraim. *Humanism and Tyranny: Studies in the Italian Trecento.* Cambridge, 1925.

Enciclopedia italiana. Vol. 10. Milan, 1935.

Ensslin, Wilhelm. *Theoderich der Grosse.* Munich, 1942.

d'Entrèves, A.P.D. *The Medieval Contribution to Political Thought: Thomas Aquinas, Marsilius of Padua, Richard Hooker.* Oxford, 1939.

————. *Dante as a Political Thinker.* Oxford, 1952.

Ermini, Giuseppe. *Storia della Università di Perugia.* Bologna, 1947.

————. "Fattori di successo dello studio perugino delle origini," *Storia e arte in Umbria nell'età comunale* 2, Perugia, 1969, pp. 289 ff.

Ettlinger, L.D. *The Sistine Chapel before Michelangelo: Religious Imagery and Papal Primacy.* Oxford, 1965.

————. "Hercules Florentius," *Mitteilungen des Kunsthistorischen Instituts in Florenz* 16 (1972): 119-142.

Evans, E.P. *Animal Symbolism in Ecclesiastical Architecture.* London, 1896.

Fabretti, Ariodiente. *Cronache e storie inedite della città di Perugia,* 5 vols. Torino, 1887.

Faina, M.C. *I palazzi comunali umbri.* Milan, 1954.

Fasola, G. *La Fontana di Perugia.* Rome, 1951.

Felges-Henning, Uta. "The Picture Program of the Sala della Pace: A New Interpretation," *Journal of the Warburg and Courtauld Institutes* 35 (1972): 145-163.

Fischer, C.B. "The Pisan Clergy and Its Awakening of Historical Interest in a Medieval Commune," *Studies in Medieval and Renaissance History,* ed. William M. Bowsky. Lincoln, 1966, pp. 141-176.

Folena, G. "La cultura volgare e l'umanesimo cavalleresco." *Umanesimo europeo umanesimo veneziano.* Florence, 1963, pp. 141-158.

Foligno, Cesare. *The Story of Padua.* London, 1910.

de Francovich, G. *Benedetto Antelami* I. Milan-Florence, 1952.

Freyhan, R. "The Evolution of the 'Caritas' Figure in the 13th and 14th Centuries," *Journal of the Warburg and Courtauld Institutes* 11 (1948): 68-90.

Gage, John. "La Victoire impériale dans l'Empire Chrétien," *Revue d'Histoire et de Philosophie Religieuse* 13 (1933): 24-39.

Garber, Joseph. *Wirkungen der Frühchristlichen Gemaldezyklen der Alten Peters-und-Pauls-Basilken in Rom.* Berlin and Vienna, 1918.

Gardner, Edmund, G. *The Arthurian Legend in Italian Literature.* London-New York, 1930.

Garrison, E. *Studies in the History of Medieval Italian Painting,* vol. 1, pp. 10 ff.; vol. 3, pp. 33 ff., 89 ff., 169 ff., 183 ff.; vol. 4, pp. 117 ff., 201 ff., Florence, 1953-1962.

Garzelli, Annarosa. *Sculture toscane nel Dugento e nel Trecento.* Florence, 1969.
Gay, Peter, *Art and Act: On Causes in History-Manet, Gropius, Mondrian.* New York, 1976.
Gewirth, A. *Marsilius of Padua,* 2 vols. New York, 1951.
Gierke, Otto. *Political Theories of the Middle Ages.* Cambridge, 1900.
Gilbert, Felix, *Machiavelli and Guicciardini: Politics and History in Sixteenth-Century Florence.* Princeton, 1965.
Gilmore, Myron P. "The Renaissance Conception of the Lessons of History," *Humanists and Jurists: Six Studies in the Renaissance.* Cambridge, 1938, pp. 1—38.
Gnoli, A. *Catalogo della mostra d'antica arte umbra a Perugia.* Perugia, 1907.
Goldschmidt, A. *An Early Manuscript of Aesop Fables of Avianus and Related Manuscripts.* Princeton, 1947.
Gower, Milton S. "Symbolic Animals at Perugia and Spoleto," *Burlington Magazine* 32 (1918): 152-163.
Grabar, André. *L'Empereur dans l'Art Byzantin.* Publications de la Faculté des Lettres de l'Université de Strasbourg 75, Paris, 1936.
Graf, A. *Roma nella memoria e nelle immaginazioni del medioevo.* Turin, 1923.
Green, Louis. *Chronicle into History: An Essay on the Interpretation of History in Florentine Fourteenth Century Chronicles.* Cambridge, 1972.
Green, Rosalie, B. "Ex Ungue Leonum," "*De Artibus Opuscula xl.,*" *Essays in Honor of Erwin Panofsky.* New York, 1961, pp. 157-161.
_____. "The Adam and Eve Cycle in the *Hortus Deliciarum,*" *Late Classical and Medieval Studies in Honor of Albert Mathias Friend,* ed. Kurt Weitzmann, Princeton, 1955.
Gregorovius, Ferdinand. *Geschichte der Stadt Rom im Mittelalter,* vol. 2. Wurtemburg, 1926.
Grossato, Lucio, "La decorazione pittorica del Salone," *Il Palazzo della Ragione di Paduva,* ed. Guido Mor. Venice, 1964, pp. 47-69.
Guardabassi, M. *Indice-Guida dei monumenti pagani e cristiani dell'Umbria.* Perugia, 1972.
Guardabassi, M., and Santi, F. *Il Portale Maggiore del Palazzo dei Priori.* Perugia, 1953.
Guillot, Lucien, *Le Cheval dans l'art.* Paris, 1927.
Gurrieri, Ottorino. *La cattedrale di S. Lorenzo in Perugia.* Perugia, 1961.
_____. *Agnelo da Orvieto, Matteo Gattapone e i palazzi pubblichi di Gubbio e Città di Castello.* Perugia, 1962.
_____. *Il Palazzo dei Priori à Perugia: Guida Illustrata.* Perugia, 1962.
Hanning, Robert W. "The Social Significance of Twelfth Century Chivalric Romance," *Medievalia et Humanistica,* n. 3, 1973, pp. 3—31.
Hanson, Anne Coffin. *Jacopo della Quercia's "Fonte Gaia."* Oxford, 1965.
Hartlaub, G.F. "Giotto's Zweite Hauptwerke in Padua," *Zeitschrift fur Kunstwissenschaft* 21 (1950): 23-45.
Haskins, Charles Homer, *The Renaissance of the Twelfth Century.* New York, 1959.
Heimann, Adelheid. "The Capital Freize and Pilasters of the *Portail Royal:* Chartres," *Journal of the Warburg and Courtauld Institutes* 31 (1968): 95-103.
Herlihy, David. *Medieval and Renaisance Pistoia: The Social History of an Italian Town.* New Haven and London, 1967.
Hamoan-Maclean, R. "Das Ikonographische Problem der 'Friedberger Jungfrau," *Marburger Jahr für Kunstwissenchaft* 10 (1937), p. 65.
Hermanin, G. "Due pitture inedite di Pietro Cavallini," *Rivista di Roma* II (1923): 34-39.
_____. *Le Gallerie Nazionali Italianne.* Rome, 1902.
Herter, F. *Die Podestàliteratur Italiens im 12. und 13. Jahrhundert.* Diss. phil. Leipzig, 1910, pp. 43 ff.
Heywood, William. *A History of Perugia.* Ed. R. Langston Douglas. London, 1910.
Hind, Arthur M. *Early Italian Engravings,* vol. 1. London, 1938.

Hirn, Yrjö. *The Sacred Shrine: A Study of the Poetry and Art of the Catholic Church.* London, 1958.

Hoffmann-Curtius, Kathrin. *Das Programm der Fontana Maggiore in Perugia.* Dusseldorf, 1968.

Holbrook, R.T. *Dante and the Animal Kingdom.* New York, 1902.

Huizinga, J. *The Waning of the Middle Ages.* New York, 1954.

Hyde, J.K. *Padua in the Age of Dante.* Manchester, 1966.

————. *Society and Politics in Medieval Italy: The Evolution of the Civic Life, 1000-1350.* London and Basingstoke, 1972.

————. "Commune, University and Society in Early Medieval Bologna," *Universities in Politics.* Ed. J.W. Baldwin and R.A. Goldthwaite. Baltimore, 1972.

Ivanoff, Nocola. "Il problema iconologico degli affreschi," *Il Palazzo della Ragione di Padova.* Ed. Carlo Guido Mor. Venice, 1964, pp. 71-99.

Jacobson, B. *Umbrische Malerei des vierzehnten, funfzehten, und sechzehnten Jahrhunderts.* Berlin, 1914.

Janson, H.W. *The Sculpture of Donatello,* vol. 2. Princeton, 1957.

Johnstone, Mary A. *Perugia and Her People.* Perugia, 1956.

Kantorowicz, Ernst H. *"Laudes Regiae": A Study in Liturgical Acclamations and Medieval Ruler Workship.* Berkeley and Los Angeles, 1946.

————. *Frederick II.* New York, 1954.

————. *The King's Two Bodies: A Study in Medieval Political Theology.* Princeton, 1957.

————. "'Pro Patria Mori' in Mediaeval Political Thought," *Selected Studies.* Locust Valley, 1967, pp. 308-325.

Kantorowicz, Hermann. *Studies in the Glossators of the Roman Law.* Cambridge, 1938.

Katzenellenbogen, Adolf. *Allegories of the Virtues and Vices in Mediaeval Art.* London, 1939.

————. *The Sculptural Programs of Chartres Cathedral: Christ, Mary, Ecclesia.* New York, 1959.

Klibansky, Raymond, Erwin Panofsky, and Fritz Saxl. *Saturn and Melancholy: Studies in the History of Natural Philosophy, Religion and Art.* London, 1954.

Klingender, Francis. *Animals in Art and Thought.* London, 1971.

Krautheimer, Richard. "Introduction to an 'Iconography of Medieval Architecture,'" *Studies in Early Christian, Medieval, and Renaissance Art,* New York, 1969.

Krautheimer-Hess, Trude. "The Original *Porta dei Mesi* at Ferrara and the Art of Niccolò," *Art Bulletin* 26 (1944): 152-173.

Kurth, B. "Ein Frescenzyklus ins Alterum zu Trient," *Jahr. d. Kunsth, Inst. d. k. Zentralkommission f. Denkmalpflege* 5 (1911): 9-51.

de Laborde, A. *La Bible moralisée,* vol. 1. Paris, 1911.

Larner, John. *Culture and Society in Italy, 1250-1420.* New York, 1971.

Leach, Edmund, *Claude Levi-Strauss.* New York, 1970.

Lee, Sherman E. "Two Medieval Ivories in the Seattle Art Museum," *Art Quarterly* 12 (Spring 1912): 192-201.

Léjeune, Rita and Jacques Stiennon. "La Légende arthurienne dans la sculpture de la Cathédrale de Modene," *Cahiers de Civilisation* 6 (1963): 281-287.

————. *The Legend of Roland in the Middle Ages.* 2 vols. New York, 1971.

Levey, Michael. *Painting at Court.* New York, 1971.

Ligota, C. "Constantiniana," *Journal of the Warburg and Courtauld Institutes* 26 (1963): 178-192.

Longhi, Roberto. "La pittura umbra della prima metà del trecento: Lezioni di Roberto Longhi nell'anno accademico 1953-1954 attraverso le dispense redatte da Mina Gregori," *Paragone,* Ns. 281-283, 1973.

Loomis, Roger Sherman. *Arthurian Legends in Medieval Art.* London-New York, 1938.

————. *The Development of Arthurian Romance.* New York, 1963.

_____. "The Heraldry of Hector, or Confusion Worse Confounded," *Speculum* 42 (1967): 32-35.

Lopez, Robert S. *The Commercial Revolution of the Middle Ages, 950-1350.* New York, 1971.

Lothrop, Stanley. "Pietro Cavallini," *Memoirs of the American Academy in Rome* 2 (1918): 77-91.

Lupatelli, V. *Storia di Perugia.* Perugia, 1950.

MacMulle, Ramsay. "Some Pictures in Ammianus Marcellinus," *Art Bulletin* 46 (1964): 441-449.

Mâle, Emile. "L'architecte et la sculpture en Lombardie à l'époque romain à propos d'un livre recent," *Gazette des Beaux-Arts* 60 (1918): 41-42.

_____. *L'Art religieux en France au XIIe siècle.* Paris, 1922.

_____. *The Gothic Image: Religious Art in France of the Thirteenth Century.* New York, 1958.

Marchini, G. *La Pinacoteca Comunale di Ancona.* Ancona, 1960.

Mariana, Ugo. "Egidius Colonna," *Enciclopedia Italiana* 13, pp. 534-536.

Mariotti, A. *Saggio di memorie istoriche ed ecclesiastiche della città di Perugia e suo contado* 1. Perugia, 1806.

van Marle, R. *The Development of the Italian Schools of Painting* 1. The Hague, 1923-1938.

_____. "L'Iconographie dans la décoration profane des demeures premières en France et en Italie aux XIVe et XVe siècles," *Gazette des Beaux-Arts* 68 (1926): 163-178.

_____. *Iconographie de l'art profane au moyen âge et à la renaissance.* The Hague, 1932.

Maroaldi, O. *Sui palazzi pubblici di Fabriano.* Fabriano, 1870.

Martines, L.(ed.). *Violence and Civil Disorder in Italian Cities, 1200-1500.* Berkeley and Los Angeles, 1972.

Martini, Carlo. "Il Palazzo dei Priori a Perugia," *Palladio* 20 (1970): 39-72.

Masi, G. *La "pittura infamante" nella legislazione e nella vita del comune fiorentino.* Rome, 1931.

Mattingly, Garrett. *Renaissance Diplomacy.* Oxford, 1955.

Meiss, Millard. *Painting in Florence and Siena After the Black Death: The Arts, Religions and Society in the Mid-Fourteenth Century.* New York, 1964.

Meyer, Paul. "Les Premières compilations françaises d'histoire ancienne," *Romania* 14 (1885): 1 ff. and 36 ff.

Milton, John, *Paradise Lost.* Books I and XII. New York, 1952.

Mommeson, Theodor E. "St. Augustine and the Christian Idea of Progress: The Background of *The City of God,*" *Medieval and Renaissance Studies.* Ed. Eugene F. Rice, Jr., Ithaca, 1966, pp. 265-281.

Morpurgo, S. "Bruto 'il buon giudice', nell'Udienza, dell'arte della lana di Firenze" in *Miscellanea di Storia dell'arte in onore de I.B. Supino,* Florence, 1930.

Morrall, John B. *Political Thought in Medieval Times.* New York, 1962.

Muñoz, A. *L'arte a Roma nel tempo di Dante.* Milan, 1926.

Mussato, Albertino. *Ecernis.* Ed. L. Padrin, Bologna, 1900.

Nessi, S. "Documenti sull'arte umbra," *Commentari* 18-19 (1967): 76-81.

Nicolini, Ugolino. "Le mura medievali di Perugia," *Storia e arte in Umbria nell'età comunale,* vol. 2. Perugia, 1969, pp. 695 ff.

Oberman, Heiko A. *The Harvest of Medieval Theology: Gabriel Biel and Late Medieval Nominalism.* Cambridge, 1963.

Olschki, Leonardo. *La Cattedrale di Modena e il suo rilievo arturiano.* Florence, 1935.

l'Orange, H.P. *Art Forms and the Civic Life in the Late Roman Empire.* Princeton, 1975.

Orsini, B. *Guida della città di Perugia.* Perugia, 1784.

Ortalli, Gherardo "La pittura infamante nei secoli XIII-XVI," Rome, 1978.

Ottakar, Nicola. *Il comune di Firenze al fine del dugento.* Torino, 1973.

Otto, Bishop of Freising. *The Two Cities: A Chronicle of Universal History to the Year 1146 A.D.* Translated by Charles Christopher Mierow. New York, 1928.

Paccagnini, Giovanni. *Il Palazzo Ducale di Mantova.* Torino, 1969.

_____. *Pisanello e il ciclo cavalleresco di Mantova.* Milan, 1972.

Pächt, Otto. "Early Italian Nature Studies," *Journal of the Warburg and Courtauld Institutes* 13 (1950): 13-45.

Panazza, G. *L'arte mediovale nel territorio bresciano.* Bergamo, 1942.

_____. "Affreschi medievali nel Broletto di Brescia," *Commentari dell'Ateneo di Brescia,* 1946/7, pp. 102-109.

Panofsky, Erwin. *Renaissance and Renascences in Western Art,* vol. 1. Uppsala, 1960.

Panofsky, Erwin, and Fritz Saxl. "Classical Mythology in Medieval Art," *Metropolitan Museum Studies,* New York, vol. 4(1933): 250-303.

Partner, Peter. *The Lands of St. Peter: The Papal State in the Middle Ages and the Early Renaissance.* Berkeley and Los Angeles, 1972.

Patch, Howard R. *The Goddess "Fortuna" in Medieval Literature.* Cambridge, 1927.

Paul, J. *Die Mittelalterlichen Kommunalpaläste in Italien.* Dresden, 1963.

Pellini, Pompeo. *Dell'Historia di Perugia.* 3 vols. Venice, 1664.

"Perugia," *Enciclopedia Italiana,* vol. 10. Milan, 1935, p. 305.

Peyer, H. *Stadt und Stadtpatron im mitelalterlichen Italien.* Zurich, 1955.

Pietrangeli, C. *Le prime fase architettoniche del Palazzo del Senatorio.* Rome, 1959.

Pincus, Debra. *The Arco Foscari: The Building of a Triumphal Gateway in Fifteenth-Century Venice,* New York and London, 1976.

Pirenne, Henri. "Northern Towns and Their Commerce," *The Cambridge Medieval History,*, vol. 6, pp. 505-520.

Plumb, J.H. *Death of the Past.* Boston, 1970.

Pope-Hennessy, John. *Italian Gothic Sculpture.* London, 1955.

Porter, Arthur K. *Lombard Architecture,* 3 vols. New Haven-London, 1917.

Portioli, A. "Monumenti a Virgilio in Mantova," *Archivio Storico Lombardo* 4 (1877): 536-552.

Post, Gaines. "Two Notes on Nationalism in the Middle Ages," *Traditio* 9 (1953): 281-293.

Prodi, Paolo. "The Structure and Organization of the Church in Renaissance Venice: Suggestions for Research," *Renaissance Venice,* Ed. J.R. Hale. Totowa, 1973, pp. 409-432.

Pullan, Brian.*A History of Early Renaissance Italy from the Mid-Thirteenth through the Mid-Fifteenth Century.* London, 1957.

Quintivalle, Arturo. Carlo. *La Cattedrale di Modena: Problemi di romanico emiliano.* 2 vols. Modena, 1971.

Raggio, Olga. "The Myth of Prometheus, Its Survival and Metamorphoses up to the Eighteenth Century," *Journal of the Warburg and Courtauld Institutes* 21 (1958): 44-53.

Randall, L.M.C. "*Exempla* as a Source of Gothic Marginal Decoration," *Art Bulletin* 29 (1957): 97-120.

Rapone, M.M. *Peruse: Le Palais des "Priori."* Paris, 1950.

_____. *Guida di Perugia.* Perugia, 1950.

Rashdall, Hastings. *The Universities of Europe in the Middle Ages,* vol. 1. Oxford, 1936.

Réau, Louis. *Iconographie de l'Art Chrétien,* vol. 2. Paris, 1956.

Reinach, S. *Epòna.* Paris, 1895.

Reinhardt, T. *Umbrische studien.* 2 Berlin, 1914.

Ricci, Ettore. "La piazza del comune et le logge di Braccio Fortebraccio," in *Il Tempio di San Francesco al Prato a Perugia.* Perugia, 1927.

_____. *La piazza del comune et le logge di Braccio Fortebracci.* Perugia, 1927.

_____. *La Chiesa di San Prospero e i pittori del duecento in Perugia.* Perugia, 1929.

Ridolfi, Alfredo. "Alcuni documenti e notizie sulla costruzione del Palazzo Comunale (1288-1289)," *Rassagna d'arte senese* 13 (1920): 84-89.

Riesenberg, Peter. "Civicism and Roman Law in Fourteenth Century Italian Society," *Society and Government in Medieval Italy: Essays in Honor of Robert L. Reynolds.* Ed. David Herlihy. Kent, 1969, pp. 237-254.

Riess, Jonathan. "French Influences on the Early Development of Civic Art in Italy," *Annals of the New York Academy of Sciences*, 314 (1978), 285 ff.

Rodolico, F., and G. Marchini. *I Palazzi del Popolo nei comuni toscani del medio evo*. Florence, 1962.

Rosand, David. "Titian's *Presentation of the Virgin in the Temple* and the Scuola della Carità," *Art Bulletin* 58 (1976): 55 ff.

Rosati, Franco Panvini. "La monetazione delle città umbre nell'età dei Comuni," *Storia e arte in Umbira nell'età comunale*, vol.. 2 Perugia, 1969, pp. 239-252.

Rosenau, Helen. *The Ideal City in Its Architectural Evolution*. London, 1959.

Ross, David J. A. *Alexander Historiatus*. London, 1963.

Rossi, G.B.S. *Il Palazzo del Popolo*. Perugia, 1864.

Rowley, George. *Ambrogio Lorenzetti*, vol. 1. Princeton, 1958, p. 489.

Rubinstein, N. "The Beginnings of Political Thought in Florence," *Journal of the Warburg and Courtauld Institutes* 5 (1942): 198-223.

_____. "Political Ideas in Sienese Art: The Frescoes of Ambrogio Lorenzetti and Taddeo di Bartolo in the Palazzo Pubblico," *Journal of the Warburg and Courtauld Institutes* 7 (1944): 65-81.

_____. "Some Ideas on Municipal Progress and Decline in the Italy of the Communes," in D.J. Gordon (ed.), *Fritz Saxl: A Volume of Memorial Essays*. London, 1957, pp. 165-181.

_____. "Vasari's Painting of the *Foundation of Florence* in the Palazzo Vecchio," *Essays in the History of Architecture Presented to Rudolf Wittkower*. London, 1967, pp. 97-113.

_____. "Notes on the Word *'Stato'* in Florence Before Machiavelli," *"Florilegium Historiale"*: *Essays Presented to Wallace K. Fergusen*. Ed. J.G. Rowe and W.H. Stockdale. Toronto, 1971, pp. 313-317.

Runciman, Steven. *A History of the Crusades: The Kingdom of Acre and the Later Crusades*, vol. 3. Cambridge, 1954.

Rushforth, G.M. "Magister Gregorius, *De Mirabilius Urbis Romae:* A New Description of Rome in the Twelfth Century," *Journal of Roman Studies* 9 (1919): 14-58.

Sacconi, G. "Un antiquario del secolo XIV," *Giornale di erudizione artistica* 1 (1872): 184-186.

Salvian. *On the Government of God.* Translated by Eva M. Sanford. New York, 1930.

Santi, Francesco. *Perugia: Guida storico-artistica*. Perugia, 1950.

_____. *Galleria Nazionale dell'Umbria: Dipinti, Sculture, e oggetti d'arte di età romanica e gotica*. Rome, 1969.

_____. "Note sul Palazzo dei Priori a Perugia," *Bollettino della Deputazione di Storia Patria per l'Umbira* 69 (1972): 49-53.

Saxl, Fritz. "The Troy Romance in French and Italian Art," *Lectures*, vol. 1. London, 1957, pp. 125-138.

_____. "The Revival of Late Antique Astrology, *Lectures*, vol. 1. London, 1957, pp. 73-85.

_____. "The Belief in Stars in the Twelfth Century," *Lectures*, vol. 1. London, 1957. 85-97.

Saxl, Fritz and Hans Meier. *Catalogue of Astrological and Mythological Illuminated Manuscripts of the Latin Middle Ages; Manuscripts in English Libraries*. London, 1953.

Scalvanti, G. "Un opinione del Bartolo sulla libertà Perugina," *Bollettino della Deputazione di Storia Patria per l'Umbria* 2 (1887): 59-73.

Schade, H. "Adam und Eva," *Lexikon der Christlichen Ikonographie* (in progress). Ed. Hans Aurenhammer, Vienna, 1959.

Schapiro, Meyer. *Words and Pictures: On the Literal and the Symbolic in the Illustration of a Text*. The Hague-Paris, 1973.

_____. "On the Aesthetic Attitude in Romanesque Art," *Art and Thought:* Issued in honor of Dr. Ananda K. Coomerswamy on the occasion of his 70th birthday, London, 1947.

Scheller, R.W. *A Survey of Medieval Model Books*. Haarlem, 1963.

Schlosser, J. "Giustos Fresken in Padua," *Jahrb. der Kunsthist. Sammlg. in Wien* (1896): 47-69.

Schneider, P. *The Story of Perugia.* London, 1952.

Scholz, R. *Die Publizistik zur Zeit Philipps des Schonen und Bonifaz VIII.* Stuttgart 1908.

Schrader, J.L. *The Waning of the Middle Ages: An Exhibition of French and Netherlandish Art from 1350 to 1500 Commemorating the Fiftieth Anniversary of "The Waning of the Middle Ages" by Johan Huizinga.* The University of Kansas Museum of Art, November - December 1, 1969.

Schramm, P. E. "Das Herrscherbild in der Kunst des Mittelalters," *Vortrage der Bibliothek Warburg* 1 (1924): 198-272.

Segolino, Daniele. 'Bartolo da Sassoferrato e la Civilitas Perusiana," in *Bartolo da Sassoferrato: Studi e documenti per il VI centenario,* vol. 2. Perugia, 1962, pp. 513-673.

Selbie, J.A. "Lamech," *Dictionary of the Bible,* vol.3. Boston, 1903, p. 19-20.

Seznec, Jean. *The Survival of the Pagan Gods: The Mythological Tradition and Its Place in Renaissance Humanism and Art.* New York, 1953.

Seymour, Charles. "Invention and Revival in Nicola Pisano's 'Heroic Style,' " *Acts of the Twentieth International Congress of the History of Art,* vol. 1. Princeton, 1963, pp. 207-218.

Siegel, Jerrold E. "Civic Humanism' or Ciceronian Rhetoric," *Past and Present,* No. 34, (July, 1966): pp. 3 ff.

Sinding-Larsen, Staale. *Christ in the Council Hall: Studies in the Religious Iconography of the Venetian Republic,* with a contribution by A. Kuhn. Institutum Romnum Norvegiae, Acta ad archaeologiam et artivm historiam, vol. 5. Rome, 1975.

Sindona, C. *Pietro Cavallini.* Florence, 1958.

Skinner, Quentin. *The Foundations of Modern Political Thought, I: The Renaissance.* Cambridge, London, New York, Melbourne, 1978.

Smalley, Beryl. *The Study of the Bible in the Middle Ages.* Oxford, 1952.

Smart, Alastair. *The Assisi Problem and the Art of Giotto.*Oxford, 1971.

Southard, E.C., *The Frescoes in Siena's Palazzo Pubblico, 1289-1539: Studies in Imagery and Relations to other Communal Palaces in Italy,* New York, 1978.

Starn, Randolph. "Meaning-Levels in the Theme of Historical Decline," *History and Theory: Studies in the Philosophy of History,* 14 (1975): pp. 1-31.

Stenton, Sir Frank Merry et al. *The Bayeux Tapestry: A Comprehensive Survey.* London, 1957.

Strayer, Joseph R. "France, the Holy Land, the Chosen People, and the Most Christian King," *Action and Conviction in Early Modern Europe: Essays in Memory of E.H. Harbison.* Ed. Theodore K. Rabb and Jerrold E. Seigel. Princeton, 1969, pp. 3 ff.

Souvay, Charles L. "Aaron," *The New Catholic Encyclopedia,* vol. 1. London, 1907, p. 3.

Swarzenski, Georg. "The Song of the Three Worthies," *Bulletin, Museum of Fine Arts,* Boston, 56 (1958): 30-49.

Tarchi, U. *L'arte medievale dell'Umbria e della Sabina,* vol. 2. Milan, 1938.

Tassi, Roberto. *Il Duomo di Fidenza.* Milan, 1974.

Taylor, Henry Osborn. *The Medieval Mind.* 2 vols. New York. 1919.

Thaon di Revel, M. "Perugia," *Enciclopedia Italiana,* vol. 26. Rome, 1932, p. 907.

"The Liber Augustalis,"or the Constitutions of Melfi Promulgated by the Emperor Frederick II for the Kingdom of Sicily in 1231. Translated and introduced by James M. Powell. Syracuse, 1971.

Thiele, A. *Der illustrierte Lateinische Aesop.* Leyden, 1905.

Thorndike, Lynn. *A History of Magic and the Experimental Sciences,* vol. 2. London, 1923.

Tiberi, T. "Il Palazzo Comunale," *Il giornale dell'esposizione provinciale umbra* 1 (1879): 2-4.

Tikkanen, J.J. *Die Genesismosaiken von S. Marco in Venedig.* Helsinki, 1889.

Toesca, Pietro. *La pittura e la miniatura nella Lombardia.* Milan, 1912.

———. *Il Trecento.* Turin, 1951.

de Tolnay, Charles, *Michelangelo: The Tomb of Julius II.* Volume 2. Princeton, 1944.

Toscano, B. "La fortuna della pittura umbra e il silenzio sui primitivi," *Paragone* 193 (1966): 3-32.

Trachtenberg, M. *The Campanile of the Florence Cathedral: "Giotto's Tower."* New York, 1971.

Trilling, Lionel. *Sincerity and Authenticity,* Cambridge, 1971.

Troeltsch, Ernst. *The Social Teaching of the Christian Churches,* vol. 1. London and New York, 1956.

Ugolino, Francesco A. *Annali e cronaca di Perugia dal 1191 al 1336.* Perugia, 1962.

Ullmann, Walter, *Principles of Government in the Middle* Ages. New York, 1961.

_____. *A Short History of Political Theory.* London, 1965.

_____. *The Carolingian Renaissance and the Idea of Kingship.* Birkbeck Lectures, 1968-1969, London, 1969.

Van Cleve, T.C. *The Emperor Frederick II: "Immutator Mundi."* Oxford, 1972.

Vasari, *Le Opere,* Vol. 1. Ed. G. Milanesi. Florence, 1906, p. 400.

Venturi, A. *Storia dell'arte italiana,* vol. 3. Milan, 1901-1940.

Venturi, L. "Opere di sculture nelle Marche," *L'Arte* 19 (1916): 25-50.

Vermiglioli, G.B. *Della zecca e delle monete perugine.* Perugia, 1816.

Volpe, C. *Il medioevo.* Rome, 1926, pp. 294 ff.

de Voragine, Jacobus. *The Golden Legend.* Translated by Granger Ryan and Helmut Rippenger. New York, 1969.

Vossler, Karl. *An Introduction to Dante and His Times.* 2 vols. London, 1929.

Waley, Daniel. *The Papal State in the Thirteenth Century.* London, 1951.

_____. *Medieval Orvieto: The Political History of an Italian Town, 1157-1334.* Cambridge, 1952.

_____. "The Army of the Florentine Republic from the Twelfth to the Fourteenth Century," *Florentine Studies: Politics and Society in Renaissance Florence.* Ed. Nicolai Rubinstein. London, 1968, pp. 70-97.

_____. *The Italian City-Republics.* New York and Toronto, 1969.

Walter, Christopher. "Papal Imagery in the Medieval Lateran Palace,"*Cahiers Archéologiques* 20 (1970): 155-176; 21 (1971): 109-136.

Warburg, Aby. "Italienische kunst und internationale Astrologie im Palazzo Schifanoia zu Ferrar" *L'Italia e l'arte straniera. Atti del X congresso internazionale di storia dell'arte.* Rome, 1922, pp. 101 ff.

Webster, J.C. *The Labors of the Months in Antique Medieval Art.* Princeton, 1938.

Wedel, Theodore Otto. "The Medieval Towards Astrology," *Yale Studies in English,* vol. 60. New Haven, 1920, pp. 41-63.

Weinberger, M. "Remarks on the Role of French Models within the Evolution of Gothic Tuscan Sculpture," *Acts of the Twentieth International Congress of the History of Art,* vol. 1. Princeton, 1963, pp. 198-210.

Weiss, R. "La cultura preumanistica Veronese del tempo di Dante," *Dante e la cultura veneta.* Ed. V. Branca Florence, 1966, pp. 263-272.

_____. *The Renaissance Discovery of Classical Antiquity.* Oxford, 1969.

Weitzmann, Kurt. *Illustrations in Roll and Codex.* Princeton, 1947.

_____. *Ancient Book Illumination.* Cambridge, 1959.

Westfall, C.W. *In This Most Perfect Paradise: Alberti, Nicholas V, and the Invention of Conscious Urban Planning in Rome, 1447-1455.*University Park and London, 1974.

White, John. *Art and Architecture in Italy, 1250-1400.* Baltimore, 1966.

_____. "The Reconstruction of Nicola Pisano's Perugia Fountain," *Journal of the Warburg and Courtauld Institutes* 33 (1970): 70-83.

Wieruszowski, Helene. "Art and the Commune in the Age of Dante," *Speculum* 19 (1944): 14-33.

_____. "Arezzo as a Center of Learning and Letters in the Thirteenth Century," *Traditio* 9 (1953): 321-391.

Wilde, Johannes. "The Hall of the Great Council in Florence," *The Journal of the Warburg and Courtauld Institutes* 7 (1944): 65-81.

Wilkins, E.H. *A History of Italian Literature.* London, 1954.

Wilks, Michael. *The Problem of Sovereignty in the Later Middle Ages: The Papal Monarchy with Augustinius Triumphus and the Publicists.* Cambridge, 1964.

Wilpert, Joseph. *Die Romischen Mosaiken und Malerein der Kirchlichen Bauten vom IV-XIII Jahrhundert,* vol. 1. Freiburg, 1917.

Wind, Edgar. "Donatello's *Judith*: A Symbol of 'Sanctimonia,'" *Journal of the Warburg Institute* 1 (1937-38): 62-63.

Wingate, S.D. *The Medieval Versions of the Aristotelian Scientific Corpus.* London, 1931.

Witt, Ronald. "The Rebirth of the Concept of Republican Liberty in Italy," *Reniassance Studies in Honor of Hans Baron.* Anthony Molho and John Tedeschi. Florence, 1971, pp. 173-190.

Wittkower, Rudolf, "Chance, Time and Virtue," *Journal of the Warburg Institute* 1 (1937-38): 313-321.

Wittkower, Rudolf and Margot Wittkower. *Born Under Saturn: The Character and Conduct of Artists: A Documented History from Antiquity to the French Revolution.* New York, 1969.

Wixon, William D. *Treasures from Medieval France.* The Cleveland Museum of Art, Cleveland, 1969.

Wolters, W. *La scultura veneziana gotica (1300-1400).* Venice, 1976.

Woolf, C.N.S. *Bartolus of Sassoferrato.* Cambridge, 1913.

de Wulf, Maurice. *Philosophy and Civilization in the Middle Ages.* New York, 1953.

Yates, Francis. *Astraea: The Imperial Theme in the Sixteenth Century.* London and Boston, 1975.

Zanotto, F. *Il Palazzo di Venezia,* vol. 1. Venice, 1853-1861

Zdekauer, L. *La vita pubblica dei senesi nel dugento.* Siena, 1897.

―――. "'Iustitia,'immagine e idea,"*Bollettino senese di storia patria* 20 (1913): 384-425.

Figure 1a.   Plan of the Sala dei Notari, Palazzo dei Priori, Perugia;
             location of frescoes of 1297

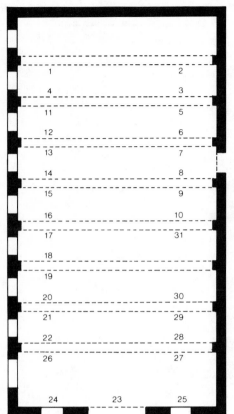

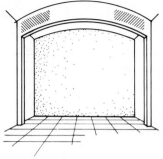

Figure 1b.
Cutaway view of the Sala dei Notari, Palazzo dei Priori,
Perugia, showing placement of the murals of 1297 on one
transverse arch

Key to Figure 1

Placement and Subjects of the Frescoes in the Sala dei Notari (1297)

1. Gideon Squeezes Dew from the Fleece at
   the Command of an Angel
2. God Appears to Moses in the Burning Bush
3. Moses and Aaron before the Pharoah
4. The Pursuit of the Israelites by the Egyptians
5. The Creation of Adam
6. The Creation of Eve
7. The First Labor of Adam and Eve
8. The Offering of Cain and Abel
9. The Death of Cain
10. Slaying of Abel
11. The Wolf and the Lamb
12. Saint George and the Dragon
13. The Dog Carrying Meat
14. The Wolf and the Crane
15. The Fox and the Crow
16. The Fox and the Grapes

17. The Old Lion and the Fox
18. The Dog and the Wolf
19. The Fox and the Dog
20. The Fox and the Eagle
21. The Hog and the Dog
22. The Thief and the Dog
23. January and February
24. Battling Knights
25. Battling Knights
26. The Contemplative Man
27. The Man with the Rearing Horse
28. The Knight in Prayer
29. The Soldiers Crossing a Bridge
30. The Knight Battling a Dragon
31. The Woman Riding a Horse
32. Bull and Boar

Figure 2.   *Isola del Comune, Perugia, c. 1300* (after Tarchi)

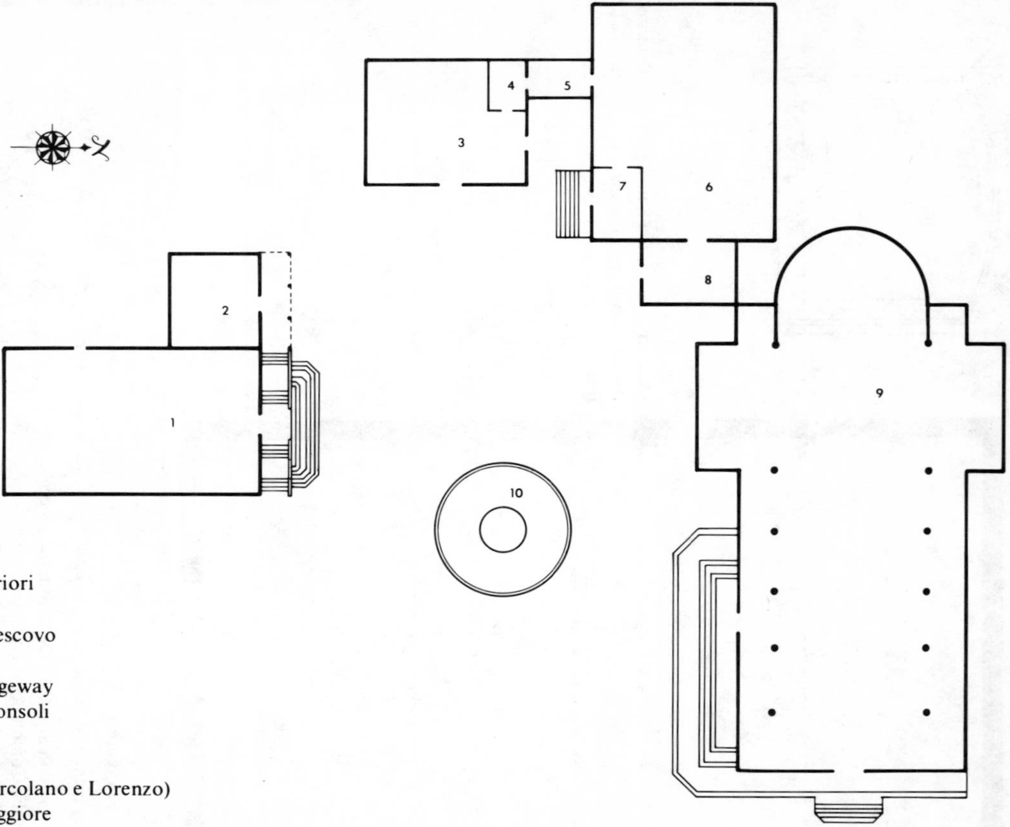

Key to Figure 2

2.1.   Palazzo dei Priori
2.2.   S. Severo
2.3.   Palazzo del Vescovo
2.4.   Tower
2.5.   Vaulted passageway
2.6.   Palazzo dei Consoli
2.7.   Stair ramp
2.8.   Canonica
2.9.   Duomo (Ss. Ercolano e Lorenzo)
2.10. Fontana Maggiore

Figure 3. Reconstruction of the first nucleus of the Palazzo dei Priori and S. Severo, Perugia, c. 1300 (north elevation; after Martini)

Plate I.   Sala dei Notari, Palazzo dei Priori, Perugia (Photo: Alinari)

Plate II.   Piazza IV Novembre, Perugia (Photo: Alinari)

Plate III. *Fontana Maggiore,* Perugia, 1278 (Photo: Alinari)

Plate VII. The Pursuit of the Israelites by the Egyptians, Palazzo dei
            Priori, Perugia, 1297 (Photo: Luigi Artini, Villa I Tatti,
            Florence)

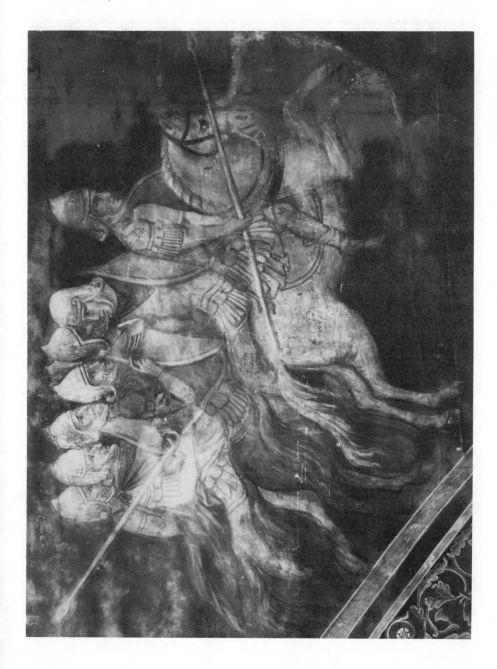

Plate VIII. The Creation of Adam, Palazzo dei Priori, Perugia, 1297
(Photo: Luigi Artini, Villa I Tatti, Florence)

Plate X. The First Labor of Adam and Eve, Palazzo dei Priori,
Perugia, 1297 (Photo: Luigi Artini, Villa I Tatti, Florence)

Plate XI. The Offering of Cain and Abel, Palazzo dei Priori, Perugia,
1297 (Photo: Luigi Artini, Villa I Tatti, Florence)

Plate XII.   The Slaying of Abel, Palazzo dei Priori, Perugia, 1297
            (Photo: Luigi Artini, Villa I Tatti, Florence)

Plate XIV. Saint George and the Dragon, Palazzo dei Priori, 1297
(Photo: Luigi Artini, Villa I Tatti, Florence)

Plate XV. The Wolf and the Lamb, Palazzo dei Priori, Perugia, 1297
          (Photo: Luigi Artini, Villa I Tatti, Florence)

Plate XVI.   The Dog Carrying Meat, Palazzo dei Priori, Perugia,
             1297 (Photo: Luigi Artini, Villa I Tatti, Florence)

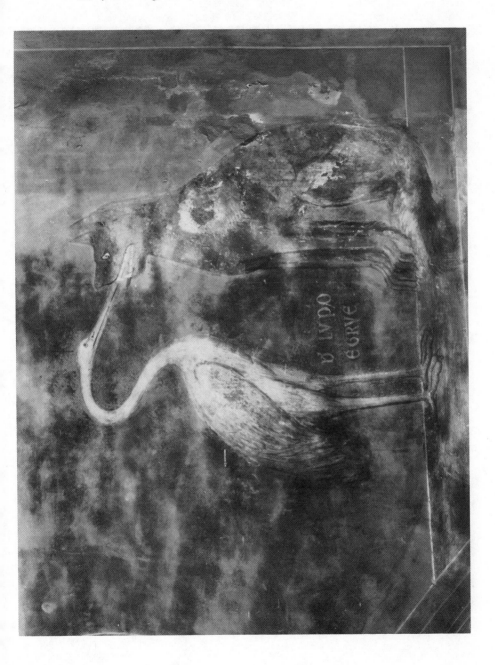

Plate XIX. The Fox and the Grapes, Palazzo dei Priori, Perugia, 1297 (Photo: Luigi Artini, Villa I Tatti, Florence)

Plate XXI.   The Dog and the Wolf, Palazzo dei Priori, Perugia, 1297
            (Photo: Luigi Artini, Villa I Tatti, Florence)

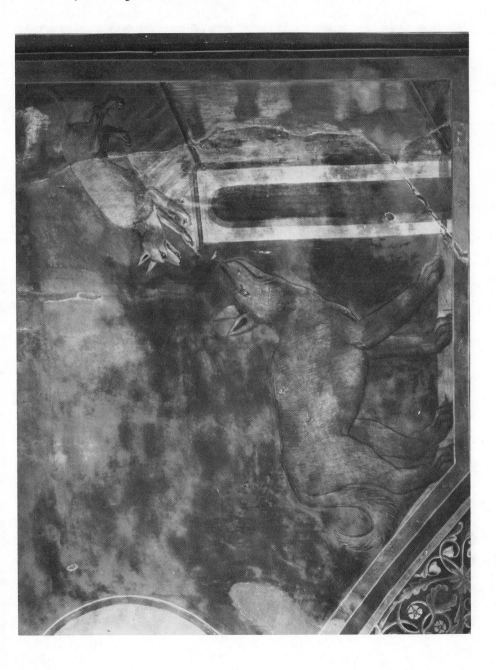

Plate XXIII.   The Fox and the Eagle, Palazzo dei Priori, Perugia, 1297
(Photo: Luigi Artini, Villa I Tatti, Florence)

Plate XXIV.   The Hog and the Dog, Palazzo dei Priori, Perugia, 1297
            (Photo: Luigi Artini, Villa'I Tatti, Florence)

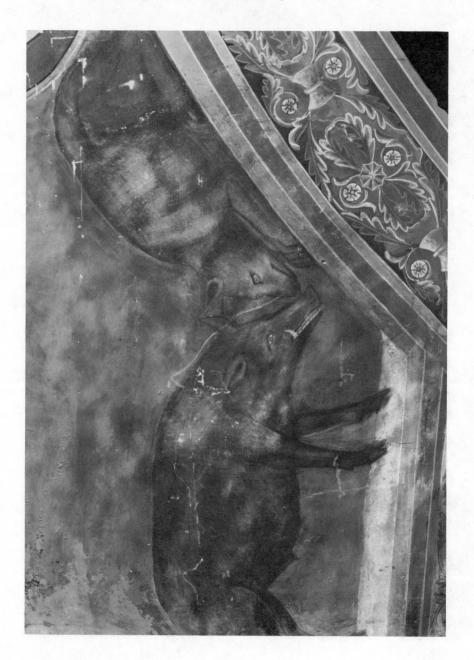

Plate XXV.   The Thief and the Dog, Palazzo dei Priori, Perugia, 1297
            (Photo: Luigi Artini, Villa I Tatti, Florence)

Plate XXVI.　January and February, Palazzo dei Priori, Perugia,
1297 (Photo: Luigi Artini, Villa I Tatti, Florence)

Plate XXVIII. The Contemplative Man, Palazzo dei Priori, Perugia,
1297 (Photo: Luigi Artini, Villa I Tatti, Florence)

Plate XXIX. The Man with the Rearing Horse, Palazzo dei Priori,
Perugia, 1297 (Photo: Luigi Artini, Villa I Tatti,
Florence)

Plate XXXI. The Soldiers Crossing a Bridge, Palazzo dei Priori, Perugia, 1297 (Photo: Luigi Artini, Villa I Tatti, Florence)

Plate XXXII. The Knight Battling a Dragon, Palazzo dei Priori, Perugia, 1297 (Photo: Luigi Artini, Villa I Tatti, Florence)

Plate XXXIII. The Woman Riding a Horse, Palazzo dei Priori, Perugia, 1297 (Photo: Luigi Artini, Villa I Tatti, Florence)

Index